THE BLITZKRIEG ERA AND THE GERMAN GENERAL STAFF, 1865–1941

LARRY H. ADDINGTON

THE BLITZKRIEG ERA AND THE GERMAN GENERAL STAFF, 1865–1941

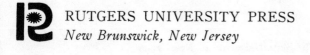
RUTGERS UNIVERSITY PRESS
New Brunswick, New Jersey

To My Parents

Contents

List of Maps   ix

Preface   xi

Introduction *by Theodore Ropp*   xiii

Chapter 1. The Kesselschlacht Heritage   3

Chapter 2. Birth of the Blitzkrieg   28

Chapter 3. Prologue to War   47

Chapter 4. Poland: The First Test   61

Chapter 5. France: Victory in the West   83

Chapter 6. England: The Narrow Sea   125

Chapter 7. The Balkans: An Interlude   139

Chapter 8. North Africa: To Aid an Ally   159

Chapter 9. Russia: Climax of the Blitzkrieg   177

Epilogue   213

Notes   219

Selected Bibliography   257

Index   267

Maps

1. Central and Western Europe, 1866–1870.   1

2. Campaign in Bohemia, 1866.   5

3. Franco-Prussian War, 1870.   7

4. The Schlieffen Plan of 1905.   13

5. The March of the First and Second German Armies to the Marne, 1914.   18

6. Campaign in East Prussia, 1914.   24

7. Europe in 1935.   48

8. German Deployment for the Invasion of Czechoslovakia, 1938.   55

9. Campaign in Poland, 1939.   63

10. The Ardennes Breakthrough and the Western Front, 1940.   103

11. The Battles of the Somme and the Aisne, 1940.   118

12. OKH Invasion Plan for England, July, 1940.   128

13. The Invasion of Yugoslavia and Greece, 1941.   153

14. General Map of the Mediterranean Theater of War, 1941.   160

15. Rommel's First Offensive in North Africa, 1941.   164

16. Planned German Thrusts for the Invasion of Russia.   181

17. The Bryansk-Vyazma Encirclements, October, 1941.   205

18. The Battle of Moscow, November–December, 1941.   210

Preface

This book does not pretend to be an exhaustive history of the evolution of German military doctrine and performance since the mid-nineteenth century. It does seek to offer some new interpretations of the origins and nature of the blitzkrieg and to place the German army's performance in the Second World War in a better historical perspective. Most of the book is devoted to the period from September, 1939, to December, 1941, a period which in my view was the climax of the blitzkrieg era. The focus is on the Army General Staff and the soldier at its head, General Franz Halder. Halder not only played a key role in the functioning of the blitzkrieg army, he maintained a war journal which is an indispensable document for understanding the workings of Hitler's war machine.

The army of the Third Reich was never the motorized, mechanized juggernaut of popular legend but a mixture of modern and old-fashioned elements whose combination is the key to understanding the army's successes and final failure. Basically, the so-called blitzkrieg doctrine was a final step in the evolution of the old nineteenth-century Prussian doctrine of *Kesselschlacht* (battle of encirclement and annihilation), modified not only to take advantage of new weapons—such as the airplane and the tank—but to allow the traditional infantry-artillery divisions to escape in part the tyranny of railroad and horse-drawn logistics—logistics that hampered Moltke's army in the wars of the mid-nineteenth century and brought disaster to the Kaiser's army in the First World War. The modified doctrine and organization gave Hitler's army a greater strategic range and striking power than its German predecessors, but before 1939 time had been too short and resources too scarce to permit a complete transition to modern forms. Behind a thin veneer of panzer and motorized divisions was an army composed in the main of old-style infantry-artillery divisions—divisions hampered by logistical limits similar to those which had afflicted the armies of Moltke and the Kaiser.

The consequences of the limits of this "semimodern" army were fatal for Hitler's expansionist policies. Equipped with a doctrine and organization suitable only to central and western Europe, the blitzkrieg army was not prepared for overseas operations or for campaigns in the vast land-areas of Russia. The weaknesses in both doctrine and organization revealed themselves decisively in the crucial battle of Moscow in November–December, 1941. That defeat, coming as it did almost simultaneously with the Japanese attack on Pearl Harbor and the forging of the grand alliance between Soviet Russia, the United States, and Great Britain, really finished the blitzkrieg era for Germany. Great battles were still to be fought over the next three years, but the global military potential of the United Nations was so great that the final outcome was almost certain. Stalingrad, El Alamein, and the Normandy Invasion were the nearly inescapable conclusions to a conflict which in Europe at least had already passed its climax. The high tide of the German army had crested and we are left to ponder the conseqences.

Introduction

This fine book focuses on how modern or post-Napoleonic officers thought commanders should fight their planned campaigns and battles. A generation after the latest events he describes, Professor Addington tells the supposedly familiar story of the German Army's blitzkrieg victories during the first years of the Second World War. But he tells it from the standpoint of a Chief of Staff, Franz Halder, whom he sees as an unwitting prisoner of the ideas and techniques which had been developed and first used by Helmuth von Moltke during the nineteenth century. Moltke had been Prussia's and Germany's organizer of more than Napoleonic victories over Austria in 1866 and France in 1870–71. Otto von Bismarck's diplomatic genius in limiting both wars had helped to make William the Great's Second Reich the strongest military and—eventually—the strongest industrial power in Europe, but at the cost—for which Moltke was partly responsible—of "permanent" French enmity and a Bismarckian political settlement within Germany that only a Bismarck could sustain.

Professor Addington makes it clear that many of Germany's successes in the two great wars of the twentieth century—wars which finally ended with her "permanent" dismemberment—were based on careful staff work, her ability repeatedly to seize the initiative through faster mobilization, her central position, and the weaknesses of her enemies. She exploited the strategical initiative for major tactical victories by surrounding portions of the enemy forces and making them surrender or attempt to fight their way out against overwhelming infantry and artillery firepower. But tactical and strategic concepts which had brought victory in 1866 and 1870–71 did not finally win the European "peoples' wars" of the twentieth century.

In assessing the blame for Germany's defeats, other historians have focused on weapons, on the courts of William II and of Adolf Hitler, and on the reserves of space, men, matériel, and morale which, ironically, political rhetoric and early victories of these courts scared their enemies into throwing into the scales against Germany. Dr. Addington sees all these factors, but adds another: how the German Army's dependence on railroads and horse-drawn supply transport fatally hampered its offensive capabilities in two world wars. In the case of World War I, the role of logistics has gone largely unnoticed because of the preoccupation of historians with the mistakes of the younger Moltke in attempting to execute the Schlieffen Plan in 1914, with the general failure in tactical weapons evaluation which resulted in the long agony of the trenches, and with Ludendorff's shifting aims in the spring–summer offensives of 1918. These preoccupations have tended to conceal the vital role in German defeats played by a logistical system which was incapable of advancing marching infantry and horse-drawn artillery for more than one short-ranged punch at a time.

After World War I, German military planners—and certain military planners in other countries—correctly observed that tanks, motorization and mechanization, and tactical aircraft could solve some of the tactical puzzles of the trenches. The German Army was the first to add substantial numbers of motorized-mechanized infantry and artillery to aid armored units in springing strategic encirclements to hold the enemy within effective striking range of the marching infantry and artillery.

Other historians have concentrated on the vital role of the mechanized-motorized forces in the early German successes in World War II and on Germany's lack of trained men, oil, and time in preparing adequately for this kind of war or any other. Dr. Addington is well aware of these factors, but he is the first historian to concentrate on the role of the nonmotorized and semimotorized

forces in the German Army—by far the largest part of the Army—
and his is the first clear description of the effects of the logistical
weaknesses of this "semimodern army" in both its successes and
failures. He describes the German system as basically a modified
version of that which had served the elder Moltke and the Kaiser,
with increased range and striking power. The World War II model
could support a series of 300-mile monthly or bimonthly jumps, followed by long lulls for the system to rejuvenate itself. This system
reminds one of Louis XIV's French armies in the late seventeenth
and early eighteenth centuries; they advanced their fortified bases
and then threw men and supplies into them for the next annual
offensive. But Hitler's armies, like Louis', depended upon good
roads, the capture of local supplies, and the rapid circumvention or
reduction of strong points in order to achieve final success. Neither
was prepared for winter campaigning or dealing with spring thaws
and rains, and the need for horses and fodder was fundamental to
both. When faced by natural or man-made barriers which it could
not swiftly circumvent or overcome, the logistics of the German
Army were vulnerable to rapid disintegration.

Like most historical analogies, the comparison of Louis XIV's
military logistics with those of the German Army in the nineteenth
and twentieth centuries cannot be pushed too far. But the similarities do suggest what happened to the military forces of the Second
and Third Reich and offer new explanations for both their successes
and final failures. Dr. Addington does not challenge the traditional
explanation that German success early in World War II was due in
large measure to German exploitation of mechanization, motorization, tactical airpower, and Allied matériel and organizational weaknesses. But he suggests that the German Army in World War II
was only "semimodern" and that the new elements in warfare were
seized upon to revive a traditional doctrine which was more suited
to the limited German goals of the nineteenth century than to Hitler's totalitarian goals of the twentieth. Hitler's boldness and early
military success are again analogous to those of Louis XIV and
inclined him to follow up his too easily won diplomatic gains with
too great a reliance on force. He, like Louis perhaps, never understood the limits of his own military instrument and set political goals
which overtaxed its inherent strength. At the end of this book the

German Army is as thoroughly stalled before Moscow as were Louis' armies before the dikes and canals of the Low Countries.

An English translation of Halder's diary exists in mimeographed copies, too long and too few to be used except by researchers on particular topics. Dr. Addington's years of research bring Halder himself front and center, as the typical staff officer—careful, sober, rational, and cautious—of an army which had both retained and lost parts of the Moltkean staff tradition. There is no evidence here that Halder ever had an original idea about anything on the staff officer's chessboard, and he was cool towards and perhaps jealous of more brilliant and enterprising officers such as Erich von Manstein. Moreover, while an expert on the possibilities of land warfare in the German tradition, he had a limited grasp of the strengths and weaknesses of sea and airborne operations. He retained grave doubts about Hitler's strategy in the Mediterranean and was caustically critical of the Italian performances in North Africa and the Balkans, yet he lacked the courage and determination to use what influence he had to prevent the Mediterranean warping of German strategy. On the other hand, his operational and logistical planning in this area was positively brilliant. Perhaps more technically competent than the younger Moltke of World War I, Halder, like him, seldom intervened in operations or challenged the decisions of the "all highest." His influence was almost solely exercised within the confines of the Army High Command. He was quick to point out to Brauchitsch, the Army Commander-in-Chief until December, 1941, the Fuehrer's operational errors, but he avoided direct confrontations with Hitler whenever possible. More surprising, this expert on *Kesselschlachten* showed little interest in extending the range of tactical air power in midrange interdiction to hold the enemy inside the blitzkrieg's armored, artillery, and infantry "kettles."

Whether another kind of professional staff planner would have fared any better than the younger Moltke or Halder in the courts which ran Germany at the beginning of her Great Wars is problematical. In Halder's defense, it must be noted that Hitler's court was less like those of William II and the aging Louis XIV than like that of Louis' younger contemporary Peter the Great. Both Peter's and Hitler's were full of adventurers, ideologues, traders, and professional soldiers intriguing for shares in the absolute power of a charismatic and ruthless leader who might sacrifice any or most of them for his own political purposes. Halder survived as long as he did by deliberately remaining a technician, one whose occasional doubts and warnings had little influence on German policy.

This is an important book because it adds depth and breadth to the understanding of a major problem in modern European history. Why did the German Army of 1914, the most professionally prepared in Europe, reach but not sustain its high tide at the Marne? And why did an even better led German Army in World War II reach two high tides—at Dunkirk and at Moscow—and fail to sustain both of them? No single, comprehensive answer can be offered to these complex questions, but this book affords a new perspective on the historical reasons for Germany's eventual defeat by powers which were, each in its own way and time, intellectually and morally prepared for survival. That German military action and political rhetoric also inspired Germany's enemies to add substantially to their strength in both world wars is not, of course, something which can be blamed wholly on Germany's planners, but all these factors, like the analogous ones from the long wars of Louis XIV's age, do help to explain what happened in history.

Theodore Ropp

THE BLITZKRIEG ERA
AND THE GERMAN
GENERAL STAFF,
1865–1941

1. Central and Western Europe, 1866–1870.

CHAPTER ONE

The Kesselschlacht Heritage

Moltke and the Transformation of War

In the middle of the nineteenth century a vast technological revolution transformed the waging of war by introducing rifled weapons in quantity for the first time, by developing the railroad as a potential instrument of strategic movement, and by offering the telegraph as a potential instrument of strategic command. The appearance of rifled weapons enormously increased the range and accuracy of both artillery and infantry firearms, while the railroad and telegraph reduced both time and distance and permitted the rapid movement, systematic supply, and centralized command of greatly increased numbers of troops. At first European commanders only dimly understood the impact that these developments would have on tactics and strategy, but in Prussia the Great General Staff [1] under Helmuth von Moltke slowly groped its way through the 1860s toward a doctrine of war compatible with the new conditions.

Prussia was not involved in the first wars of the mid-nineteenth century—the Crimean War (1854–1856) and the first Wars of Italian Unification (1859–1861)—and the General Staff paid little attention to the American Civil War, the first real test of the new technology. [2] But Prussian experience in the minor Danish War of 1864, coupled with Moltke's searching mentality, provided insight into one of the Civil War's principal lessons, namely that the new firepower had chiefly benefitted tactical defense and that the railroad had greatly increased the speed and power of strategic offense. Not long after Lee surrendered at Appomattox in 1865, Moltke wrote that to attack a position was becoming notably more difficult than to defend it. A skillful offensive in the future, Moltke reasoned, would consist in forcing a Prussian foe to attack a position chosen by the Prussians, and only when casualties, demoralization, and exhaustion had drained the enemy of his strength should the Prussians take up the tactical offensive.[3] Moltke was approaching the heart of the future Kesselschlacht doctrine when he concluded that Prussian strategy must be offensive, Prussian tactics defensive.[4]

Moltke's views at the time were quite unorthodox. Since the Napoleonic Wars the prevailing military opinion in Europe was that both tactical and strategic offensives were normally the stronger forms of war. The essence of Napoleon's tactics had been an offensive concentration of fire and shock at the weakest point of the enemy's front to create a fatal rupture. Not once in his entire career did Napoleon engage in a purely defensive battle, and rarely did he allow the foe the tactical initiative.[5] Although Wellington invented a defensive remedy for the French system of fire and shock under certain conditions and in certain kinds of terrain, the end of the Napoleonic Wars in 1815 found the European armies in the main thoroughly converted to Napoleonic principles.

The great change in weaponry at mid-century caused a sudden and striking reversal in the trend favoring the tactical offensive. Claude Minié's development of the "expandable bullet" made the insertion of ammunition in muzzle-loading rifles as rapid as in smoothbores, and Alexander Forsyth's experiments with fulminate of mercury led to the invention of the percussion cap, a much more reliable ignition system than the flintlock. The "cap and ball rifle" (Minié's cylindro-conoidal bullet was still referred to as a "ball") could fire up to five times as far as the smoothbore musket of Napoleon's day and with much greater accuracy. Rifled artillery and breech-loading weapons followed in due course. Increasingly, when entrenched and well-protected, troops armed with the new weapons could deliver such defensive fire at long ranges that even greatly superior numbers of attacking troops and guns could not successfully storm their positions from the front. This phenomenon was first fully demonstrated in the great slaughter of attacking troops during the American Civil War, but episodes in the Danish War of 1864 suggested the same unpalatable fact.[6] Just when the railroad and telegraph permitted strategic speed and concentration on a scale never dreamed of in Napoleon's time, weapons development took a contrary turn to give tactical defense the upper hand.[7] These puzzling and contradictory trends led Moltke to reach that insight already described.

Before the Austro-Prussian War in 1866, Moltke tried to get his strategic and tactical ideas approved by the Prussian king, William I, but he was only partly successful. William gave Moltke a free hand over strategy, but Moltke's tactical ideas seemed too radical to the monarch. William, in line with most military opinion of his day, still believed that Napoleonic massed frontal attacks would penetrate the enemy's defense with a combination of fire and cold steel. Accordingly, at the decisive battle of Königgrätz, the Prussian troops relied primarily on fire but attacked the Austrian front in

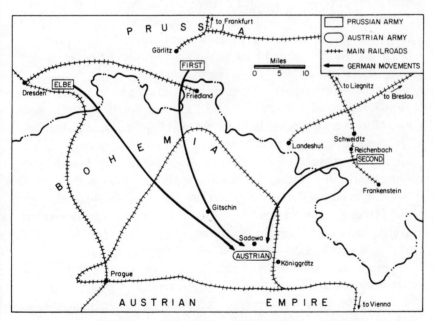

2. Campaign in Bohemia, 1866. The Prussian Advance Culminating in the Battle of Königgrätz.

close-packed masses.[8] Fortunately for the Prussians, the Austrians did not exploit their infantry firepower fully or that of their superior artillery, and made a worse mistake by attempting to counterattack the Prussian front with the bayonet. Although the Prussian infantry was equipped with the Dreyse rifle—an early breech-loader —and the Austrian infantry still used the muzzle-loading Lorenz, this advantage was partly cancelled by premature offensive tactics and the technical inferiority of Prussian artillery.[9] The battle raged indecisively until a second Prussian army finally arrived on the field and attacked the exposed Austrian flank. Königgrätz was really won by "good luck and hard fighting," [10] but it drove Austria to sue for peace without another major test of arms. Prussia was permitted to annex the other German states north of the Main river and to form the North German Confederation, a political unit controlled by Berlin and about equal to France in population and industrial power. The first great step toward German unification had been taken.

The experience of the Austro-Prussian War gave Moltke sufficient support to bring about a change in Prussian tactical doctrine in 1869. In that year he issued the *Regulations for the Higher Troop Commanders,* in which he warned against the futility of frontal attacks and urged that wherever possible Prussian troops should attack the flanks of the enemy position.[11] The *Regulations* stressed movement to get better firing advantage; and flanking (and by implication encirclement) became a key element in Prussian doctrine. Moreover, wherever the enemy could be enticed into attacking a strong Prussian position frontally, Moltke was inclined to exploit the advantages of the tactical defensive before launching a counterattack. But ideally he preferred to keep the initiative and offset the enemy's defensive power by strategically directing separate forces to converge simultaneously for encirclement. Herbert Rosinski has summed up the matter by writing that Moltke intended that the actual tactical encounter should be clearly predetermined in advance and should serve merely to confirm the decision already achieved by his strategy of encirclement.[12]

Moltke also hastened to correct the technical weaknesses revealed in the 1866 campaign—especially in artillery. Upon the urging of General Gustav Eduard von Hindersin, the Army Inspector Gen-

eral of Artillery, the Prussian field batteries were entirely re-
equipped with improved steel breech-loading rifled fieldpieces from
the Krupp works.[13] With unprecedented range and firepower, the
new guns played an important role in the new doctrine.[14] Horse-
drawn artillery could operate more effectively on the defensive when
firing from fixed positions and with unlimbered ammunition wagons,
a situation that was to remain true throughout the horse-drawn era.
Moltke foresaw the advantage of maneuvering his guns so that
the enemy would eventually face a circle of artillery fire against
which even massed infantry and cavalry assaults would be powerless.

The test of the revised Prussian doctrine and its new weaponry
came the following year with the outbreak of war between the
Prussian-dominated North German Confederation and Napoleon
III's Second French Empire. This war was also a test of the Ger-
man Nation in Arms [15] against the professional long-service army of
France. Much to the surprise of the French High Command, the

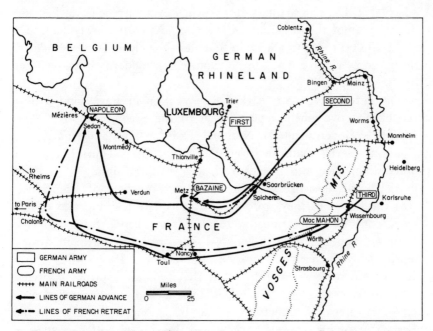

3. Franco-Prussian War, 1870. The German Advance Culminating in the
Battle of Sedan.

Prussian General Staff mobilized the German civilian reservists speedily and efficiently (as a result of careful prewar planning and organization), and the German mass mobilizable armies were ready when the French attempted to invade the Saar. Despite Moltke's *Regulations* and his intention of luring the enemy into a Kesselschlacht trap in the Rhineland, impulsive subordinates moved too soon and the enemy fell back into the Lorraine Gap. At the battles of Spicheren and Wörth, the Prussians tried frontal assaults only to find that sheer numbers and enthusiasm were no match for French defensive fire. Accordingly, they changed their tactics; both battles were finally won by German flanking maneuvers.[16] In the battles deeper in France the German armies had to learn the same lesson repeatedly and sometimes with heavy loss,[17] but Moltke's armies finally trapped one French army at Metz and with fire beat back all its attempts to break out of the ring around it. The truly climactic moment for the new doctrine came at Sedan in September, when Moltke's armies encircled a second French army endeavoring to relieve Metz. In an almost classical performance of the Kesselschlacht, German artillery fire repelled every French attack made in the attempt to break out of the ring. After his army had suffered 17,000 casualties in vain assaults, Napoleon III surrendered the largest field force yet to be captured in modern times—a total of 104,000 men.[18]

The defeat at Sedan sparked a revolution in Paris, and a new republican government replaced that of the Second Empire.[19] The republic's Government of National Defense sent a delegation to Tours as the Germans encircled Paris, and from Tours it tried to breathe new life into French resistance by proclaiming a *levée en masse*.[20] This measure soon brought large numbers of Frenchmen into the field, but they were without adequate training and equipment. The German armies were also large, better trained, better equipped, and better led. Even so, French resistance with its armed horde delayed German victory until January, 1871, when Paris fell. This experience taught Moltke that even an improvised citizen mass army was more formidable than a badly led, smaller professional force.[21] With better training, leadership, and equipment the French mass army might have turned the tide of battle or at least fought the Germans to a stalemate. Instead, a united Germany emerged beyond the Rhine and the Prussian General Staff assumed control over a new *Kaiserheer* (Imperial Army).

Although the experiences of 1866 and 1870 had proved his doctrine of encirclement, Moltke did not delude himself into believing that he had found a magic formula for victory. His understanding of war was too profound for him to believe that any single tactical pattern or strategic system could insure success. He was fond of reminding his officers that "in war as in art there is no general rule," [22] at least none that would hold true regardless of time and circumstance. But Moltke was also aware that both the 1866 and 1870 campaigns had revealed the Army's logistical limits and how those limits might govern the success or failure of the Kesselschlacht doctrine for the future. In 1866 supplies had been rushed to the railheads in such abundance that they quite overwhelmed the capacity of the old-fashioned horse-drawn wagons to move them quickly to where the marching armies needed them. As it happened, the Austrians played into Prussian hands by massing so near the frontier that their main forces could be engaged before the strain proved too severe. The Prussian system was improved in 1867 by the establishment of a Supply Transportation Inspectorate, which greatly improved the co-ordination of the movement of supplies to the front; but the Prussians could not entirely escape the consequences of having to rely on horse-drawn supply transport beyond the railhead. Upon mobilization against France in 1870, the Prussian-German Army established three (later four) Route Inspectorates, each having its own Inspector General of Communications responsible for the transportation of supplies and reinforcements to the three German armies. Nine trunk lines led to the frontier, and between July 24 and August 3 a total of 1,200 trains passed over them, carrying 350,000 men, 87,000 horses, and 8,400 wagons and guns. [23] Generally speaking, the troop deployment went smoothly, but (as in 1866) the bottlenecks at the railheads constricted the flow of supplies. Many cars were immobilized by the long delays resulting from having to wait for wagons to make the staged trips to the advancing army corps. By September 5, just after the battle of Sedan, the Second Army's railroads had 2,300 loaded cars standing idle on sidings with 16,830 tons of provisions—enough to supply the Second Army for twenty-six days—while many soldiers of the

Second Army were living off captured enemy supplies. In the case
of the First Army, its Route Inspectorate began with a reserve of
2,000 wagons in July, but wear and tear reduced the reserve to
just twenty wagons by mid-October.[24] Shortages in horses and
wagons, their relatively low load capacities compared with the
railroads, and their low speed relative to that of marching troops
repeatedly created logistical difficulties for Moltke's armies; at times
only the capture of supplies from the French on a large scale kept
the Germans going.[25] The logistical strain continued for some time
even after Paris was invested; by then Moltke's armies were over
two hundred miles from German railheads, and most of the rail
lines in northeastern France had been destroyed or sabotaged.[26] Only
one line was in full operation during the fall of 1870—a railway
running from Strasbourg—and, as a result, the supplies delivered
from Germany met only half the requirement.[27] However, the mobile
phase of German operations was largely over and the troops invest-
ing Paris could forage off the countryside. Still, Moltke could hardly
avoid the conclusion that the tenuous nature of German logistics
deep in France might have brought about a different result against
a more resolute, better armed, and better led opposition. The 1866
and 1870 campaigns left him with an enlarged understanding of the
relatively short striking range, the limited endurance, the logistical
inflexibility of the German Army beyond the railheads, and the
need to tailor doctrine and strategy to logistical limitations.

Moltke was also aware that special circumstances—both military
and diplomatic—had played a vital role in Prussia's victories over
Austria and France. Bismarck's diplomacy had allowed the Prussian General Staff to concentrate the whole of German strength on
one front at a time; enemy leadership had proved greatly inferior
to the Prussian, especially in the realms of prewar planning and
mobilization; and in neither Austria nor France had the Germans
faced a Nation in Arms from the outset of hostilities. But in the
years after the Franco-Prussian War the development of the European alliance systems made single-front wars unlikely for the future,
and political developments forced the military planners of Imperial
Germany to be increasingly preoccupied with the possibility of a two-
front war with France and Imperial Russia. Furthermore, after
1871 both France and Russia adopted their own versions of the

Nation in Arms and some form of a general staff on the Prussian model; Moltke could no longer count on a clear superiority in leadership or organization. Finally, a rising line of French frontier fortifications made a decisive German strategic stroke in the West, à la 1870, increasingly unlikely, while the vast territories and human resources of Russia also made rapid victory in the East unlikely. In brief, the unique military and diplomatic circumstances of 1866 and 1870 no longer obtained, and without them much of Prussian Germany's former military advantage was lost.

Moltke grasped the implications of the new circumstances in which Imperial Germany found itself. He pragmatically accepted the conclusion that German manpower and resources would be inadequate to defeat France and Russia completely in a two-front war. Believing that military strategy, like political strategy, must be "the art of the possible," Moltke planned operations which might create a favorable military situation in which to negotiate a compromise peace. From 1879 to 1890 Moltke based all his strategic planning on the assumption of a limited victory over France and Russia, a goal also in line with Bismarck's policy, which sought no more territorial gains in Europe. The German Army would remain on the strategic defensive in the West at the outset of hostilities in order to take advantage of the narrower and therefore more defendable frontier with France, which had been greatly strengthened by the annexation of Alsace-Lorraine. In the East, Moltke planned a limited "spoiling" offensive against the enemy in Russian Poland, a stroke that could be co-ordinated with an attack by Germany's new Austrian ally on the exposed Polish bulge in Russian territory.[28] Yet Moltke did not expect a total victory in the East; he was aware that geography favored Russian withdrawal to avoid encirclement and that the operating radius of the German Army was too short to allow it to pursue the enemy armies into the Russian interior. He declared in 1879 that to follow up a victory in Poland by a pursuit into the Russian interior would be of no interest to the Germans, but that a Polish victory would enable the General Staff to move the greater part of its forces to the Rhine, using suitable railway connections. Once the German armies were concentrated in the West, Moltke probably hoped to draw the French armies into a trap in Lorraine (his original plan in 1870 for the Rhineland), but this time he did not expect a total victory. After beating and repelling the enemy, Moltke believed that it must be left to diplomacy to achieve a compromise peace settlement.[29]

Schlieffen and the Doctrine of Encirclement

Moltke's assumptions and limited aims after 1879 were not shared by all members of the General Staff, and by 1890 a strongly dissenting view had appeared whose principal representative was General Alfred von Schlieffen. Schlieffen believed that Germany could totally defeat France and Russia even in a two-front war, provided the proper strategy was followed, and he had enormous faith in the doctrine of encirclement. He had a distressing tendency to divorce military from political problems and to look at Germany's dilemma almost as a strategic exercise. His enormous absorption with his profession won him the respect of younger General Staff officers who, toward the end of Schlieffen's career, tended to revere him as the "grand old man." The General Staff's tendency to seek a total military solution to the problem of a two-front war was restrained while Moltke remained Chief of the General Staff, but the death of the cautious Kaiser William I in 1888 and the accession to the throne of his headstrong grandson, William II, brooked ill for the future of the Second Reich. William II's clashes with Bismarck over policy led to the dismissal of the Iron Chancellor in 1890, and the new Kaiser gave himself over to unabashed militarism and an uncritical faith in the military superiority of the Imperial Army. As a result of these influences both within and without the Army, Moltke perceived in his final years a new and disturbing spirit among younger General Staff officers—a spirit of arrogance and narrow-minded professionalism which gave him anxiety until the night of his death in 1891. By that date Moltke had already retired and the new Kaiser had appointed Schlieffen as his successor.[30]

From 1891 to 1905 Schlieffen remolded German strategy in the image of his own cast of thought. He departed from Moltke's ideas first by setting the goal of total victory in the event of a two-front war with France and Russia. Schlieffen readily saw some of the great difficulties such an aim imposed, but he believed total victory was possible if the German Army could rapidly overwhelm one foe

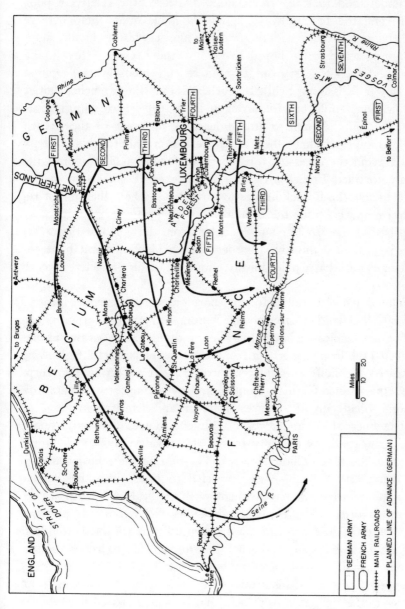

4. The Schlieffen Plan of 1905.

at the outset and then quickly reconcentrate to deal with the second. He understood that the tremendous distances, the relatively poor roads, and the few railways in Russia made quick victory there unlikely, and, after considering various alternatives, he finally chose a strategy whereby he hoped to destroy the French Army in the West and then to carry out a rapid redeployment by rail against the slower Russians. Schlieffen believed that the French frontier fortifications could be circumvented by a surprise wheeling movement through Belgium to attack the flank and rear of the French armies mobilized along the Franco-German frontier. This strategy would avoid the necessity for a German frontal assault against the highly fortified French frontier, which, even if successful, would merely drive the French armies toward Paris, where they might reorganize and continue the struggle. But if the French armies were surprised at the frontier and encircled from the north at the outset or driven against the Swiss border, then Schlieffen might hope for a super-Sedan that would quickly eliminate further effective French resistance.[31]

Schlieffen's plan called for an enormous concentration of forces opposite the Belgian-Luxembourg border—thirty-five corps divided among five armies—while only five corps divided between two armies protected the Franco-German frontier. Once the powerful right wing advanced, Schlieffen would reinforce it by transferring two corps from the Franco-German frontier and by adding six "Ersatz" divisions (made up of reserves of older and semitrained men) to protect lines of communication. This enormous right wing, finally numbering perhaps eighty infantry and cavalry divisions,[32] would pivot on the Metz-Thionville area. The two northernmost armies—the First and Second—were expected to break into the Belgian plains and spring the envelopment west of the Meuse with sixteen infantry corps and five cavalry divisions. Schlieffen was prepared to violate the so-called Maastricht Appendix of the Netherlands in order to give his two northernmost armies plenty of room for maneuver and to bypass the Liège bottleneck. He hoped to secure the unopposed passage of his armies through Belgium by offering guarantees to the Belgian government, but he was prepared to use force if necessary. The small Belgian Army could not long delay the German advance, and the British might be less likely to intervene in fulfillment of their pledges to Belgium if presented with a *fait accompli*. If a British army did appear in Belgium, Schlieffen knew it was bound to be small and thought it could be driven along with the Belgian Army to the coast or to Antwerp, where it could be cooped up as securely as if it were in its own island.[33]

Schlieffen's plan was nothing if not breath-taking, and not a small consideration in its success would be logistics. Gerhard Ritter has pointed out that when the chain of obstacles in Belgium had been overcome and the flank threat from Antwerp was warded off, the Germans still faced the enormous problem of sufficiently supplying the right wing, on whose rapid advance everything really depended. This wing had to achieve prodigious feats of marching and fighting, and there was great danger that it might become quickly exhausted. From the time that Schlieffen conceived of his plan, this had been one of his major worries.[34] The problem of logistics had actually increased since Moltke's day, not diminished, and Schlieffen was planning a strategic march that dwarfed anything that Moltke had conducted. The scope of Schlieffen's logistic dilemma may be understood by reviewing the logistics of the age. As has already been seen, in the mid-nineteenth century the railroad had permitted the movement of troops and supplies on an unprecedented scale and at an unprecedented speed, but this advantage ended at the railhead. Beyond the railhead, unless one's own railways could be extended or the enemy's railroads exploited, the troops had to depend on their legs, and guns and supply wagons had to be drawn by horses. As early as 1866 the Germans introduced a system of staged supply to improve the efficiency of the movement of supplies from the railhead to the front, but soon found that the efficiency of even this system began to decline beyond a certain distance from the railhead. The chief problem was that the animals themselves consumed such great quantities of bulky foodstuffs that the farther from the railhead the supplies had to be transported the more they consisted of food for the horses. Food and ammunition for the troops had to be reduced proportionately, and, as any eighteenth-century soldier knew, a point could be theoretically reached where the animals were hauling only their own fodder. Since the quantity of supply needed by the troops was in direct ratio to the size of the armies and the firing speed of their weapons, the distance over which animal-powered transport could maintain an adequate flow of supply was actually diminishing by the beginning of the twentieth century. The results of this trend have been well treated by G. C. Shaw in his study of supply. Shaw wrote on the eve of World War II that down to his day the supply system used by the great manpowered armies had shackled real maneuverability to the steadily dwindling distance between the railhead and the troops. Advancing forces were tied to a constantly shortening "umbilical cord of supply." [35] By Schlieffen's day the ammunition requirement had sharply mounted with the appearance of repeating rifles, machine guns, and rapid-fire artillery. The growing ammunition requirement in turn increased the need for more wagons and horses to operate beyond the railhead for a given number of men, with a corresponding increase in the demand for animal fodder. By 1914 the German First Army alone—the northernmost in Schlieffen's plan—used 84,000 horses with a fodder requirement of 1,848,000 pounds *per day,* or enough to fill nearly eighty boxcars or 924 wagons. This requirement was, of course, in addition to enough food to feed 260,000 men, and enough ammunition to supply as many rifles, 784 artillery pieces, and 324 machine-guns.[36] The result of this supply burden was that an army corps could not operate at peak efficiency over twenty-five miles from the nearest railhead, nor could even minimal supply requirements be met from the rear at distances greater than fifty miles.[37] For the Schlieffen plan to work logistically, the Germans would have had to seize the Belgian and French railroads as they advanced and repair them fast enough to keep the railheads within efficient operating range of the advancing armies. But the risk would have been tremendous and even the excellent *Eisenbahntruppen* (Railroad Troops) might find the problem insoluble for the two northernmost armies if numerous rail repairs were required or if the armies simply marched too rapidly for extensions of the rail lines to keep up. Yet speed was the essence of Schlieffen's planned envelopment maneuver.

Hardly a lesser logistical consideration in Schlieffen's plan was the march distances involved. The First Army on the extreme right was to march on Brussels, then wheel southwest toward Abbeville, and finally to cross the Seine between Paris and the Channel coast. By the time it reached the Seine it would have covered three hundred miles. To its left, inside the wheel, the Second and Third armies would have covered about two hundred miles apiece by the time they reached the Marne just east of Paris; the Fourth Army about a hundred and fifty miles; and only the Fifth Army—the hinge of the Metz-Thionville pivot—would have less than one hundred miles behind it before the main enemy body would be theoretically encountered. Normally, a corps could march fifteen miles a day for three days and then required a day of rest.[38] But, in order to give the French no time to redeploy their armies to counter his encirclement, Schlieffen allowed the First Army no days of rest and a schedule of about three weeks' marching time at not less than fifteen miles a day. Such marches were bound to prove grueling and especially hard on the reservists, who might have had no more than two weeks after mobilization to acclimate themselves before marching. Inherent in Schlieffen's plan was the danger that the right wing armies would be simply too exhausted to give a good account of themselves when the decisive battle finally took place.

The March to the Marne, 1914

Schlieffen retired at the beginning of 1906 and was succeeded as Chief of the General Staff by Helmuth von Moltke the younger, nephew and namesake of the famous Moltke. The younger Moltke modified Schlieffen's plan by increasing the forces protecting the Franco-German border to eight infantry corps plus the six Ersatz divisions originally intended for the right wing armies. He also cancelled the planned transfer of two corps from the Franco-German border to reinforce the right wing as it advanced. Under the original plan, the ratio had been seven to one in favor of the right wing; Moltke's changes reduced it to three to one in favor of the right wing.[39] Moltke also dropped the idea of violating Dutch neutrality in order to have more room to maneuver at the Liège Gap, thus requiring the First and Second armies to make an initial advance through a narrow funnel. Finally, he subtracted one division from the ten divisions that Schlieffen had assigned to the Eighth Army to delay the Russians in the East. Schlieffen was willing to strengthen the armies protecting the Franco-German border but not at the expense of the forces he had planned to use in the right wing, and he died in January, 1913, uttering, according to legend, a final warn-

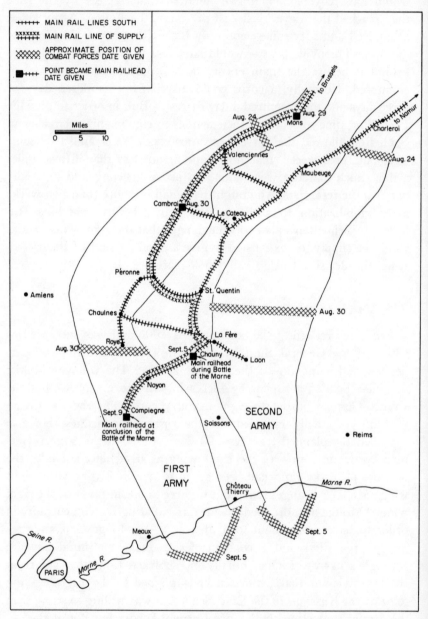

5. The March of the First and Second German Armies to the Marne, 1914.

ing: "It must come to a fight. Keep the right wing strong!" The First World War broke out in August, 1914, and during the August–September campaign the younger Moltke further weakened the right wing armies by detaching two corps as reinforcements for the East, where the Russians had launched an unexpected early offensive.[40] Thus the later legend that the younger Moltke's changes in Schlieffen's "master plan" and errors in execution led to German failure at the Marne in September. But neither changes in the original plan nor errors in execution were chiefly responsible for the 1914 failure. That failure was inherent in the logistical, speed, and endurance limits of the 1914 Army and the blindness of both Schlieffen and his successor to those limits.

In August, 1914, the German armies, after detraining along the Belgian-German border, made their way through Belgium by forced marches as planned, but not quickly enough to prevent the French High Command from shifting its armies (earlier defeated in their own frontal attack against the German frontier) westward on the excellent rail network between the frontier and Paris. While the Germans moved on foot into northern France, many French divisions rode to their new deployment areas along the Marne, where in September they and the British Expeditionary Force (BEF) engaged the exhausted Germans in a battle that wrecked all of Schlieffen's expectations. Directly involved in these events were General Alexander von Kluck, Commanding General, First Army; his Chief of Staff, General Hermann Joseph von Kuhl; and the First Army's Deputy Chief of Staff for Supply and Logistics, Colonel Walter Friedrich Adolf von Bergmann.

After the war Kuhl and Bergmann composed a monograph (to which Kluck wrote the introduction) on the logistics of the First Army in the 1914 Marne campaign.[41] The Kuhl-Bergmann document provided much of the source material for at least two U.S. Army War College analytical studies in the 1930s,[42] the implications of both being that Schlieffen's plan (or Moltke's version of it) was impracticable on logistical grounds. The analytical studies stressed that the Germans had been too dependent on the railroads and animal-drawn supply transportation and that only a much more motorized army could have been successful from the strategic point of view.

The First Army's march from the Meuse to the Marne via Brussels was approximately three hundred miles in length. The average daily distance covered was slightly over sixteen miles, an average that includes days of fighting such as occurred at the Gette River, at Mons, and at Le Cateau. The problems of supplying an army moving this fast and over such a distance proved tremendous. Although the Germans had elaborate supply procedures, in their postwar monograph Kuhl and Bergmann admit that special difficulties arose on account of the extraordinary rapidity of the advance, with which the reconstruction of the railways could not keep up. One of these special difficulties was, of course, the unco-operative attitude of the Belgians, who demolished their railroads as they retreated and tenaciously defended the fortress guarding the key rail center of Namur. Fortunately for the Germans, most Belgian demolitions on the line from Liège to Brussels were hasty and crude, and energetic work by the Eisenbahntruppen restored service. Nevertheless, after the fall of Brussels and the beginning of the German wheel to the south, the shorter line from Liège to Maubeuge via Namur was still blocked, and the First and Second armies found themselves depending primarily on a single trunk rail line from Brussels. This continued to be the case even after the two armies reached French territory. This line ran from Brussels south through Mons, Valenciennes, and Cambrai, and the Eisenbahntruppen had it in operation as far south as Chauny when the battle of the Marne was fought. But at that point the principal German railhead for the First and Second armies was nearly fifty miles from the scene of action. The Kuhl-Bergmann monograph also makes clear that for much of the time over the preceding two weeks the First Army had been beyond the range of efficient supply from the railhead. For instance, by August 24 when it was forcing the Mons Canal, the railhead supplying it had only reached Louvain, a situation which placed the First Army about forty miles (or three animal-marches) from its life-line. On August 30, when the railhead was advanced to Cambrai, the distance was reduced to twenty-five miles, but at this distance the First Army was just on the edge of full operating efficiency, and for nearly a week previous it had been at distances too great to provide supplies efficiently. The chief problems, besides oc-

casional enemy demolitions along the railroad and the defense of
rail centers, were that the supply system depended too much on the
use of animal transportation and that the amount of ammunition
to be transported was much greater than had been foreseen. These
problems constituted an insupportable burden for the whole transport service.[43]

With the increasing demand for ammunition, food for the troops
and fodder for the horses had to be proportionately reduced. In
any other season of the year this situation might have produced a
German logistic collapse far north of the Marne, but the Germans
were lucky in that the war had broken out in late summer and the
First Army was passing through the Belgian plain. Kuhl and Bergmann write that it was a decided advantage to the Germans that the
advance took place in a rich country and during a favorable season
of the year. As a rule the oat-shocks that stood in the field or other
standing forage could be fed to the horses, and whenever possible
the troops loaded as many sheaves on their wagons as the latter had
room for.[44] Thus, in an improvised fashion, fodder was supplied to
the horses. Nevertheless, this experience shows that had the Schlieffen plan been attempted as originally designed or at a less favorable
time of the year, the results would have been almost certainly cata-
strophic for German horse-drawn supply.

Food for the troops was also improvised, according to Kuhl and
Bergmann. Increasingly the troops foraged at night around their
bivouac areas and used all the food they could find in towns and
cities en route. On August 22, the Germans ordered the city and
province of Brussels to furnish enough food supplies to cover at
least one day's requirements for four army corps. Still, bread supplies
failed to keep pace with the advance as the field bakeries had been
unable to halt long enough to complete the process of baking at the
various places where they were set up.[45] In consequence, the food
supply was uncertain and sometimes inadequate, adding to the attrition in strength and energy caused by the incessant marching.

The Great General Staff was not unaware of the First Army's
logistical problems and those of its neighboring armies, and from
his headquarters at Coblentz the Chief of the General Staff tried to
exploit every resource to aid the advance. The German Army began

the war with only 4,000 motor vehicles, but, as the advantages of motor transport were increasingly apparent during the drive to the Marne, the Germans pressed into service civilian motor vehicles of every description.[46] These improvised motor columns repeatedly bridged the gap between marching troops and the railheads—much as they did on an enormously expanded scale during World War II— but in 1914 the motor industry was in its infancy, and nothing like enough motor transport was available to supply the needs of a million men and half a million horses.

If the German supply situation was precarious during the march to the Marne, the exhaustion of the troops was perhaps even more critical for the outcome. Kuhl and Bergmann testify in their monograph that there is no doubt but that the troops suffered from over-exertion. Ever increasing march performances were exacted from them in order to maintain schedule, and the IV Reserve Corps, although its troops were not seasoned for the road, had to keep up with the active corps of the First Army. This grueling ordeal went on without remission from August 17, when the First Army completed its crossing of the Belgian border, until September 4, when it approached the Marne. On the eve of the battle of the Marne, the troops were so played out that, according to Kuhl and Bergmann, the various unit commanders pointed out to their superiors, with increasing emphasis, the unfortunate effect on discipline and readiness for action caused by such extraordinary march performances.[47] The result is well-known, although the role of logistics in the German defeat at the Marne is not always given sufficient prominence. For not only had the German right wing armies failed to find the flank and rear of the enemy, but the masses of men and horses who composed them had outdistanced their supplies and marched themselves to the point of exhaustion.[48] German defeat was almost certain from the moment when the French had been able to disengage from the frontier and to redeploy their forces by rail, but the failures of German speed, supply, and endurance were equally important. Schlieffen's plan, in its original form or as Moltke modified it, proved to be nothing more than a huge gamble against long odds and with a blind eye for the limitations of the German foot-bound forces; the mistakes of the younger Moltke and his subordinates both before and during the campaign merely compounded the problem.

The World War after the Marne

Moltke was relieved as Chief of the General Staff after the failure at the Marne and a fifty-mile German withdrawal to the Aisne, and his successor—General Erich von Falkenhayn—took up the offensive in the West again. During the fall of 1914 the Germans and Allies tried to outflank each other toward the Channel,[49] but this so-called "Race to the Sea" ended in a dead heat on the coast above Nieuport. By the end of the year the war on the Western front had settled down to a stalemate along entrenched lines that ran from the neutral Swiss border to the North Sea. The next three years saw "war without flanks," in which the frontal assaults of both sides failed repeatedly against machine guns, barbed wire, trenches, dugouts, and great concentrations of defensive artillery. Sometimes these great frontal attacks, both Allied and German, pressed the other side back, but the defenders always restored their front somewhere in the rear. The meager gains achieved (over most of the front the line did not shift more than ten miles either way for nearly three years) usually took a fearful toll of lives. Whatever the errors in Schlieffen's ideas, the experience of war proved him right in believing that frontal attacks could not bring about a rapid decision with prewar weapons and tactics.

Actually, the opening phase of the war in the East showed the Moltke-Schlieffen encirclement doctrine was sound, given certain conditions. A single German army—the Eighth under generals Paul von Hindenburg and Erich Ludendorff—used the excellent rail system in East Prussia to foil the invasions of two Russian armies, which, in contrast, lacked adequate rail support, moved more slowly, and failed to keep in effective contact. The Eighth Army was able to surprise and encircle one Russian army near Tannenberg in late August, 1914, thereby achieving the only complete Kesselschlacht victory of World War I. Two weeks later another rapid redeployment by rail permitted the Eighth Army to defeat the second Russian army through a flanking maneuver at the Masurian Lakes.[50] These battles demonstrated that the German doctrine was workable when the Germans could use their own railways, their enemy could be brought to battle near the German railheads, and where there was

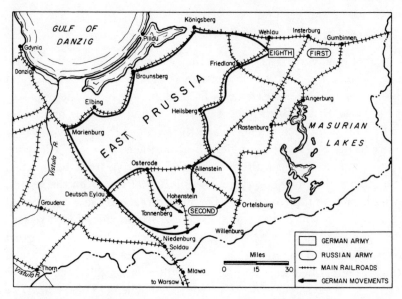

6. Campaign in East Prussia, 1914. Movements of German Eighth Army Culminating in the Battle of Tannenberg.

plenty of room for maneuver. A German offensive in Poland during 1915 inflicted still another severe defeat on the Russians, but, as the elder Moltke and Schlieffen had foreseen (and Falkenhayn came to realize), the enormous distances in the East, the poor roads, and the scarcity of railways made impossible a rapid pursuit of the retreating Russians and a quick conclusion to the Eastern campaign.[51] Thus, in the East, logistical limitations on the German Army made encirclement and annihilation of the Russian armies impossible, while in the West a tactical stalemate blocked German success. The 1914–1918 War turned into a dreaded struggle of attrition that gradually drained Germany's resources in men and matériel.

The Germans struggled valiantly with these problems during the course of the war and eventually made important progress toward tactical solutions. The unwieldy 1914 "square" divisions with their cumbersome brigade headquarters and four infantry regiments were gradually streamlined to the "triangular" divisions of three infantry regiments of three battalions each and one artillery regiment. The smaller, more maneuverable divisions helped restore a necessary degree of tactical flexibility, and by April, 1917, a total of 241 triangular divisions had been put into the field.[52] The Germans also experimented with technical solutions such as poison gas, which they introduced in 1915, but that weapon created about as many problems for the attacker as the defender. The British introduced the tank in 1916, which was a far better move in the direction of breaking the stalemate, but the early tanks—like the early airplanes—were mechanically unreliable, relatively slow and short-ranged, and there was no fully developed doctrine for their use.[53] The Germans made much greater progress in improving the performance of the traditional infantry and artillery arms for assault roles against fortified zones. General Oskar von Hutier experimented with infiltration tactics on the Eastern front, and, after Hindenburg and Ludendorff succeeded to supreme command in the fall of 1916, the development of such tactics accelerated. At the same time the Germans put great emphasis on more mobile infantry weapons, and during 1916 and 1917 they re-equipped their foot soldiers with light machine guns, light trench mortars for indirect firing, and flamethrowers—weapons which in general increased the offensive capabilities of infantry against strong defensive positions. As terrible as episodes such as Verdun proved to be, the Germans learned many useful lessons from them about the employment of artillery and infantry.[54] By the fall of 1917 the new tactical system had been developed sufficiently for a major test on the Italian front at Caporetto. Using the new techniques, twelve German and Austrian divisions broke through the enemy lines and advanced fifty miles. In the spring of 1918, when, after Russia's final collapse from internal revolution, Ludendorff was at last able to concentrate most of the German Army in the West, the threat to the Allies lay not only in the concentration of German forces but in vastly improved German assault tactics, organization, and weapons.[55]

The early successes of the "Ludendorff Offensives" in the spring of 1918 demonstrated that the Germans had finally hit upon methods which under certain conditions permitted large-scale breakthroughs on the Western front. The German recognition that attacking infantry must now be organized into "combat teams" of all arms had led the General Staff to create special battalions of Storm Troops to lead the attack, using the new weapons and infiltration tactics. In addition to light machine guns, flamethrowers, and light mortars, each battalion was supported by two batteries (that is, eight guns) of light artillery for direct firing which could be maneuvered over the battlefield by hand. The Storm Troops did not seek at once to achieve wide breakthroughs in the enemy front but sought to make narrow penetrations at weak points in his lines between enemy machine-gun nests. When they had infiltrated the enemy's trenches at these points, they attacked the enemy strong points from flank and rear. The Storm Troop assaults were preceded by intense but relatively short artillery barrages so as not to give away the place of intended attack. When a breach in the enemy lines opened, German reserves moved through to turn a tactical success into the beginnings of a strategic victory. The General Staff had not forgotten the Kesselschlacht doctrine: one of the breakthrough experts of the Ludendorff era wrote after the war that the breakthrough was "only a preparatory move, which may inflict heavy penalty upon the enemy," but "the final victory can only be achieved by subsequent operations of encirclement." [56]

The new fire and maneuver tactics of the German infantry, supported by brief, intense, but accurate artillery barrages, nearly won the war in the West between March and June, 1918. On March 21 in the first of the Ludendorff Offensives, 6,100 German guns overwhelmed 2,500 British guns; this was followed by an attack of forty-one German infantry divisions against eleven and a half British divisions. Such odds could have been resisted earlier in the war, but so much weight, intensified by the new tactics and weapons, ripped open the British front in less than a day and permitted a German advance that nearly reached the vital rail junction at Amiens. If the German drive could have been sustained and Abbeville reached at the mouth of the Somme, the Allied front would have been split, the British and Belgian armies separated from the French, and the British and Belgian troops pinned inside a great beachhead on the coast—a situation remarkably similar to that of 1940 before Dunkirk. But, as in 1914, failing logistics robbed the Germans of complete success. The Allies shifted forces by rail to seal off the breach faster than German reinforcements and supplies could exploit it on foot. Once more human and animal speed and endurance were prime factors in the outcome. Horse-drawn wagons and guns had trouble negotiating the broken terrain, and the problem of rapidly extending the railways was as great as ever.[57] After driving a salient into the enemy's lines forty miles deep, the German offensive faded out in early April.[58] Attempts to revive it during the rest of the month also failed, and by May Ludendorff was planning to take advantage of the fact that the enemy had shifted so much of his strength to that sector that a surprise blow against the French along the Aisne might be successful. On May 27 a second great offensive caught the Allies by surprise; the Germans crossed the Aisne and advanced forty miles in three days.[59] But exhaustion, lagging supply, and, this time, American reinforcements along the Marne finally brought the offensive to a halt in June. A last offensive was attempted in July, but the German Army was played out.[60] Thereafter, the Allies had the initiative. Nevertheless, the new German assault tactics had been proved, and Ludendorff's drives came close to winning the war; only the same limits on endurance and supply that had wrecked German operations in 1914—plus heavy American reinforcement of the Allied armies—denied the German Army final victory in the spring of 1918.

After the initiative passed to the Allies in July, the new Allied generalissimo, Ferdinand Foch,[61] struck back with the enormous advantages of a growing stream of American reinforcements [62] (two million U.S. troops were in Europe by November), a growing matériel superiority, and the knowledge that the German Army had been exhausted by its own offensives. Foch did not attempt massive breakthroughs followed by deep penetrations, but rather grinding, methodical battles of attrition, which placed no insurmountable burden on Allied logistics.[63] By September, the German Army in the West, although still on foreign territory, was heavily outnumbered, poorly supplied, and had little hope of final victory. In the same month an Allied offensive in the Balkans shattered the forces of Germany's Bulgarian ally, and in October an Italian offensive routed the exhausted Austro-Hungarian Army. By then the four-year old British naval blockade had brought the German economy to a near standstill, and hunger stalked the land. Unable to hold the Western front and support its allies at the same time, and near the point of economic exhaustion, the Second Reich collapsed with great suddenness in early November. Internal revolution drove the Kaiser into exile. The new republican government hastily sought peace on Allied terms. All that remained of the defeated Kaiserheer was the old Officer Corps and an imperfect but promising doctrine of war.

Birth of the Blitzkrieg

Seeckt and the Revised Doctrine

The task of organizing the postwar German Army or *Reichsheer* [1] was entrusted to General Hans von Seeckt, a member of the old General Staff and a soldier determined to save as much of the old military tradition for the new army as possible. The Treaty of Versailles forbade the Great General Staff or any similar institution for the Reichsheer, but Seeckt saw that neither the treaty nor the nature of the institution made impossible the use of the General-Staff-with-Troops concept in the new army. [2] He proceeded to organize the new *Heeresleitung* (Army Command) so that a professional soldier rather than the head of state (as formerly under the Kaiser) should command the Army, while an army general staff disguised as the *Truppenamt* (Troop Office) was concerned with purely operational and training matters and with assisting the *Chef der Heeresleitung* (Chief of the Army Command) and the higher field commanders.

In the postwar period the Truppenamt tried to understand the causes of the great catastrophe that had overtaken Germany in the First World War. Clearly, that war had turned unexpectedly into an unwanted struggle of attrition, and this extended struggle had resulted in turn from German failure to defeat the French quickly and decisively in 1914. German inquiry therefore began with the war plans of 1914 and their execution. Eventually, in reconsidering German performance up to the battle of the Marne, the Truppenamt saw the Kaiserheer's failure in terms of instrumentation rather than in doctrine. It did not challenge the Schlieffen view that total victory had been possible, nor did it reconsider the wisdom of the elder Moltke's strategy for limited victory. Instead, it assumed that technical failure, not faulty strategy or doctrine, was the chief cause of the initial defeat. The failure of 1914 seemed due to three major errors or limitations: (1) the failure to interfere with French mobilization; (2) the failure to prevent French redeployment; and (3) the failure to recognize the limits on foot-bound and horse-drawn armies for carrying out encirclement maneuvers. If the Moltke-Schlieffen doctrine was to be applied successfully in the future, the leadership of the new Reichsheer believed, these limitations would have to be overcome.[3]

While attempting to work out answers to these three problems of the Kesselschlacht, the Truppenamt was also led, by the restrictions of the Treaty of Versailles, to place emphasis on speed and maneuver. The treaty temporarily made a mass army of the traditional type impossible and thus pushed German planners in the direction of a mobile warfare for defensive purposes, for it restricted the Reichsheer to 96,000 enlisted men and 4,000 officers, and allowed the formation of no more than seven infantry divisions and three cavalry divisions. The treaty also prohibited fixed fortifications in western Germany and heavy artillery as well as airplanes and tanks. But the new army command saw that prototype tanks and planes might be covertly developed despite the scrutiny of the Inter-Allied Military Control Commission, and trucks could be used for experiments with motorized infantry. In addition, the Germans hoped that a tight concentration of their limited but mobile forces would somewhat offset their inferiority in trained numbers while the treaty was in effect. The Truppenamt was encouraged in this direction by the personal views of Seeckt while Chief of the Army Command from 1921 to 1926. Seeckt minimized mass as a factor and doubted that giant armies of the traditional type could even be maneuvered in accordance with a strategy that sought a rapid decision. He even questioned whether the World War had not proved the Nation in Arms had outlived its usefulness.[4]

Seeckt believed that German experience in both 1914 and 1918 had proved that an effective regular army must in future meet three demands: (1) higher mobility by the fullest possible use of motor transport; (2) a logistical system strengthened by increased motorization which was capable of a continuous replacement of men and material at the front; and (3) a greater degree of independence from the civilian reserves so that the Army might mobilize more rapidly, take the initiative, and perhaps strike before the enemy's Nation in Arms could mobilize.[5] Regarding mobilization, Seeckt held that the call-up of the reserves should follow rather than precede the beginning of hostilities. In this way, he believed, a military force could be constituted which, though unsuited to take part in a war of movement and encirclement, would be well able, after a hurried completion of training and the supply of suitable equipment, to discharge the duties of home defense and to provide from its best elements a continuous reinforcement to the forces in the field.[6] The role of the reserves was rather academic as long as the Treaty of Versailles remained in effect, but, as will be seen, Seeckt's thought in this area powerfully influenced Army leaders after open German rearmament began in 1935.

Seeckt also placed great emphasis on the development of offensive aviation to complement the mobile ground striking force that he had in mind. He had little regard for the more extreme air-power schools of thought of the 1920s, which emphasized either terrorizing the enemy's civilian population or disrupting his economy through industrial bombing. If Seeckt's thinking was tied too securely to traditional concepts for these schools to have much impact, he saw clearly aviation's potential for disrupting an enemy's mobilization, attacking troop concentrations at the front and immediately behind it, and for gaining command of the air at the outset by destroying the enemy air force while at its most vulnerable on the ground. He gave priority to the destruction of the opposing air forces by sudden air attack and believed that once command of the air was assured the German air forces should concentrate their attacks on major troop concentrations, which should prove to be easy and important targets, with the disruption of the enemy's mobilization as the primary objective.[7]

Seeckt's concepts did not, however, have a clear field. There was much discussion in the Reichsheer as to whether the world war had not proved that the day of decisive maneuver was over. Some Reichsheer officers were impressed by the French postwar doctrine of offense, under which lines of tank-supported infantry formed a continuous front of advance. With their flanks protected by natural obstacles and never moving beyond the range of heavy guns, the French lines were always ready to deploy immediately into a defensive position. Though this system allowed only slow movement and required complicated orders so that the artillery could be periodically limbered and moved forward (while the infantry-tank lines halted), some argued that the French system presented no vulnerable flanks, while the nearly deployed infantry-tank lines, supported by massed artillery in the rear, would have tremendous firepower with which to repel any frontal attack. Some German officers claimed that the German tradition of keeping troops in marching order until the main enemy force was encountered (to facilitate maneuver) would now be fatal. They thought that French firepower would shatter the German columns as they tried to deploy and attack without the support of equal masses of artillery. The best thing for the German Army to do, they maintained, was to recognize, as did the French, that fire rather than movement dominated the modern battlefield.[8] As for disrupting the enemy's mobilization and preventing him from getting his mass army into the field, the critics pointed out the uncertainty of weather suitable for air strikes and the difficulty of ground forces penetrating the enemy's frontier fortifications fast enough to disrupt his mobilization. How was it possible, they asked, to carry out encirclement battles under such conditions?

British Solutions

The problem of how to restore maneuver to war interested others besides the Germans, and it was in fact a small group of British military theorists who made the first progress along these lines. The most important for the German Army were General J. F. C. Fuller, Captain B. H. Liddell Hart, and Colonel Giffard Martel. While their ideas differed at points, they shared the conviction that the mechanization, including motorization, of war was the "wave of the future" and contained the answer to the problems of maneuver war. The ideas contained in their books and articles attracted more interest in

Germany than in Britain, however, for British military planners did not expect ever again to send a large British expeditionary force to fight on the European continent.

While General Fuller did not initiate the postwar interest in mechanization in Germany, he did introduce radically new notions about how the tank might be used.[9] Certain German officers found their horizons broadening when, in 1928, Fuller pointed out that until then the tactical employment of the tank had been hampered by trying to harmonize its powers with existing infantry and horse artillery tactics. Fuller suggested that if the tanks were released from such ties, they might be able to exploit their constantly improving speed and striking power to break through the enemy's lines on narrow fronts and to disorganize the enemy's further defense by overrunning his divisional, corps, and army headquarters.[10] Fuller predicted that without co-ordinated command the enemy's front would collapse.

Captain Liddell Hart's ideas also aroused German interest. The keynote of his *The Remaking of Modern Armies* was mobility, for he held with Napoleon that the strength of an army, like the quantity of motion in mechanics, is estimated by the mass multiplied by the velocity. Liddell Hart maintained that the armies of the First World War had become masses without impulsion and that there was urgent need of research for the causes of this stagnant condition and for the speedy application of a remedy.[11] Like Fuller, he foresaw the strategic possibilities of the tank, but unlike Fuller he emphasized motorized infantry as well. He went so far as to say that the invention of the six-wheel truck was a landmark in military evolution, and he argued during the last years of the 1920s that only motorized infantry could keep up with the tanks in their new strategic role. He predicted that the future role of infantry would be as a species of "land-marines," fully integrated into completely mechanized and motorized units for the duties of "mopping-up" and for hill and wood fighting. Above all, he cautioned that motorized movement should not be tied to the pace of the slowest foot-soldier.[12]

Colonel Giffard Martel, whose postwar experiences with various British attempts in mechanization gave him a solid practical as well as theoretical knowledge of mechanical warfare, displayed prophetic powers when in 1931 he wrote that, just as the First World War tank had been developed as an answer to the machine gun, tank design in the future would have to take into account the development of antitank weapons. More striking was his championship of the small tank, or tankette, with which he proposed to put the infantry-man on tracks.[13]

These British thinkers did not produce all the ideas which the German Army used in its pre-1939 mechanized and motorized development, but the dean of the German tank school in the Second World War, General Heinz Guderian, has admitted their importance to German thinking. Guderian, formerly a junior officer of light-infantry, had been transferred in 1922 to the Inspectorate of Transport Troops for his first experience with motorized infantry.[14] The emphasis on mobile defensive war in the event of foreign attack in the early years of the Reichsheer led Guderian to investigate the question of protection for motorized transports and thus into the developing field of tank warfare. The experiments of the British and particularly the writings of the British thinkers cited above caught his attention. Their books and articles excited his interest, for he realized that even then they were trying to make of the tank something more than just an infantry support weapon and to relate it to the growing motorization of the age.[15]

The ideas of Liddell Hart impressed Guderian chiefly because this British writer had emphasized the use of armored vehicles for long-range strokes, operations against the opposing army's communications, and a proposed type of armored division combining tanks and motorized infantry. Guderian was so deeply impressed by these ideas that he tried to develop them in a way practicable for their adoption in the German Army.[16]

Guderian's Solution

Applying British solutions to German problems was not as easy as it might have sounded. The British peacetime army was traditionally small, and after 1918 British military planners prepared it primarily for garrisoning Britain's overseas empire in the tradition of the nineteenth century. Units of motorized infantry and light tanks might be both useful and economical in places such as India, and belated converts from the cavalry could envision such mechanized units sharing the role formerly belonging to the mounted forces.[17] But despite Seeckt's depreciation of mass, any realistic approach to the problems of Continental armies had to be premised on the likelihood that large armies would be needed in the next general European war and that it was unlikely that any European state in the foreseeable future could afford a large all-motorized and mechanized army. Guderian and other Continental soldiers had the task of not only deciding what combination of motorized forces would be most effective, but also of considering what relationship they would have to the nonmotorized or semimotorized forces, which were likely to constitute the mass.

By 1929 Guderian had hit upon the general formula which characterized German armored warfare in the Second World War and which pointed the way toward the proper relationship between the motorized and semimotorized components. Convinced that the trend in the British and French armies of subordinating armor to old-fashioned concepts of infantry and cavalry was wrong, Guderian saw that neither Fuller's solution (tanks alone) nor Liddell Hart's solution (tanks with motorized infantry) was the complete answer. Instead, Guderian conceived of a complete armored, motorized team of combat components of all branches of the Army designed to allow the tanks to fight with full effect.[18] The similarity between this "combat team" concept and the 1918 Storm Troop assault force is not accidental, but Guderian was thinking not only of breakthroughs but of deep strategic penetrations unhindered by the logistic limits of the past. In his vision the panzer division would have every Army combat component represented in some form, but all components would have great range, speed, and stamina. The supporting motorized artillery, infantry, and cavalry were to be so constituted as not to impede the tanks in their natural offensive roles, and ideally they should have the same speed and cross-country performance as the tanks.[19] Guderian was not able to realize his dream immediately or even later in every respect, but he gave the German Army the correct doctrinal insight at a crucial moment. By the time Adolf Hitler came to power in Germany in 1933, further German armored development only awaited support from the government and conversion of Guderian's superiors to the panzer division idea.

Guderian's "armored combat team" idea finally took concrete form when, in 1935, after long debate, the Army High Command permitted Guderian to organize the first three panzer divisions. Each panzer division centered on a tank brigade supported by a motorized infantry brigade, motorized artillery, and other motorized arms and services. Since only light tanks were available in 1935, the two armored regiments in each armored brigade contained a total of 561 machines. The motorized artillery regiment contained towed 105-mm. howitzers, while an antitank battalion was equipped with towed 37-mm. antitank guns. The new divisions also contained armored car battalions for the role of cavalry reconnaissance as well as motorcycle troops. Richard Ogorkiewicz, an armor expert, has written that the panzer division was thus a self-contained combined arms team in which tanks were backed by other arms brought up, as far as possible, to the tanks' standards of mobility.[20]

Between 1938 and 1939 another three panzer divisions were added, and, with the appearance of more powerful tanks, reorganized. Infantry strength was increased from three to four battalions, tank battalions were reorganized into one medium and two light tank companies, and on the eve of the Second World War each panzer division had an authorized strength of 320 tanks. Further reorganizations occurred as the war went on, but in concept the panzer division remained the same, a further evolution of the assault team of World War I but with a strategic as well as tactical capability.[21]

Beck's Role

Conservative soldiers also influenced the German Army's doctrine and organization between the world wars, the most important of them being General Ludwig Beck, Chief of the Truppenamt, beginning in 1933, and then Chief of the Army General Staff during the crucial years of German military expansion between 1935 and 1938. After open rearmament began in March, 1935, the Reichswehr was retitled the *Wehrmacht* (armed forces) and divided into three services: the *Heer* (Army), the *Kriegsmarine* (Navy), and the *Luftwaffe* (Air Force). The Chief of the Army Command became the *Oberbefehlshaber des Heeres* (Commander in Chief of the Army), the Truppenamt became the *Generalstab des Heeres* (Army General Staff), and perforce the Chief of the Troop Office became *Chef des*

Generalstabes des Heeres (Chief of the Army General Staff). The *Oberkommando des Heeres* (Army High Command, or OKH), which included the Army General Staff, along with the high commands of the other two services, fell under the new *Kriegsminister-ium* (War Ministry) and the Minister of War, Field Marshal Werner von Blomberg. General Werner von Fritsch became the Commander in Chief of the Army.

As Chief of Staff of the most important of the three services, Beck's influence was bound to be important. He has been described by one of his deputy chiefs as an overly devout disciple of Schlieffen and the elder Moltke and difficult to persuade to change old methods. Whenever something new had to be done, according to this source, he asked himself how it would have been handled in the past.[22] Beck was at first skeptical about Guderian's proposals for large armored formations, and after the war Guderian claimed that he had to win a long-drawn-out fight with General Beck before he would agree to the setting up of panzer divisions.[23] Beck was more interested in developing the use of conventional arms—especially infantry and artillery—but he was no reactionary, as proved by the famous *Truppenfuehrung* (*Troop Command*), the official statement of Army doctrine produced by a committee of officers chaired by Beck between 1931 and 1932 and officially issued in the fall of 1933.

Troop Command preserved the best facets of the old pre-1914 doctrine and drew sound lessons from the experiences of World War I; its reasoning foreshadowed a good understanding of the future role of armor. The German method of attack contrasted with the slow and formal methods emphasized by the French in their postwar doctrine, as *Truppenfuehrung* shows. Attacking troops were urged to advance quickly and energetically and not to allow hostile artillery fire from considerable distances to hold them up. The hostile batteries were to be silenced quickly by air attacks, counterbattery fire, and armored penetrations. As a rule, the attack was to be carried out by battalion-sized *Kampfgruppen* (combat teams) composed of infantry and artillery, and, where appropriate, of tanks. Whenever possible, these combat teams were to circumvent enemy strong points so as not to hold up the general advance and to permit the strong points to be attacked on their flanks and rear.[24] Guderian had little quarrel with *Troop Command*'s version of the proper relationship between armor and other arms. That version held that tanks might be integrated with infantry for attack under some circumstances, depending upon the nature of the terrain and the character of enemy resistance, but it emphasized that tank forces tend to lose the advantage of greater speed and striking power when they are tied too closely to infantry. Normally, tanks should attempt deep penetrations of the enemy's position in order to put out of action the hostile units—especially artillery—stopping the infantry's attacks, and they should be finally employed with the infantry and supporting artillery to encircle and destroy the enemy. (P. 63)

Beck believed that the Army could not do without the old-fashioned infantry divisions, with their marching troops and horse-drawn guns and wagons, for the foreseeable future because they still provided the necessary "mass of decision." But he too understood that the panzer and other all-motorized maneuver divisions must not be hampered by being too tightly tied in with the old-fashioned elements, however necessary the latter might still be. Within the flexible limits of the emerging doctrine and organization there was still room for Seeckt's and Guderian's relatively small "army of quality and maneuver" to spring the encirclements as well as Beck's "army of mass and defensive firepower" to fight the battles of annihilation. Beck thus fruitfully championed the older forms of war as Seeckt and Guderian championed the new.[25]

These two schools of thought tended to produce relatively few panzer and other motorized divisions and a much larger number of infantry divisions.[26] The comparatively few all-motorized divisions of all types were so geared to the old-fashioned mass that by 1939 the German Army had greater striking power and range than any other in Europe, an advantage achieved not through superior resources but through a better doctrine and better organizational concepts. Indeed, lack of resources in certain respects was in part responsible for this double development. A large, all-motorized army was out of the reach of any European power in the 1920s and 1930s,[27] but in Germany's case the financial and industrial limits were reinforced by a shortage of oil, the life-blood of the gasoline engine. The creation of large armored units would also place heavy requirements on Germany's limited steel production. Beck's qualified enthusiasm for the panzer division idea was prompted by the realization that the concentration of so much of Germany's resources in such units would retard the re-equipping of the infantry divisions [28] and condemn them to continued weak logistics and relatively weak offensive power. Their condition, in turn, might severely limit the application of the revised Kesselschlacht doctrine. Beck was keenly aware that the doctrine of encirclement called not only for forces capable of piercing the enemy's front or quickly turning an exposed flank and then penetrating deeply into his rear, but also for infantry divisions capable of following up quickly to close the encirclements and powerful enough to fight decisive battles. Finally, the Chief of the Army General Staff knew that the Army's competition for Germany's limited resources would have to be waged against the rival claims of Goering's Luftwaffe, Erich Raeder's navy, and (later) Heinrich Himmler's "private army," the *Waffen SS* (Armed SS). [29]

Hitler's Influence

Still another factor which played a major role in shaping the German Army's doctrine and organization on the eve of the Second World War was Hitler's political decision to expand the armed forces as quickly as possible. When Hitler became Chancellor in 1933, the Reichsheer still numbered only seven infantry and three cavalry divisions, possessed no air force, and lacked most of the armaments necessary for a modern army. [30] The Army did possess plans and designs for an expanded force in line with Seeckt's vision of a great German army gradually built up on the firm foundations of the Reichsheer, but neither Seeckt nor his successors as Chief of the Army Command favored a "crash program" of expansion. Because of his need to proceed cautiously at first lest rearmament alarm the Anglo-French powers prematurely, Hitler accepted the Army plans for a covert expansion of the Reichsheer to twenty-one divisions in three years and limited production of armaments outlawed by the Treaty of Versailles. But before these three years were up, Hitler's impatience led him to risk open violation of the treaty. In 1935, he reinstituted conscription, announced the existence of an independent Air Force, and set a new goal for the Army of thirty-six divisions. [31] Hitler's abandonment of caution and his setting of new goals were not wholly welcome to the Army High Command, which believed that a too rapid expansion would result in serious internal defects.[32] Hitler's resulting impatience with this cautious outlook strained relations with the Army still further when even the new goals were substantially increased to fifty divisions.[33] Although Hitler strongly backed motorization and the development of large armored units, his insistence on rapid expansion magnified the oil and steel shortages and limited industrial production for those very purposes. On the other hand, the planned increase in infantry divisions improved Germany's defensive strength and reassured the more conservative generals that the Fuehrer was not betting Germany's entire resources on the as yet untested theories of airplane and tank warfare.

The Blitzkrieg Army

The German Army entered its final form in 1935, after Hitler reintroduced conscription. At that time the German Army had no reserves of the traditional type, and the rotation of conscripts through the regular training program would take a long time to create a true "mass, mobilizable army." The classes of men born in 1901–1913 had received no compulsory training because of the restrictions of the Treaty of Versailles, and there were no facilities for training many age groups at one time.[34] An imperfect but feasible solution was summer and weekend training courses for the older age groups, which were then assigned to *Landwehr* (militia) divisions. Even by 1939, however, only a small proportion of the older age groups had received any training at all,[35] and the twenty-one Landwehr divisions formed in 1936 were of relatively poor quality.[36] In time these divisions would have been filled out by the trained 1914 class and its successors, others would have been added, and all transformed into genuine reserve divisions of the traditional type. But Hitler did not grant this dispensation of time, and, as the danger of war increased from the dictator's own actions, the Army High Command had to reckon with the fact that the reserves were composed largely of inadequately trained and ill-equipped older age groups.

Despite this weakness in the Army's reserves, the Army High Command elected to base its mobilization plans on the time-tested pre-1914 system of *Wehrkreise* (military districts), numbering seven in Germany until 1933. The Wehrkreis commander handled routine administration and training for the active and reserve divisions assigned to his district in peacetime, and upon mobilization he relinquished his territorial responsibilities to a deputy and led his corps (mobilized from the active and reserve infantry divisions in his district) in the field.[37] As more active, reserve, and Landwehr divisions were added, the number of Wehrkreise was increased until by the beginning of 1938 there existed thirteen military districts and three elite nonterritorial corps. These elite corps were composed exclusively of active panzer, motorized infantry, and "light" divisions,[38] and provided the active Army with an offensive potential which was not tied to the slow mobilization of the reserve. The Wehrkreise were responsible to the Army High Command for routine matters and to six *Heeresgruppenkommandos* (Army Group Commands) for tactical control in peacetime. In the event of war and mobilization, the Army Group Commands would be activated as numbered field army headquarters and the mobilized corps would be divided among them for operations.[39] This organization preserved in the new army the traditional elitism found in the former Kaiserheer's Imperial Guard divisions and later in the Storm Troops of World War I by transferring it to the motorized divisions and associating them with an offensive role. Thus quality and quantity were associated with specific tasks and made the new army organization in certain respects highly suitable to the uses of an opportunistic political leadership. This organization was also a faithful reproduction of the blueprint that Seeckt had laid down for the future during his time in office.

From March, 1935, to the beginning of 1939, the number of divisions in the Army increased dramatically from only 21 to 103. The number of active divisions rose from 21 to 52 (5 panzer divisions, 8 other motorized divisions, 38 infantry divisions, and 1 cavalry division), while the various types of reserve divisions (reserve and Landwehr) rose from zero in 1935 to 51 by 1939.[40] Only the 13 panzer, motorized infantry, and light divisions had complete "organic" motor transport for men and supplies. The 38 infantry divisions of the active Army and the 51 infantry divisions of the reserves were dependent for strategic movement on the railroads. Beyond the railheads, their strategic movement had to be carried out on foot while their supplies were hauled in horse-drawn wagons, in motor transport left over from the motorized divisions, and in horse-drawn and motor transport improvised from the civilian economy.[41] Thus the divisions that made up the mass of the 1939 army were in respect to logistics still similar to the German infantry divisions of 1870 and 1914. By September, 1939, on the eve of the outbreak of war, the situation had not materially changed. The only completely motorized divisions in the German Army were 7 panzer divisions,[42] 5 motorized infantry divisions, and 4 so-called "light" divisions.[43] The remainder—90 divisions—were in varying degrees dependent on the railroads and horse-drawn transport for strategic movement.[44]

The Army High Command was sensitive to the logistic weaknesses of the semimotorized infantry divisions and did everything possible to help offset their insufficient motor transport. The Army was empowered upon mobilization to employ the motor vehicles of other government agencies and even those privately owned. For this purpose, every Wehrkreis maintained a current list of all motor vehicles in its district, including those of the German postal service, business corporations, and privately owned automobiles. Another list was maintained of the available horses and horse-drawn transport. The infantry divisions had to rely heavily upon such improvisation to reach their authorized strength in both motorized and horse-drawn transport.[45]

The emphasis generally placed on the motorized and mechanized forces of the German Army not only obscures the fact that the mass of the Army was rather old-fashioned, but does not always make clear how vital motorization was to a strong logistical system. As explained earlier, reliance on the railroad and animal-drawn transportation shackled the fighting elements of every army to a constantly shortening "umbilical cord of supply," to use G. C. Shaw's words. The situation for motorized forces is far more favorable. Internal combustion engines move troops and supplies both faster and more economically relative to the distance covered for a given quantity of fuel. The greater hauling power of any individual engine reduces the number of units and road-space required to move a given quantity of supplies and, with its speed, provides motorized forces with efficient transportation. In addition, the strength and energy of

the troops in the mechanized or motorized division are better con-
served for the task of fighting.[46] The distances over which the mechanized-motorized division may operate from the railhead are vastly
greater and provide a strategic range and flexibility unknown to
divisions wholly or partly dependent on horse-drawn supplies beyond
the railhead. The divisions of the German Army in World War II
that were still partly dependent on the railroad- and horse-drawn
supply system suffered from the same kind of logistic limitations
imposed on the German armies of 1870 and 1914. And because that
part of the Army in 1939 was still by far the most numerous, the
Army High Command did not contemplate the substitution of the
modern, motorized forces for the traditional infantry divisions, but
rather hoped that fast-moving and long-ranged armored and motorized units could spearhead the attack, break through the enemy's
front and penetrate quickly and deeply into his rear, block the
enemy's moves to counter encirclement or escape, and sever his communications. The infantry divisions could then take advantage of the
enemy's disorder and paralysis to reinforce the motorized divisions
in his rear and complete the encirclement from the front. The final
phase would be a battle of annihilation, fought well within the
limited range of the infantry divisions and under conditions that
favored their defensive firepower and offset their relatively weak
logistics.[47] Such was the essence of the revised Kesselschlacht doctrine and the state of the vaunted blitzkrieg army on the eve of the
Second World War.

The Luftwaffe

The organization and doctrine of the German Army on the eve
of the Second World War cannot be completely understood without
at least a cursory discussion of its chief ally and sister-service, the
Luftwaffe. The close co-operation between the Army and Air Force
on the tactical level greatly contributed to the Army's victories in
World War II, but the Luftwaffe's limitations undoubtedly contributed to later Army defeats. Like the Army, the Luftwaffe was a
mixture of strengths and weaknesses.

The Luftwaffe was not made into a completely independent service
until 1935, when Hitler formally denounced the arms limitations of

the Treaty of Versailles, and thus was only four and a half years old when the Second World War began. Only ten years elapsed between its birth and its death, yet it aroused for a time the terror of the world. What were the nature and means of this performance?

The Luftwaffe from its beginnings was much more closely associated with the Nazi movement than either of the two other services, the Army or the Navy. It owed its independence from the Army in part to the fact that its commander in chief, Hermann Goering, was at the same time second only to Hitler as a power in the Nazi Party and in the German government. For such a figure to have taken orders from the Army was inconceivable, and before 1938 Goering showed his independence of his nominal superior, Field Marshal von Blomberg, the Minister of War. After the 1938 reorganization, Goering was in theory as well as in fact responsible only to Hitler, who at that time assumed the title of *Oberbefehlshaber der Wehrmacht* (Commander in Chief of the Armed Forces). Goering was an empire-builder too, and in 1935 he secured for the Luftwaffe control of the *Flakartillerie* (antiaircraft artillery) and in 1938 the *Fallschirmtruppen* (parachute troops).[48]

The doctrine of the emerging Luftwaffe was based on German experience in World War I, and the most influential officers in its fashioning were former commanders in the Kaiserheer's air arm. In 1934 a special staff of the Air Ministry, headed by General Helmuth Wilberg and advised by General Hermann Thomsen, drew up a statement of air doctrine intended to guide the Luftwaffe's development in peace and its employment in war. This doctrinal statement, entitled the *Luftkriegfuehrung* (*The Conduct of Air War*) and issued in 1935 as *Luftwaffe Field Manual No. 16*, recognized four major offensive air missions: air superiority, strategic or independent air operations, interdiction of the battlefield, and close support of the Army. The doctrine rejected the idea that strategic attacks on enemy industry or the terrorizing of his civilian population could alone defeat the enemy—an idea popular in some Western aviation circles—but recognized the value of strategic bombing to disrupt enemy armament production and thereby to assist the Army in gaining a decisive ground victory. The *Luftkriegfuehrung* also stressed the importance of assisting the Army by interdiction of enemy communications (attacks on reserves and supplies moving to the battlefront) and close support (direct attack on the enemy ground forces in co-ordination with Army operations). In essence, the 1934 statement called for an air force that would serve as part of a team rather than as one which would operate independently of the Army and Navy. The *Luftkriegfuehrung* summed up its position on that matter by flatly declaring that decision in war could be brought about only through the combined efforts of all three branches of the military forces.[49]

The first Chief of the Luftwaffe General Staff, General Walter Wever, tried to implement the *Luftkriegfuehrung* doctrine by developing a balanced air force capable of carrying out the four major types of offensive air operations,[50] including destruction of the enemy air forces sufficient to give the Luftwaffe command of the air, and work was begun on a four-engined long-range bomber for strategic operations as well as on medium bombers for interdiction, attack aircraft for close support, and fighters for air superiority. But Wever's influence was removed by a fatal air crash in 1936, and in the same year Ernst Udet, a former stunt flyer and a crony of Goering's, was appointed Chief of the Luftwaffe Technical Office. Udet was fascinated by the possibilities of the dive-bomber, and he influenced both Goering and Albert Kesselring, Wever's successor as Chief of the Luftwaffe General Staff, to cancel work on the strategic bomber and shift emphasis to dive-bomber development. The first dive-bomber models were tried out in the Spanish Civil War during 1937 and 1938, and the Junkers 87 (JU-87), the famous gull-winged, fixed-gear dive-bomber, was selected for mass production. In November, 1938, the first four dive-bomber groups were formed.[51] Enemy air opposition had been weak in Spain, however, and the Luftwaffe failed to take into sufficient account that its bombers tested there had not met with real aerial opposition and that their light defensive armor and armament had not been really probed.[52]

The Army leaders were not unhappy with the new Luftwaffe emphasis on tactical aircraft. They were little interested in a strategic air force for waging a lengthy war of industrial attrition, and like the Luftwaffe's founders they dismissed quick victory by independent air operations as visionary. But they (and the Luftwaffe leaders as well) failed to connect the possibilities in strategic bombers with strategic interdiction of the battlefield. Perhaps this gap in their thinking was due to the small land areas of Germany's most immediate neighbors in the late 1930s (Czechoslovakia, Poland, and France), which reduced range as a factor. Indeed, the Luftwaffe's development (like the Army's) was clearly intended for operations in Central and Western Europe. Neither the Army nor the Luftwaffe leaders gave much thought to the problems of operating outside this theater of operations or how to subdue an enemy protected by water ramparts (Britain) or great land areas (Russia). In this respect at least, the principal Wehrmacht leaders before 1939 could honestly plead not guilty to the charge of preparing aggressive war; if anything, they had prepared too little.

By 1939, besides the dive-bomber, the backbone of the Luftwaffe consisted of short-range medium bombers such as the Dornier 17 (DO-17), the Heinkel 111 (HE-111), and powerful but short-range fighters such as the Messerschmitt 109 (ME-109), and later the light-medium Junkers 88 (JU-88) bomber and the twin-engined Messerschmitt 110 (ME-110) fighter. During the first phases of World War II the Luftwaffe achieved air superiority at the outset of operations simply by launching surprise air strikes and destroying the enemy air forces on the ground; the weaknesses in its defensive bomber armament and armor were not probed because there were really no great air battles. But this system for gaining air superiority faltered against the British in their home island, protected as it was by a small but fine fighter command and an early-warning radar system. The Luftwaffe successfully combined close support with interdiction of the battlefield in the early campaigns, where range was not a major factor and where ground operations were decisive within a few days or weeks. But the breadth and depth of the front in Russia combined with the relatively short striking range of the Luftwaffe resulted in serious failures. Although the Soviet Air Force was caught and destroyed on the ground in the opening round, most of its personnel were successfully evacuated to the East, where Soviet factories out of Luftwaffe range equipped them with better aircraft than that lost at the frontiers. As early as the fall of 1941 the Luftwaffe increasingly encountered an enemy air force that challenged its tactical domination of the battlefield. The attempt to combine close support with interdiction resulted in the Luftwaffe's failing to hit the Russian rail system hard enough at the right places and at the right time, even at the frontier.[53] The Luftwaffe's performance was in part responsible for the successful withdrawal of Russian ground units from the frontier to the interior during the summer of 1941, thus reneging on its promise to be the Army's "third arm of encirclement."

In sum then, the Luftwaffe, like the Army, had more punch than range or versatility, and the two together, in Telford Taylor's words, were "like a skillful and enormously powerful prize fighter, with a short reach and poor endurance."[54]

CHAPTER THREE

Prologue to War

The Hossbach Conference[1]

On November 5, 1937, Adolf Hitler called a secret military conference with the commanders in chief of the armed forces at the Reich Chancellery and there revealed to them for the first time his intention to set out on a deliberate program of territorial expansion that would again make Germany the greatest power in Europe. Hitler told his listeners that unless Germany acquired greater living-space and resources, she was bound to pass out of the ranks of the great powers. The belt of relatively weak East European states created by the 1919 Paris Peace Conference out of the defunct Russian, German, and Austrian empires seemed to Hitler a natural area for German expansion. Hitler admitted that such a policy ran some danger of involving Nazi Germany in war with Britain and France, since neither democracy could afford a German colossus astride Central and Eastern Europe, but he proposed to move against his victims one at a time and at opportune moments when crisis elsewhere prevented their intervention. If quick success could be achieved, Germany's war potential could be greatly increased for a final struggle, if one were necessary, against Britain and France. On Hitler's time-table, Austria and Czechoslovakia came first.[2]

Hitler's announced intentions thoroughly alarmed at least two members of his audience, Field Marshal Werner von Blomberg,

7. Europe in 1935.

the Minister of War, and General Werner von Fritsch, Commander in Chief of the Army. Neither Blomberg nor Fritsch believed that Germany was yet militarily prepared to take grave risks, and both raised objections at the end of Hitler's remarks. They pointed out to Hitler that the Czechs were French allies, and that an attack on Czechoslovakia might lead to war with France and a French invasion of the Rhineland. They also rated the Czech fixed defenses as very strong. Though Hitler replied that he did not intend to move against either Austria or Czechoslovakia until it was clear that intervention by France or Britain was unlikely, the meeting ended on a note of mutual distrust between Hitler and two of his military subordinates.[3]

After the Hossbach Conference, Fritsch informed General Ludwig Beck, Chief of the Army General Staff, of what had happened, and Beck quickly agreed with Fritsch's view that Hitler must be dissuaded from his course if at all possible. With the complicity of the German Foreign Minister, Baron Constantine von Neurath, who shared the views of the two Army leaders, they arranged for Fritsch to meet with Hitler privately on November 9 in order to convince him of the danger of his schemes. This interview went badly, for Hitler was angered by Fritsch's stubborn opposition to his will.[4]

Late in January, 1938, Hitler found sufficient pretexts to dismiss both Blomberg and Fritsch from their offices [5] and on February 4 announced a complete reorganization of the military command levels. The War Ministry was abolished and in its place Hitler created the *Oberkommando der Wehrmacht* (OKW, High Command of the Armed Forces) with himself as *Oberbefehlshaber* (Supreme Commander). He appointed General Wilhelm Keitel his deputy and Chief of the OKW,[6] and somewhat later he made Colonel (later General) Alfred Jodl the Chief of the *Wehrmachtfuehrungsamt* (OKW Operations Office).[7] For Fritsch's replacement as Commander in Chief of the Army, Hitler chose Walter von Brauchitsch, then a corps commander.[8]

The reorganization also extended to the Army General Staff. Although Beck was retained as Chief of the Army General Staff, General Erich von Manstein was transferred from his position as *Oberquartiermeister I* (Deputy Chief for Operations and Planning) to the command of a division in the field. Franz Halder was promoted to the rank of *General der Artillerie* (Lieutenant General) on February 1, and was appointed to Manstein's post on February 4, thus becoming Beck's deputy and his closest coworker on the Army General Staff.[9]

Operation Otto

The reorganization had hardly taken place when Hitler began a campaign of threats and intimidation to force Austria into *Anschluss* (union) with Germany. In 1934 the Fuehrer had attempted a coup to overthrow the Austrian government from within, but Mussolini's Italy had intervened and prevented a Nazi takeover. This time Hitler had prepared his way more carefully, and Mussolini agreed to stand aside. The Anglo-French powers likewise failed to take action, and this campaign reached its climax in March. On March 11, 1938, the first of many OKW directives was issued to the Army High Command (OKH). The opening paragraph began with Hitler's declaration that if other measures proved unsuccessful, he intended to invade Austria with armed forces.[10] The directive caught the

OKH off guard. The previous year the now-defunct War
Ministry had directed the General Staff to prepare plans to prevent
a restoration of the Austrian Hapsburgs (Operation Otto), but
the need for such a contingency plan had seemed so unlikely to the
OKH that, as Halder said, the whole matter was allowed to slide
under the table.[11] The day before the new directive was issued, Jodl
of the OKW Operations Office had asked Beck what preparations
had been made for Operation Otto, and the Chief of the General
Staff had been forced to admit that none at all had been made.
Beck then hastily drafted General Manstein (who had not yet left
the OKH for his new duties) to plan an improvised operation. Beck
and Manstein arranged to mobilize the two Wehrkreise along the
Austrian border and to employ the Second Panzer Division of General Heinz Guderian's XVI Panzer Corps. Under the threat of German invasion, Chancellor Kurt von Schuschnigg of Austria capitulated without war, and Operation Otto turned into a peaceful occupation of the Austrian state. But the hasty mobilization of the
Eighth Army showed that preparations for calling up the reserve
had made slow progress, and technical weaknesses were detected
even in the panzer forces mobilized.[12] Operation Otto was the first
real operational movement of the still experimental panzer division
and revealed weaknesses in equipment and organization which
Guderian hastened to remedy. The subsequent advance into Czechoslovakia also revealed shortcomings. Both "peaceful" occupations
tested and strengthened the Army's internal organization on the eve
of war, a result of "appeasement" not always appreciated.

The German occupation of Austria also had important strategic
implications. It uncovered Czechoslovakia's southern flank, surrounded it on three sides by German territory, and jeopardized its
vulnerable east-west communications. By ingesting one victim,
Hitler had prepared the way for another.

Hitler's next target was to be Czechoslovakia, but he needed a pretext to justify the German use of force and to divide the Czechs
from their French allies. Austria had been without friends, and,
except for the possibility that Italy might intervene as once before,
Hitler's tactics had not run the risk of involving other powers. The
case of the Czech state was altogether different. The French, and
perhaps the British and Russian, attitude might be decisive. Hitler

therefore sought to exploit the internal situation of Czechoslovakia as a means of preventing foreign involvement.

Case Green

The campaign against the Czechs began soon after the conquest of Austria. In April and May, Hitler opened a drumfire of propaganda on the alleged persecution of the German minority in the Sudeten area with proposals for solving the Sudeten situation on different lines than before. The Sudeten Nazi Party leader, Konrad Henlein, apparently worked hand in glove with Berlin and demanded either "autonomy or separation" from Prague.[13] Subsequent riots and disorders in the Sudetenland moved tension between Berlin and Prague toward the breaking point. The threat of war seemed so ominous that on May 21 France solemnly warned that if German troops crossed the Czech frontier, France would come to the aid of her ally.[14] Britain declared herself under no obligation to defend the Czechs, but Soviet Russia announced its willingness to aid in the resistance to Hitler. The Army General Staff in Berlin believed that an attack on Czechoslovakia would lead to a dreaded war against at least two powerful states simultaneously. Hitler seems to have hesitated in the face of these developments, but sometime during the last week of May he made the momentous decision that the Sudeten situation was to be settled in 1938 even at the risk of war.

The first formal indication to the OKH that Hitler had made up his mind came in the form of an OKW directive to the German armed forces on May 30. The directive began with Hitler's declaration that it was his unalterable decision to destroy Czechoslovakia by military action in the near future. It went on to say that from a military as well as a political standpoint the most favorable course was a lightning blow. The most important factor contributing to success would be surprise, to be assured by appropriate preparatory measures and by rapid execution. It was also essential that within the first four days of the campaign the Czechoslovakian military situation should be rendered hopeless in order to discourage other powers from intervening. Since too much time would be consumed by the mobilization and rail movement of the reserve infantry divisions before the attack, the initial assault forces would be formed from active divisions stationed near the Czech frontier and from those which could be brought rapidly to the scene by their motorization. Supported by Luftwaffe air strikes, the Army's assault columns were to break through the Czechoslovakian fortifications at numerous points. The motorized units were to pass through these gaps with utmost speed in order to prevent the Czechoslovakian Army from withdrawing eastward into Slovakia and to destroy it quickly by encirclement in Bohemia and Moravia.

Against the possibility of foreign intervention, the OKW directive ordered specific measures to be taken. The Army was to allocate as few troops against the possibility of a French attack as the state of the West Wall fortifications would permit. The actual mobilization of troops to man them would be executed only on order from the OKW. Russian attempts to aid the Czechs were to be expected mainly in the air, if at all. Russian ground forces would have to receive permission from Poland to cross the thin strip of Polish territory that lay between the nearest Russian border and Czechoslovakia, and the poor relations between Moscow and Warsaw made this unlikely. Germany's borders with the Low Countries, Poland, and Yugoslavia were to be weakly manned since intervention was unlikely by these powers.[15]

The OKW directive for Czechoslovakia was given the code-designation "Case Green," and its reception by the OKH led to a new crisis in German military leadership. Earlier in the year, General Beck had ordered operational studies of a two-front war with France and Czechoslovakia in which other powers such as Great Britain, Soviet Russia, and even the United States were supposed to intervene. Since the results produced by this worst of all possible situations had been clearly negative, Beck had concluded that a German attack on Czechoslovakia would run too much risk of foreign intervention and eventual German defeat. When the OKW directive for Case Green was received, Beck reacted by putting the results of the Czech operational studies in a memorandum to the OKW, which concluded with his personal opinion that a military proceeding against Czechoslovakia would automatically lead to a general European conflict or even a world war. The results of such an involvement, Beck prophesied, would be not only military defeat for Germany but a general catastrophe for Europe.[16]

In July, Beck read his memorandum in the presence of Brauchitsch before a specially convened body of the top German field commanders. When he had finished, the commanders endorsed Beck's views unanimously. Beck then entrusted the memorandum to Brauchitsch for delivery to Hitler. Subsequently, while visiting a special assault-training school, Hitler made caustic remarks about the pessimism shown in the General Staff. Beck took Hitler's remarks to mean that his views had been rejected and decided that there was no longer any way to dissuade the Fuehrer. Unwilling to serve under these conditions, Beck submitted his resignation to Brauchitsch in August.[17]

Halder's Rise to Chief of the General Staff

Beck's resignation forced the appointment of a successor, and the new first deputy chief, Franz Halder, was next in line. When Brauchitsch approached Halder on the matter, Halder was not eager to accept the post of Chief of the General Staff since he had worked with Beck for several months and had himself been involved in the operational studies and knew their results. His view of the situation was the same as Beck's, and, like Beck, he had convinced himself that reasoning with Hitler was futile. Though he doubtless yearned, like all General Staff officers, to reach the pinnacle of professional success, this honor would mean little if he was about to preside over the military defeat of Germany. Halder talked with Beck about Brauchitsch's offer and eventually reached agreement with him. Then Halder informed Brauchitsch that he would accept the post of OKH Chief of Staff on the condition that he would try to balk Hitler's war policy if possible. Brauchitsch, who seems to have shared Beck's views if not his moral courage, quickly accepted Halder on this somewhat equivocal basis. Hitler was doubtless ignorant of Halder's views, for he confirmed Brauchitsch's choice with the proviso that Beck's resignation be kept *in camera* for a time. Halder assumed his new duties on September 1, 1938.[18]

The man who assumed the duties and responsibilities of Chief of the Army General Staff and upon whose shoulders the Moltke-Schlieffen traditions now rested was born on June 30, 1884, the son of a distinguished Bavarian general and a French mother. Halder had chosen an officer's career in the Bavarian contingent of the Imperial Army, trained for service in the artillery, and was finally selected to attend the War College on the eve of World War I. During that struggle he held several staff and command positions on both the Western and Eastern fronts, and eventually served in the headquarters of the Supreme Commander, East. In the postwar period, Halder's talents opened his way into the elite Officer Corps of the Reichsheer, and during the 1920s he served for five years in the Truppenamt, the "General Staff" of the period. By 1933 Halder was chief of staff of a military district, and in 1936 he was appointed chief of the armed forces maneuver staff. In October, 1937, Beck personally chose Halder for the post of Deputy Chief for General and Officer Training in the OKH General Staff. By this time Halder had risen to the rank of *Generalleutnant* (Major General).[19] His subsequent promotion to Lieutenant General and assignment as Beck's first deputy have been described.

In appearance, Halder has been likened to the old-fashioned schoolmaster, an impression heightened by his habit of wearing pince-nez. From his picture, one gathers that his height was moderate and his frame well knit but not stocky. His grey hair is cut close to the scalp in the Prussian fashion, his nose is small but slightly hooked, his eyes piercing, his jaw lantern-shaped. His mouth is a straight, dark line on a fair complexion. The face reflects both intelligence and an indefinable inner tension. The total effect is unprepossessing, yet somehow memorable, and although a picture of the more debonair Brauchitsch gives the impression of greater personal attractiveness, somehow one never doubts that of the two Halder possessed the more dominating mind. Both mentally and physically, Halder was well suited to be the last Chief of the General Staff to represent the old German military tradition.[20]

Since Halder already believed that persuading Hitler was impossible, he realized the necessity of removing the Fuehrer from power. Yet Halder could not bring himself to accept the possibility of having to shed blood to this end, a factor that may well have tended to dilute his resolution. In this morally ambiguous situation, he contacted the resistance movement, with which Beck was already associated, of civilians and soldiers who for various reasons opposed the Nazi regime. This resistance movement had already begun to formulate plans to arrest Hitler and other key Nazi figures and to create some form of interim military government until a regularly constituted government could be elected. It was evident by September, 1938, that unless Hitler was removed quickly from power, Germany might be plunged into war. The members of the resistance movement decided that the plot would be executed when Hitler gave the General Staff the signal to move up the forces for Case Green. This so-called "Green Plot" never took place because Hitler's triumph at Munich in late September left the plotters powerless, and Halder was not again actively associated with the resistance until after his retirement in 1942.[21]

The Czech Crisis

Even while plotting Hitler's overthrow, Halder had to develop an operational plan to carry out the Case Green directive in time to meet Hitler's deadline of October 1. The OKW directive had made very clear that a general mobilization could not take place before the actual attack and that a plan would have to be improvised using mostly active units. As explained earlier, the Army was so organized that partial mobilization was quite feasible, providing

8. German Deployment for the Invasion of Czechoslovakia, 1938.

mobilization plans had been designed for such a contingency. Beck
had made no such arrangements either before or after the Austrian
crisis, and Halder was forced to improvise since there was no time
left in which to work out a new mobilization scheme. With the aid
of General Karl Heinrich Stülpnagel, the new *Oberquartiermeister I*
(O.Qu.I.), and the OKH Operations section, such a plan was hammered out for Halder to present to Hitler on September 9 at Nuremberg, where Hitler was attending a Nazi Party rally. In the presence
of Wilhelm Keitel and Brauchitsch, Halder explained that evening
to the Fuehrer that the General Staff plan called for the concentration of four field armies along the three Czechoslovakian frontiers,
using mostly active divisions. Two pincer thrusts were to be delivered on the flanks by the Second Army from Silesia and the
weaker Fourteenth Army from Austria. The Second Army was expected to break through the Czech defenses and advance south to
Olomoue in two days, while the Fourteenth Army was striking northward in the direction of Brno. These two thrusts would sever the
communications between Bohemia–Moravia in western Czechoslovakia and Slovakia in the east and would insure a Kesselschlacht
in the frontier area. While these two pincer thrusts of panzer and
motorized divisions were taking place, two German armies composed
of infantry divisions—the Twelfth Army operating out of Thuringia
and the Tenth Army from Franconia—would attack the mountainous
western frontier of Czechoslovakia in order to complete the encirclement.[22]

Hitler was generally satisfied with Halder's proposals, but he
asked for changes on specific points. He criticized the concentration
of strength in the Second Army and argued that, if the northern
pincer became stalled, the Fourteenth Army might be too weak to
sever the enemy's line of retreat. Halder replied that German intelligence on the Czech frontier fortifications in front of the Second
Army indicated that many of the forts had unarmed gun cupolas
and that wide gaps existed at intervals along the fortified belt
through which German units might penetrate. Since, in any case,
the Austrian railroads could not support a greater number of divisions for the Fourteenth Army, Hitler had to be satisfied with a
transfer of panzer and motorized infantry divisions to the Tenth
Army to insure the early fall of Prague for political reasons.[23] These

changes jeopardized the Kesselschlacht plan that Halder and the General Staff had offered, and this session gave Halder his first unpleasant experience with Hitler's tendency to interfere even with the details of military planning.

Since the majority of the active divisions and all of the panzer and motorized divisions of the Army were to be concentrated against Czechoslovakia, the General Staff had to rely for the most part on reserve units to defend the West Wall in case of French intervention. Aside from the Landwehr divisions, there were as yet only seven reserve divisions available for this purpose.[24] But Halder knew that the French Army could not complete mobilization until after a declaration of war and that its peacetime active force was not constituted for offensive action.[25] The French regular army numbered about six hundred thousand men, but of this number 240,000 were recruits with less than one year's service, and the rest were not tactically organized for anything but defense to cover a general mobilization. In contrast, the German active army of about seven hundred thousand troops was tactically organized for offensive operations. Halder therefore believed that it was feasible to plan a campaign against Czechoslovakia which could be concluded before the French could mobilize and act.

The Czech peacetime active force numbered about two hundred and fifty thousand troops, and its reserve could further expand this figure upon general mobilization to six hundred thousand.[26] Since the German peacetime active force alone outnumbered the mobilized Czech Army, Czechoslovakia was under any circumstances at a disadvantage in respect to numbers. Still, if the Czechs could carry out their mobilization in good order, the chances were greatly increased that they could hold out against a German attack until the French mobilized and attacked Germany's western frontier. Thus it was extremely important to the Germans that an attack on Czechoslovakia be mounted in absolute secrecy in order to prevent extended Czech resistance. Also, postponement of operations in the West while the French mobilized would have given Halder and the German resistance movement some days in which to remove Hitler from power before serious fighting broke out. Hence, it is at least possible that, had the Anglo-French powers stood firmly against Hitler's demands at Munich, the Green Plot might have succeeded in preventing a general European war without abandonment of Czech freedom. In any case, by waiting until the following September to stand firm against Hitler, the Western powers permitted Hitler to improve Germany's military position and to reduce the doubts of Halder and the Army General Staff.

So there was neither a Green Plot nor a war in 1938. The mediation of British Prime Minister Neville Chamberlain resulted in the exchange of the Sudetenland for what Europe hoped would be "peace in our time" and Hitler's solemn pledge that Germany had no further territorial claims in Europe. Deserted by their French allies, who feared to act without British support, and by Russia, whose government feared to act without French participation, the Czechs were forced to surrender much of their territory and nearly all of their fortifications. If Hitler proved insincere, the Czech rump state could not long endure.

The Welle Mobilization Plan

The resolution of the Sudeten crisis at the end of September, 1938, did not immediately relieve the tempo of Army General Staff activity. The preparations for Case Green had indicated a second time that the German mobilization scheme was not appropriate to Hitler's political policy and forced an awkward improvisation whenever a speedy or partial mobilization was needed. During the remainder of 1938, Halder kept the General Staff hard at work developing a better solution, and in December the OKH adopted a new mobilization plan based on four *Wellen* (waves). This secret "Welle Plan" provided that under Wave I the higher headquarters, the active divisions, and supporting units of the Army would mobilize within three days. Under Wave II sixteen reserve divisions of the younger, trained reservists would be mobilized on four days' notice, and the military district headquarters activated into corps headquarters. Under Wave III, twenty of the former Landwehr divisions (except for one, now reclassified as reserve divisions) would be mobilized on six days' notice and used chiefly to man the West Wall defenses and to secure rear areas. Under Wave IV, fourteen divisions were to be created from units of the German training command by the seventh day. On the same day the *Ersatz*

Heer headquarters would be activated to assume responsibility for the German Zone of the Interior in order to permit the Army High Command to give its undivided attention to field operations.[27]

The advantages of the Welle Plan were significant and in line with Seeckt's views on mobilization. The plan permitted either partial or general mobilization without improvisation, and the most powerful and ready divisions, those of the peacetime active force, were now available to launch an attack without the traditional lengthy mobilization associated with mass armies in the past. The new plan exploited the dual nature of the German Army organization already discussed, and with its implementation the Army became an instrument uniquely well-designed for a policy of quick territorial aggression. While every other Continental European army required lengthy mobilization to act offensively, the German Army was in a position to strike with little delay and without the warning associated with general mobilization of the traditional type.

The Army General Staff spent 1939, until the outbreak of war, in implementing the Welle Plan, expanding the Army by adding new divisions, and re-equipping existing ones. Wave II divisions received equipment on a par with the active divisions for the first time, while Wave III divisions were specially equipped for defensive fighting appropriate to their role at the West Wall. The West Wall itself was appreciably stronger than in 1938, as the result of Hitler's crash program of construction, but still not yet completed. Nevertheless, the conclusion is inescapable that the German Army was greatly strengthened and improved between Munich and September, 1939.[28] Halder also strengthened the General Staff by adding a new deputy chief for the intelligence section in November, 1938— General Kurt von Tippelskirch. By the outbreak of war these measures had "stiffened" the Army both physically and psychologically.

The fact that war was not far off was demonstrated unmistakably in the spring of 1939. In March, Hitler cast aside his Munich pledges and ordered military occupation of the remainder of the Czech state.[29] The Czechs, earlier stripped of their fixed defenses, were unable to resist. This act of perfidy, however, alerted the British and French governments to the fact that Hitler's territorial ambitions could not be satisfied by appeasement, nor could they trust his most solemn promises. Britain retaliated by adopting the first peacetime conscription act in her history, a clear warning that the British government was about to follow a firmer policy toward German expansion. France was encouraged by this new tone in British policy. Poland was clearly Hitler's most probable next victim, and Britain and France moved to forestall a repetition of the fate meted out to the Czechs by signing defensive agreements with Warsaw, thereby encouraging the Poles to resist German demands in the future. But by then the German Army was once again the most powerful in Europe, and the new Anglo-French policy of deterrence came too late to halt the European drift toward war.

CHAPTER FOUR

Poland: The First Test

Case White

By the spring of 1939 the war clouds so briefly dispersed by the Munich agreement were lowering once more over Europe. In October, 1938, the month after the Munich crisis and the surrender of the Sudetenland to Germany, the new German Foreign Minister,[1] Joachim von Ribbentrop, informed the Polish ambassador to Berlin that the German government desired sweeping changes and concessions regarding the Polish Corridor and the Free City of Danzig. In particular, the German government desired to build a double-tracked railroad and superhighway to East Prussia. When the Polish government curtly refused to make such concessions, Hitler chose not to press the issue just then. But after the German occupation of rump Czechoslovakia in March, 1939, Hitler renewed his demands on Poland, and Ribbentrop warned the Polish government that peace between Poland and Germany would depend in large measure on Poland's attitude toward the Danzig question. When the Polish government again made clear that it would not be bullied by Nazi threats, relations between Germany and Poland moved toward the breaking point.[2]

The other powers were awake to the growing German menace by this time, for Hitler's contemptuous violation of the Munich agreement had wiped away all illusions that Hitler's word could be trusted. Almost immediately after German troops marched into Prague, negotiations began among the governments of France, Great Britain, and the Soviet Union concerning a common course of action to curb further German expansion. The time had come for these powers to stand together for the preservation of European peace, but hardly had the talks begun than they revealed mutual suspicions and uncertainties which made rapid agreement impossible. The Anglo-French-Soviet negotiations dragged on indecisively into the spring.

In contrast, Hitler was losing no time. His dispute with Poland over Danzig provided a useful *casus belli,* and on April 3 the OKW issued a directive to all three armed services to prepare a plan of campaign against Poland under the code-designation *Fall Weiss* (Case White). The directive stated that while relations with Poland were being based on the principle of avoiding friction, nevertheless should Poland adopt a threatening attitude toward Germany, a final settlement might become necessary, notwithstanding the nonaggression pact with Poland.[3] In the event of war, the German armed forces were to endeavor to destroy those of Poland as quickly as possible, while the political leadership would attempt to insure that Poland remained diplomatically isolated. The directive specified that planning should include the rapid establishment of communications between Germany and her province of East Prussia, and the possible use of Slovakia as a troop assembly area. In order to exploit the factor of surprise, general mobilization was to be announced only on the eve of the attack. Mobilization of troops at the West Wall was to depend upon the political situation vis-à-vis the Anglo-French powers.[4]

General Staff Planning

Upon receipt of the OKW Case White directive at OKH headquarters, General Brauchitsch turned the matter over to Halder, who henceforth became fully responsible for the Army's operational planning for the Polish campaign. Under his direction the OKH General Staff set to work. The General Staff officers most closely associated with Halder in this phase were General Karl Heinrich von Stülpnagel, Chief of OKH Operations; Colonel Hans von

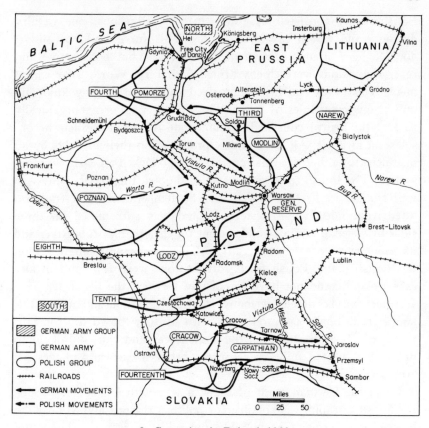

9. Campaign in Poland, 1939.

Greiffenberg, Chief of the OKH Operations section; and General Kurt von Tippelskirch, then Chief of the Intelligence section. The task of these officers and their subordinates was to assess Poland's general military capacities and to select the basic operational concepts under which the campaign would be conducted. A timetable would be prepared for the necessary concentration of forces and for subordinate levels to work out the details of the master plan.[5]

The factors considered decisive in determining the Army's overall strategy in the case of Poland were: (1) the superiority of the German forces, numerically and qualitatively, if they could be concentrated against Poland; (2) the geographical situation which made Poland's western provinces vulnerable to encirclement; and (3) the latent threat of the Soviet Union in Poland's rear.[6] The peacetime

Polish Army consisted of thirty infantry divisions, one cavalry division, and eleven cavalry brigades. This force could be almost doubled by full mobilization of the reserves, but both active and reserve divisions were chiefly armed with First World War equipment. The Poles had little motorized equipment of any kind and only a few companies of tanks. The Polish Air Force (organically part of the army) consisted of about one thousand obsolete or obsolescent aircraft. All were poorly protected on their airfields by an insufficient number of antiaircraft guns and lacked an early warning system. The Polish spirit was considered good, the Polish army was well trained in French tactics, and by temperament and tradition offensive-minded.[7] Yet western Poland was surrounded on three sides by German territory and, except for the great Vistula River and its tributaries, possessed no really suitable defense lines anywhere on the Polish plain. Polish fixed fortifications were few, and in any case Poland could not have completely fortified the perimeter of a frontier that bordered Germany for nearly a thousand miles. Poland's traditionally poor relations with Moscow posed the constant threat of Russian attack on the Polish rear and caused Poland to divide her limited military resources between eastern and western frontiers.

From the German point of view, a war with Poland had to be concluded as rapidly as possible for political reasons and as near the borders of Germany as possible for military reasons. The more quickly Poland was defeated, the less would be the time in which other powers might act. The geographical situation offered the possibility of cutting off and annihilating the Polish forces in western Poland by a pincer movement, while supply and assembly problems would be greatly simplified if the decisive battle occurred near the German railheads in Pomerania and Silesia. Finally, basic army doctrine called for immediate encirclement and annihilation.

The planned Kesselschlacht operation would have the greatest chance of success if the Germans could strike before the Polish Army could mobilize its reserves or withdraw its main forces behind the Vistula. Since a general mobilization of German reservists would surely alert the Poles, the OKH ruled out the use of most of the reserve divisions for the initial surprise attack. The Army would have to rely primarily on the panzer, motorized, and infantry divisions of the active force for the first and most crucial blows and reinforce them after the start of operations with the mobilized reserves. The OKH counted heavily on the panzer, motorized infantry, and light divisions to prevent a Polish withdrawal beyond the Vistula, effective mobilization of the Polish reserves, and any redeployment to counter encirclement. If the main Polish forces could be pinned at the frontier, the German infantry divisions could then close the trap by hard marching and annihilate the encircled Polish forces as they attempted to break out. The Luftwaffe would play a vital role by destroying the Polish Air Force at the outset by surprise attacks on its airfields, interdicting the Polish transportation systems—especially the crucial railroads—and assisting the German armored spearheads. The OKH plan counted on throwing the Polish Army into confusion, preventing it from forming a continuous front, and blocking its routes of escape.[8]

Halder and his staff decided to concentrate two armies in Pomerania and East Prussia in the north (Army Group North), and three armies in Silesia and Slovakia (Army Group South). The greater concentration of forces in the south reflected that area's superior railroad facilities for the strategic movement of men and supplies.[9] Security troops and later-mobilized reserve divisions would form the only cover for the central Polish-German frontier.[10] The general mission of the two army groups would be to strike from north and south to link up at Warsaw and thus to trap the main Polish forces in western Poland. A final and decisive battle would then be fought with the Polish front reversed and its path of retreat blocked.

On April 26–27, the General Staff plan was presented to Hitler. He immediately approved it, after showing particular interest in special projects such as the proposed coup at Tczew to prevent the Poles from destroying the main bridge over the Vistula River where it flowed through the Corridor. The Fuehrer left all questions of logistics and troop movement, as well as general strategy, to the OKH.[11]

On May 1, the OKH activated two army group headquarters and assigned planning staffs to each of them. These staffs were to study the basic plan and to make recommendations for improvement to the OKH. General Feodor von Bock was named at this time to command Army Group North, General Hans von Salmuth was made his chief of staff, and General Wilhelm Haase was appointed his chief of operations. The important post of commanding Army Group South was given to the senior ranking general of the Army, the soon-famous Gerd von Rundstedt. For Rundstedt's chief of staff, Halder chose General Erich von Manstein, perhaps the most brilliant German General Staff officer and future field commander of the war. Colonel Guenther von Blumentritt was named as his chief of operations. These planning staffs were quite small, Army Group South's *Arbeitsstab Rundstedt* consisting of only five General Staff officers, two of whom—Manstein and Blumentritt—also held other responsible positions. The former continued to command a division during the summer of 1939, while Blumentritt remained chief of an OKH training section and handled his Case White duties in his spare time. Rundstedt himself remained in retirement for most of the summer and took little part in the planning except to approve decisions from time to time. Similar planning staffs were also set up for each of the field armies.[12]

On May 7, Manstein's staff produced an "estimate of the situation" for Army Group South. It pointed out that the success of the planned operation hinged entirely on enveloping most of the Polish Army west of Warsaw and the Vistula and that a successful withdrawal behind the river and its tributaries would frustrate the whole design. While every effort should be made to prevent such a withdrawal, it was reasonable to prepare against this possibility by launching the army based in Slovakia on the extreme right to cross the upper extremities of these water courses, thereby unhinging the Vistula line at the start. If large Polish forces succeeded in escaping, their Vistula position would be already compromised.[13]

Toward the end of May both army group planning staffs submitted their recommendations to the OKH for approval and incorporation into the basic plan. The OKH approved the change suggested by Army Group South and a suggestion from Army Group North that the army in Pomerania and the army in East Prussia strike simultaneously without waiting for linkage across the Corridor. The Pomeranian army would first cross it and then wheel into line on the right flank of the Third Army, which would already be advancing toward Warsaw. The revised OKH general order was issued on June 15, 1939.[14]

Political developments in early May had meanwhile altered Hitler's plans. The negotiations among the Anglo-French powers, Russia, and Poland had broken down as the result of the negotiators' inability to reach acceptable terms for the defense of Poland. The Soviet Union had insisted that any guarantee against German aggression should cover the whole of Eastern Europe, that a practicable defense of Poland required the presence of Russian troops on Polish soil before any attack, and that the Soviet Union be informed in detail of Anglo-French war plans. The Polish government refused to allow Russian forces to be stationed on Polish soil. Britain and France suspected Russia's motives and were not sure of the combat value of the Red Army. They also insisted upon a definite alliance before discussing military terms. Perhaps fearful that the Anglo-French powers were only trying to involve Russia in a war with Germany from which they intended to withdraw, Stalin finally dropped his interest in collective security in early May and replaced Foreign Minister Maxim Litvinov with Vyacheslav Molotov. This sacking of a long-time advocate of collective security made it evident to Hitler that Stalin would consider a *rapprochement* with Germany.[15]

On May 23, Hitler called a military conference, which Brauchitsch and Halder attended, and announced his intention of exploiting the new political situation to destroy Poland. During the course of his lecture to the generals, Hitler made it clear that the issue was no longer Danzig or the Corridor but the existence of a Polish state which stood between Germany and her eastward expansion. If Russia could be removed from Poland's supporters, as now seemed possible, Hitler was willing to risk war with those Western powers which he believed to be the real obstacles to an expanded Germany. Hitler thought it possible, even probable, that the Western powers would submit to the destruction of Poland if Russia stood aside. In any case, the Fuehrer would not shrink from war with the Anglo-French powers. Whatever the cost, he declared, Poland must be destroyed.[16]

Hitler's declaration in late May led to an increased tempo of German military preparations. The OKH decided to insure surprise and to reduce its logistic problems by gradually assembling troops and supplies in Pomerania and Silesia during the summer. The movement of active divisions to the Polish frontier was to be disguised as normal summer maneuvers, and most of their supplies would be at the railheads in the East by the time of the attack. Enough of the Army reserve was to be gradually recalled to bring the active divisions to full strength. In order neither to alarm the German public nor alert the Poles and the Anglo-French powers, these recalls were officially described as necessary for refresher training.[17]

The proximity of the German railheads to western Poland was an important advantage to the OKH. By stockpiling supplies at these railheads, the Army High Command could be sure that logistical support would be quite close to the intended scene of operations. The Army's dependence on horse-drawn supply could be reduced, and both animals and trucks saved for actual campaigning. The German railroads in the East, mostly built during the pre-1914 or World War I periods for operations against the two sides of a similar Czarist salient in Congress Poland, ran directly to the proposed assembly areas and depots.[18] The German Army's logistic problems would have otherwise been difficult. The thirty-seven infantry divisions to be used had 198,875 horses; approximately 4,375,250 pounds of fodder, or the contents of 135 railroad cars, had to be provided every day.[19]

By exploiting this advantage conferred by the railroads, Halder's staff planned extensive depots from which the German armies could draw rations, forage, ammunition, motor fuel, and spare parts on the very edge of Polish territory. Each infantry division (or other divisions still relying in part on horse-drawn supply transport) would draw from these depots sufficient fodder for 140 miles and rations for ten days.[20] The panzer and other motorized divisions were to draw motor fuel sufficient for 450 miles. All divisions were to carry with them one load of ammunition, while a second load was kept at the railhead depots and two more loads were located on rail sidings for rapid movement to the depots.[21] After the start of the operation, truck and horse-drawn transport would begin stockpiling depots in Poland behind the advancing armies, while the railheads would be extended as rapidly as possible. But the General Staff recognized that in an operation based on swift movement the "umbilical cord" of supply between railhead and marching troops might fail to keep up. In that event, horses and men would have to rely on local resources for forage and food until supplies could be moved up by truck and rail.[22] The use of air transport to deliver fuel of high efficiency in relation to bulk such as gasoline was a possible stopgap measure for the motorized forces. Still, this supply situation made it imperative in 1939, as in 1914, that the enemy be decisively engaged as near the German frontiers as possible. For the blitzkrieg army to be successful, operations should not be prolonged nor too distant from good rail communications, nor should the Army meet with resistance which would draw heavily on the forces in action.

The limited range and endurance of the German Army made Polish deployment and mobilization a key factor in the General Staff's calculations. If the Poles could complete their mobilization and deploy well back of the frontier—perhaps behind the Vistula—the OKH knew that the initial and strongest German onslaught might be contained, the campaign greatly lengthened, and the German logistical system severely strained. Fortunately for the German Army, this option was not really open to the Poles. The Polish Army was a Nation in Arms, heavily dependent on its trained reserve to be fully effective. The Polish High Command had to cover the mobilization of the reserve by deploying its active forces along the frontier, particularly around railheads, making them extremely vulnerable to quick encirclement and annihilation. The Polish High Command was aware of this danger, but counted heavily on a mobilization as rapid as the German to offer a continuous front to any Wehrmacht assault —a defense which, according to Polish and French doctrine, could not be rapidly overwhelmed. The Poles also counted heavily on a French mobilization as rapid as the German and an early French offensive against the western frontiers of Germany. These miscalculations greatly contributed to the rapid Polish defeat in 1939.[23]

The Polish deployment on the eve of the German attack was, for the reasons given above, characterized by a dispersal of forces along the frontier in small groups of divisions. The Polish Corridor between Pomerania and East Prussia was defended by the Pomorze Group of five infantry divisions and a cavalry brigade, perhaps also intended to prevent any linkage of forces between the two German provinces in the north. The southeast Prussian frontier was covered by the Modlin Group of two infantry divisions and two cavalry brigades and on the east by the Narew Group of two infantry divisions and two cavalry brigades. Thus, most of the active Polish divisions in this area were strung out for 250 miles with very little depth. Similarly, the Polish central and southern frontiers with Germany were screened by the Polish active units to give the reserve time to mobilize and deploy. Four infantry divisions and two cavalry brigades were concentrated in the vulnerable Poznan province at the extreme west, for in this heavily populated area was located a sizable part of the Polish reserves. The southern frontier was protected by the Lodz Group of four infantry divisions and two cavalry brigades; by the Cracow Group of seven infantry divisions, one cavalry brigade, and one mechanized brigade; and by the Carpathian Group on the extreme left with three mountain brigades and two infantry divisions, each group covering a vital railhead and a mobilization area for reserves as well as vital industrial areas. In addition, small groups of active units were in local reserves behind each group. General reserves of eight infantry divisions, a cavalry brigade, and a tank brigade were located around Warsaw.[24]

A major calculation in the German war plan was the speed with which the Anglo-French powers could be expected to come to the aid of the Poles by launching a diversionary attack on Germany's western frontiers. By August, Halder was giving careful and detailed thought to this problem, as evidenced by the journal which he began to keep on August 14. Under the first entry, he wrote:

If the French feel sure that large German forces are being committed in the East, *they may decide to take the offensive.*

It must then be assumed that both frontier mobilizations (France and Germany) would at first run according to prearranged plans because of the technical impossibility of making material changes in mobilization plans on short notice.[25]

Proceeding on this assumption, Halder calculated that upon total mobilization the French Army would expand to 106 divisions, of which 47 would be available for offensive operations. The German Army could mobilize 33 divisions in four days to man the West Wall defenses, but these divisions would be relatively low-grade reserve units inadequately supplied with artillery and antitank guns.[26] At the end of two weeks, over 40 divisions (12 active and 31 reserve divisions) could be mobilized in the West.[27]

Under these circumstances, Halder believed that the most likely French course of action would be either an offensive through Luxembourg and the "Ardennes corner" of neutral Belgium or a drive through central Belgium toward the Rhineland further north. He ruled out an attack on the fortifications of the West Wall between Basel and Saarbrücken (the Franco-German frontier), for these were the strongest in the West; but the German extension of the West Wall northward opposite the Luxembourg, Belgian, and Dutch frontiers was less well developed and more vulnerable to attack. However, Halder considered it unlikely that the French could mobilize and concentrate for an attack on the Luxembourg area before the tenth day or move into the central Belgian plains before the fourteenth. By that time German mobilization in the West would be complete, although the question remained whether the German forces in the West could hold out with their deficiencies in equipment until help arrived from the East. Halder calculated that the divisions in the West would have only three hundred pieces of divisional artillery among them, while the French forces were expected to have about sixteen hundred pieces. In addition, the German forces would be extremely short of antitank guns.

Taking all these factors into consideration, Halder saw no real danger before the tenth day of French mobilization, except perhaps from a French flying column of a few "mobile divisions" attacking the Liège area through central Belgium by the fifth day. Thereafter, the German weakness would not be too little manpower but the lack of enough artillery, antitank guns, and good fortifications north of Saarbrücken. It seemed clear to Halder that, in order both to secure the Belgian frontier against an early French thrust and to provide against a later large-scale offensive, at least six reserve divisions should be mobilized ahead of schedule. Upon a French invasion of Belgium, the German forces in the West could then quickly advance into Belgian territory as far west as the Meuse in order to place a defensible water barrier between the advancing French forces and the German frontier.[28]

Later the same day, Halder attended a military conference with Hitler and presented his ideas on the defense of the West. Hitler agreed that there was little danger of a French attack on the Franco-German frontier, and he considered an early limited French thrust through Belgium so time-consuming that it would come too late to save the Poles. It seemed logical to him that the "men of Munich" would in the final analysis not intervene at all. The Fuehrer did agree to OKH mobilization of several reserve divisions in the West ahead of schedule as a precautionary measure against a French coup around Liège; after the Polish situation was well in hand the OKH might begin the rapid transfer of artillery and antitank guns to the West. But so far was Hitler from believing that the French really intended to fight to save Poland that he ruled out any German advance to the Meuse unless the French, in addition to declaring war, actually invaded Belgium.[29]

The remaining question mark for German military planning was the attitude of the Soviet Union, whose armies were the only forces in a position to defend Poland. By August, however, a German-Russian agreement was in sight, and, despite the desperate last-minute efforts of the French and British to patch up an agreement with Stalin, Hitler finally outbid his rivals. On August 22, Hitler dispatched Ribbentrop to Moscow to sign a Nazi-Soviet nonaggression pact, certain economic agreements, and a secret protocol for the partition of Poland. The same day he called a conference of his generals and announced that Russia was no longer an obstacle; the German attack on Poland would begin on August 26, the anniversary of the German victory at Tannenberg in 1914.[30] Hitler did not acquaint his generals with the details of his political settlement with Stalin; Halder remained unaware, until the Red Army intervened on September 17, that Russia intended to share in the loot of Poland.

Mobilization

The next few days were busy ones at OKH headquarters. In order to insure maximum surprise, the OKH had planned to postpone general mobilization until the eve of the attack and to use mostly active divisions in the opening phase and reinforce them as the operation proceeded.[31] But on August 25 the Western powers signed a military alliance with Poland just as orders for general mobilization were being issued. Hitler ordered the attack to be postponed. The OKH with great difficulty prevented the troops in the East from deploying, but it was too late to stop mobilization, and it was allowed to proceed while Hitler vainly attempted to drive a last diplomatic wedge between the Anglo-French powers and Poland. When this failed, the Fuehrer, on August 28, set a new deadline of September 1, when Case White was to begin automatically at 4:45 A.M.[32] By that date the Welle system would have permitted the German forces in the East to be fully mobilized and deployed.[33]

By the evening of August 31, all was in readiness. The OKH, which had moved its headquarters to its secret command post at Zossen, a few miles south of Berlin, had concentrated a total of 1,512,000 troops in the East. Army Group North numbered 630,000 troops, while Army Group South had 882,000.[34] The northern army group was composed of 16 infantry divisions, 2 motorized infantry divisions, 2 panzer divisions, a panzer brigade, and a cavalry brigade. The southern army group consisted of 21 infantry divisions, 2 motorized infantry divisions, and most of a third, 4 light divisions, 4 panzer divisions, and a mountain division. The OKH kept 3 infantry divisions in local reserve behind Army Group North and 5 behind Army Group South. In the West, General Wilhelm Ritter von Leeb's Army Group C was still in the process of mobilization and deployment, but, by September 1, 12 active and 21 reserve infantry divisions (6 Wave II, 12 Wave III, and 3 Wave IV) were in the West Wall defenses.[35]

The Poles in contrast had hesitated to order a general mobilization during the last critical days of August for fear of setting off a war they had every reason to avoid. The French and British governments had been desperately striving through diplomatic channels to reopen negotiations between the German and Polish governments, and a military mobilization by Poland would appear provocative if there was any chance of a reasonable settlement with Hitler. There was no chance, of course, and the delay in mobilization was fatal to what possibility Poland had of carrying out prolonged resistance. When at last on August 30 the Polish Army reserve began the slow process of mobilization and deployment, which required up to two weeks for completion, Halder was confident of the outcome even before the first shot was fired.[36]

The First Blitzkrieg

The first blitzkrieg of World War II began at dawn on September 1, 1939, as the German air fleets of Albert Kesselring and Alexander Loehr swept over the Polish frontier without warning. Within the next forty-eight hours the thousand-plane Polish Air Force was shattered, the Luftwaffe catching most of the Polish planes inadequately protected on the ground. This air blitz demonstrated how vulnerable an air force was without an early warning system, strong antiaircraft defenses around its airfields, and a strong fighter arm. No large-scale air battles were fought, and the weak defensive armament of the German bombers was not revealed. Surprise and superior numbers were sufficient to win command of the air within two days from the start of operations.[37] Once the Polish Air Force was no longer a significant factor, the Luftwaffe was free to attack Polish rail and road communications and mobilization areas and to assist the Army with the close support of "flying artillery." The ghost of Seeckt must have looked on with approval.

On the first day of the campaign, five German armies invaded Poland from north and south. General Günther von Kluge's Fourth Army (6 infantry divisions, 2 motorized infantry divisions, and 1 panzer division) entered the Polish Corridor from Pomerania and encountered 6 Polish infantry divisions supported by cavalry. Kluge's objective was to link up with General Georg von Küchler's Third Army, striking from East Prussia as quickly as possible; and his single Third Panzer Division was in the lead. The Polish troops were not equipped to deal with even the lightly armored and armed Mark I and II tanks, which were the most common in the German Army in 1939,[38] and the German armor was thus easily able to rout the Polish infantry and cavalry.[39] By the end of the day the Third Panzer's armored elements had nearly reached East Prussia, while the infantry divisions trailed behind. Some of the Polish forces managed to escape southward from the Corridor and toward Poznan, but on September 3 the Third Panzer and its supporting motorized infantry divisions encircled the remainder near Grudziadz. The Twenty-Third Infantry Division, after hard marches, caught up with the advanced units to complete and tighten the encirclement. A desperate Polish cavalry charge to break the ring was wrecked by German artillery, infantry, and tank fire, and Polish infantry attacks likewise proved futile. On September 4 the Thirty-Second Infantry Division arrived to tighten the encirclement still further and to release the motorized units. Finding their situation hopeless, the trapped Poles surrendered the same day, leaving the Corridor clear of organized Polish resistance.[40]

The easy success of Kluge's Fourth Army seems to have been due to several factors. First and basic was the tactical surprise achieved through the superior speed of German mobilization and deployment (as a result of the Welle mobilization plan developed by the OKH), and secondly the use of armor and motorized infantry, against which the Poles were poorly prepared. The Polish artillery was the only available weapon against tanks, but, because of German surprise and speed, it failed to get into action before its positions were overrun.[41] The unsupported Polish infantry and cavalry were, of course, unable to maintain continuous fronts under those conditions (indeed a really continuous front never formed), or to prevent the German panzer and motorized divisions from swinging around their rear and blocking escape; the expert marching performances of the German infantry closed the encirclements from the front. The small areas involved—the distance from the Pomeranian frontier to Grudziadz was not more than fifty miles—allowed the German infantry to come up in time and in a reasonably fresh condition to close the encirclements. According to Guderian, one infantry division made this march in three days and a second in four, both standards close to the fourteen miles a day expected of infantry veterans. The Polish attempts to break out of the encirclements permitted the German infantry divisions to use their great defensive firepower to maximum advantage.

General von Küchler's Third Army in East Prussia (seven infantry divisions, one panzer division, and a cavalry brigade) also struck on September 1, with most of its forces aimed toward Warsaw. The German experience was quite different on this front, however, for a few miles south of the frontier at Mlawa the Germans encountered the first really strong Polish fortifications in the campaign. From well-constructed concrete blockhouses, armed with artillery and machine guns, the Poles poured forth such fire that the German tank attacks were stalled and heavy losses were suffered. The Third Army's progress was arrested for two days until German troops managed to work their way around the fortifications and forced the Polish defenders to withdraw. Though the Mlawa-type defenses were the exception rather than the rule in Poland, the incident indicates that German frontal attacks were not irresistible even when supported by tanks. Contact between the Third and Fourth armies was made on September 3, and the Fourth then wheeled into line on the right flank of the Third for the drive on Warsaw.[42]

Rundstedt's army group in the south had struck on September 1 with tremendous strength. The most powerful army in this group was General Walther von Reichenau's Tenth (six infantry divisions, two motorized infantry divisions, two light divisions, and two panzer divisions) which attacked in the center toward Radom and the Vistula. On its left flank, protecting it from any Polish counterthrust from the Poznan area, was General Johannes Blaskowitz's Eighth Army (four infantry divisions, one mountain division, one light division, two panzer divisions, and part of a motorized infantry division).[43] Polish resistance along this front was quite weak at first, and the Eighth and Tenth armies drove the Poles back toward the Warta River line in their rear.

The Fourteenth Army's attack took a different direction from the remainder of the group as it sought to cross the Vistula and the San to unhinge any Polish front that might be forming along the rivers if the main Polish forces to the west attempted to escape encirclement. Despite brave Polish resistance, Wilhelm List's army rapidly pushed into the Cracow area and threatened to encircle the Poles defending the approaches to the rivers.[44]

By September 2 the Poles had begun to show signs of establishing a front on the Warta, based on such fortified towns as Kotowice and Czestochowa. It was imperative to the Germans that the Poles be denied this opportunity to stabilize the front and deploy reserves. Reichenau therefore ordered his panzer divisions to make vigorous attacks, and on the morning of September 3 they succeeded in capturing Czestochowa. Isolated groups of Polish troops continued to resist off the main highways, but the German motorized spearheads bypassed the remaining centers of resistance and thrust on toward Radom, leaving the final destruction of these groups to the following infantry divisions.[45]

During the first three crucial days of the Polish campaign, operations had followed plans so well that Brauchitsch and Halder had not been compelled to intervene. But unexpected developments were occurring elsewhere. On the day of the German attack, Britain and

France ordered general mobilization of their forces and dispatched an ultimatum to Berlin. When the time limit expired on September 3, the British and French governments declared war on Germany within a few hours of one another. These declarations of war had no immediate effect on operations in Poland, since the Allies could do nothing until their mobilizations were complete, but Halder had now to reckon on the possibility that by the middle of the month the German frontier in the West would be under attack. Still, the campaign in Poland was almost certainly going to be brief, and it was unlikely that the Allies would attack at all knowing that Poland was already lost and nearly all of Germany's strength would soon be in the West. A co-ordinated Anglo-French attack could hardly be organized in two weeks, and for political and psychological reasons Halder did not expect an independent French offensive.[46] Thus, while Hitler's political calculations had gone awry, German military operations in Poland were not immediately affected.

From September 3 on, Poland's situation became increasingly hopeless. As the result of the frontier battles, the Polish Army found itself embraced on two flanks by a giant pincer that was inexorably closing in on western Poland. Many Polish active units had been caught in local encirclements and destroyed near the frontier; the Germans had seized most of the vital railheads and overrun reserve deployment and assembly areas; the surviving active Polish forces and such reservists as were finally able to take the field were being steadily driven into two major pockets, one north of Lodz and a second around Warsaw. In the south, the breakthrough of Rundstedt's army group over the Warta had resulted in the capture of Radom and the encirclement of seven Polish infantry divisions on September 12.[47] In the north, armored formations of Bock's army group had begun to close in on Warsaw as early as September 8. Only the Polish forces in the Poznan area remained intact, but their route of retreat to the Vistula was fast being closed. Nevertheless, the last chance for a major part of the Polish Army west of the Vistula to escape total annihilation rested with the Poznan Group.

General von Manstein, the Chief of Staff of Army Group South, had been fully aware that the Poznan Group was still intact and dangerous, especially as the course of the southern prong of the German pincer exposed the left flank of the Eighth Army to a Polish attack.

Manstein also lacked complete intelligence on the location of this group and knew only that the enemy had assembled strong forces in Poznan province which had not yet come to light. As the Tenth Army pressed on to the Vistula, Manstein felt constrained to remind the Chief of Staff of the Eighth Army that he must carry out constant reconnaissance along his left flank.[48]

Brauchitsch and Halder were also becoming concerned because intelligence reports reaching Zossen indicated that the Poznan Group was moving east as rapidly as possible, and they feared that it might escape over the Vistula to be pursued by Rundstedt's Army Group. Manstein, however, was convinced that the original OKH plan of encirclement was still feasible; while messages were being exchanged between headquarters, the Poznan Group suddenly appeared on the flank of the Eighth Army on September 10 and heavily attacked its Thirtieth Division. The situation threatened to become critical, according to Manstein's account, as attempts by the Eighth Army to counterattack failed one after another. The Eighth Army wheeled both of its corps to form a defensive front facing north in order to prevent any Polish breakthrough south toward Lodz and requested that its forces be quickly reinforced by a panzer corps. Manstein, as the army group commander's principal advisor, stoutly opposed this last request, and suggested instead that the Polish attack be exploited to encircle and destroy the Poznan Group. Here Manstein's influence and training as a General Staff Officer was of great value. Through his firm insistence the common aim of the entire operation was not lost in a temporary reverse, nor was the basic doctrine upon which the success of the whole campaign rested now abandoned. Manstein believed that if the right actions were taken on the German side, the Polish attack offered the Germans the chance to achieve a giant Kesselschlacht.[49]

Rundstedt quickly agreed with his chief of staff and ordered two infantry divisions up from the rear and a light division to seal off the western flank of the Polish group. The Tenth Army was ordered to wheel about its XVI Panzer Corps, then on the outskirts of Warsaw, and also its XI Infantry Corps, and to direct them against the eastern flank of the Poznan Group. Finally, Rundstedt requested General von Bock, his counterpart in Army Group North, to direct the III Infantry Corps to close in on the Polish group from the north. When these measures were swiftly executed, the Poznan Group found itself surrounded; after a series of vain assaults to break out, the Polish group on September 18 surrendered 80,000 troops, 320 guns, 130 aircraft, and 40 tanks.[50]

The destruction of the Poznan Group left the Polish forces around Warsaw as the last organized resistance in Poland west of the Vistula. These forces could be easily compelled to surrender by clamping a tight siege on the city and by allowing hunger to force capitulation. Brauchitsch and Halder favored this course as the German columns approached Warsaw so that artillery and reinforcements could be released to Leeb's forces in the West. Hitler, however, insisted on bombardment and assault, a seemingly senseless demand, since at this point final Polish collapse was only a matter of time. When the Russians suddenly invaded eastern Poland on September 17, it dawned on the OKH that Hitler wished to present Stalin with a *fait accompli*. Even at this late date, both Brauchitsch and Halder were unaware of Hitler's partition of Poland before hostilities had opened.[51]

Warsaw held out in a heroic but vain defense until the end of September though subjected to massive artillery and aerial bombardment. It again demonstrated that stout fortifications do not easily fall before blitzkrieg methods. The fortress of Modlin north of the city gave the Germans a difficult time, and Manstein implies that it was only the indiscriminate bombardment of civilian areas of Warsaw that finally brought its garrison to terms. On September 27, after the Germans had agreed that the men of the garrison might return home and the officers might retain their swords, the Warsaw defenders capitulated.[52] Some one hundred and twenty thousand prisoners were taken.

Conclusion

With the fall of Warsaw, the Polish campaign was to all practical purposes concluded. Some fighting continued in Galicia until mid-October, but all significant fighting in terms of the outcome of the campaign had taken place during the first eighteen days. Hence the sobriquet attached to it by outside observers, blitzkrieg.[53]

The modified but essentially traditional Kesselschlacht doctrine of encirclement and annihilation had proved enormously successful

under the conditions in which the Polish campaign was fought and
certainly demonstrated that, properly organized and employed,
motorized forces of all types supported by strong tactical aviation
had returned mobility to war. The tremendous striking power of the
blitzkrieg army had been impressively shown; its range and endurance had not really been tested. Still, German thinking between the
wars had solved the essential problems that had frustrated German
designs in 1914. Whether the OKH recognized the limitations of its
doctrine and organization had still to be demonstrated.

The German reliance on active divisions in 1939 made general
mobilization and deployment to completion unnecessary before
taking the offensive, and the better training and endurance of the
active infantry divisions permitted faster marches than in 1914. At
the outbreak of the First World War, the younger Moltke had
rushed mobilized reservists into the marching columns without refresher training or physical reconditioning, and many of them had
broken under the strain during the long march through Belgium and
northern France. The OKH's reliance on active infantry divisions
in 1939 resulted in a far better performance. On September 10,
Halder noted in his journal that the performance of the troops was
"marvelous," despite the fact that "the roads are bad beyond
words." [54] Guderian and Manstein both mention specific instances of
notable infantry marches. Thus the encirclements that proved so
decisive were achieved not only by the speed and range of the all-
motorized divisions, but also by the improved speed and endurance
of the infantry divisions. It is interesting and perhaps significant
that Manstein credits the victory over the Poles to the excellent
training, spirit, and physical condition of the common soldier. [55]

The supply situation was unquestionably more favorable to the
German Army in 1939 than in 1914, and the potential weakness in
German logistics was not exposed. Only in one instance did the
Army encounter a major supply difficulty, when the Fifth Panzer
Division ran out of fuel, [56] and air drops solved this problem until
more conventional means of supply could be arranged. Many Polish
divisions were encircled within fifty miles of the frontier, and most
of the German divisions did not travel over two hundred miles
throughout the campaign; none fought major battles at this distance.
In contrast, many of the right wing divisions at the battle of the

Marne in 1914 had made forced marches at least two hundred miles before encountering the main enemy force and then were required to make frontal attacks.

Even though Polish fortifications were few and not outstandingly formidable, one of the more significant aspects of this campaign was the difficulty with which they were captured. This leads to speculation as to whether, had the Poles possessed a permanent system of fortifications along the frontier rather than at isolated points, the Germans could have so speedily encircled the active Polish units, seized the vital railheads, and disrupted the mobilization and deployment of the Polish Army reserves. Wherever the Germans encountered a modern system of fortifications on even a small scale such as existed at Mlawa or around Danzig, they were definitely slowed down. Halder's journal cryptically describes the German frustrations with one of the Danzig fortifications even after the Germans attacked with infantry, howitzers, dive-bombers, and flame-throwers:

Were twice inside. SS-Schleswig asserts it cannot smash it up [with artillery]. Dive bomber liaison man asserts they cannot hit it. At least 20 concrete pillboxes of the latest model, with subterranean communications. Many [machine guns]. One 8.8 cm. gun.[57]

Similarly, at Mlawa concrete fortifications armed with artillery inflicted heavy losses on German tank units and stalled the Third Army's advance for two days. Fortunately for the Germans, such fortifications were neither extensive nor linked into a co-ordinated system. Nor were there many field fortifications to overcome, except roadblocks and crude lines hastily thrown up as a defense against tanks. Yet these minor incidents indicate that the blitzkrieg flourished best where there were the least fortifications of any kind.

Only brief mention can be made of the advantages the Germans gained from their complete control of the air. The most obvious were offensive in nature, such as the disruption of Polish transportation systems, attacks on troop concentrations, and the bombing of artillery positions. The use of air transport has been mentioned. The close proximity of the Polish forces to the German frontiers and their quick encirclement by the German ground forces permitted the Luftwaffe to combine its roles of close support and interdiction and eliminated the need for the Luftwaffe leadership to make difficult choices between the two types of air missions.

Finally, this chapter cannot be closed without emphasizing the importance of professional planning and leadership to the outcome of the campaign, the result of excellent leadership at the top and a sound prewar training program throughout the Army. Manstein believes that the most important thing demonstrated by the campaign was that the Reichsheer had revived Germany's great tradition of training and leadership.[58] Judging by the results of this campaign, one can hardly quarrel with his conclusion.

CHAPTER FIVE

France: Victory in the West

The Allied Strategy

The fall of Poland at the end of September, 1939, was followed by large-scale transfers of German military forces to the West, where the front had remained quiet since the Anglo-French declarations of war on September 3. Except for a few probing attacks along the German frontier defenses (West Wall), the Allies had spent the month in mobilizing and deploying their forces along the French frontier from the North Sea to the Italian Alps. The defensive posture adopted by the Allied forces was in accordance with an Anglo-French staff decision taken in March, 1939. In view of the probable German superiority in the air and on the ground, the Allies had decided that in the event of war the first and primary aim of Allied strategy was to be the protection of French soil until such time as the Allied deficiencies in the air and on the ground had been made good.[1]

Until nearly the beginning of the war, the British had not anticipated sending large ground or air forces to the Continent in the event of another general European conflict, but rather returned again to the pre-1914 policy of limited liability, under which Britain's contribution was to be mostly air and naval action from the British Isles. In the spring of 1939, the British government dropped this policy in favor of conscription and a large British ground force to serve alongside the French Army if necessary, but this switch in policy came too late for the British to have ready more than four divisions and weak air forces for commitment in September, 1939. The British promised that eventually their contribution would increase to thirty divisions, but in the meantime the main burden fell to the French Army.[2]

The French ground forces in September, 1939, were numerically strong. Out of a total of 99 divisions, 81 were infantry, 2 were light mechanized, and 3 were cavalry. Since 13 were fortress or garrison divisions,[3] 10 were stationed in North Africa, and 9 were located along the Italian Alps, there remained 67 mobile divisions available for offensive action against Germany.[4] The quality of these divisions varied from unit to unit, the active divisions being best, the series "A" reserve divisions being good, and the series "B" reserve divisions being definitely mediocre. Of the 80 divisions in northeastern France, 44 were active, 20 were series "A" reserve, and 16 were series "B" reserve.[5] The French High Command concentrated its best and most mobile divisions in the northern wing of the Allied line, facing the Belgian plain, and its inferior and static divisions opposite the Ardennes and on the Maginot Line. The small British Expeditionary Force (BEF) was concentrated alongside the mass of French tank and air forces in the northern wing. The Allies trusted that the difficult terrain of the Ardennes and the stout defenses of the Maginot Line would force the Germans to make their main attack again, as in 1914, through the Belgian plain.[6]

The French lacked neither numerous tanks nor artillery, but the tanks were for the most part distributed in small units among the infantry divisions. French doctrine treated tanks chiefly as auxiliaries to infantry and supplements to cavalry. In September, 1939, the only large French all-motorized formations were two light mechanized divisions (*Divisions Légères Mécaniques* or DLMs) which consisted of two squadrons of armored cars and 220 tanks combined into a reconnaissance regiment, a motorized rifle brigade, a towed artillery regiment, and an engineer battalion. The DLMs were not very different from the German panzer divisions in their organization, but they were subordinated to a cavalry doctrine under which they served as covering and reconnaisance forces rather than as striking forces. Richard Ogorkiewicz, an expert on armored warfare, believes that this outdated doctrine was primarily responsible for preventing the

DLM from playing a more important role.[7] The French High Command had formed only three DLMs by May, 1940.

After the initial mobilization in September, 1939, and the impressive German blitzkrieg in Poland, the French High Command made some halting steps toward large armored formations, which, under a different doctrine, might have overtaken the German lead in armored organization. The French combined four battalions of type-B heavy tanks with two newly formed battalions of motorized infantry to create the first *Division Cuirasée* (DC). Again, this organization could be further developed into an armored, mobile striking force, and by May, 1940, three modified DCs had been formed. The 1940 DC had 158 tanks, a battalion of motorized infantry, and two twelve-gun *groupes* of towed artillery.[8] But the promising DCs went into action in 1940 inadequately trained and equipped and without the services and doctrine necessary to make them fully independent of the infantry divisions they supported.

Besides these light mechanized and infantry tank divisions, the French had only various mixtures of motorized and nonmotorized forces. The light cavalry divisions (DCLs) combined one motorized infantry regiment and a tank regiment with a horse brigade. Except for the DCs, tanks were not wedded to infantry divisions and corps in units larger than battalions. Most of the autonomous tank battalions were in local reserves or under the commander of the general tank reserves.[9] By May, 1940, the French had organized seven motorized infantry divisions.[10]

The French prided themselves chiefly on their artillery, but most of it was horse-drawn and suitable chiefly for siegelike operations along the lines of the First World War.[11] The French Army had tremendous firepower, but was a slow and clumsy machine unsuited for a war of rapid movement. Organizational clumsiness was accentuated by the French doctrine, which emphasized systematic, formal methods of attack and defense, and which allowed the local commander little room for initiative. The French *Instructions for Tactical Employment of Large Units* subordinated all other arms to the infantry:

The Infantry is charged with the principal mission in combat. Protected and accompanied by its own fires and by those of the artillery, perhaps preceded and supported by tanks, aviation, *etc.,* it conquers the ground, occupies it, organizes it and holds it. Its task is particularly difficult, but is glorious above all others.

In contrast to the *Truppenfuehrung,* the German doctrinal statement, the French manual of doctrine declared of tanks:

They are able to make their way through certain passive obstacles, and to neutralize or destroy active resistance that is nearby. Under certain favorable circumstances, they can temporarily interdict the terrain by their own means; *they can never hold it conclusively.* In general, their operations, even when in mass, cannot suffice to break through positions that are *very strongly organized,* without the co-operation of other arms.[12]

In the French view, tanks existed to allow infantry to fight with full effect, rather than the other way around.

Despite its organizational and doctrinal problems on the ground, the greatest weakness of the French war machine lay in its weak air defenses. The *Armée de l'Air* possessed only 1,200 first-line aircraft of which 700 were fighters, 150 were bombers, and 350 were scout and observation aircraft.[13] The French lacked an early warning system at their airfields, and there were insufficient numbers of antiaircraft guns in front and rear.[14]

The BEF sent to France at the outbreak of war was numerically weak and insufficiently supported by the Royal Air Force (RAF). By the end of September, 1939, the BEF consisted of four motorized infantry divisions and a few battalions of tanks.[15] The British air forces in France were divided between the RAF component of the BEF and the Advanced Air Striking Force (AASF), the latter not intended to help the French Army or even the BEF but to get the shorter-ranged RAF bombers within striking distance of German industry. The RAF component of the BEF consisted of only five tactical squadrons, four strategic reconnaissance squadrons, and four (later six) Hurricane fighter squadrons. All ten British bomber squadrons sent to France were concentrated in the AASF, while two additional fighter squadrons of Hurricanes were allocated to it to protect its bases in France. Although the AASF's mission was subsequently changed to direct support of the Allied armies, the

RAF command structure in France was unnecessarily complex for a force that did not exceed 400 aircraft.[16]

Limited or Total Victory?

Although the Germans were aware of Allied weaknesses in certain respects, their councils were divided at the end of September as to the proper strategy for the future. The OKH favored a postponement of any offensive operation until the following spring in order to replenish military stocks depleted during the Polish campaign and to place the German Army on a firmer economic basis. General Halder had been informed by General Georg Thomas, the Chief of the OKW Economics section, that the demands of the three armed services already exceeded Germany's productive capacity.[17] The new "waves" of draftees had to be trained and equipped, and the planned expansion of the armored and air forces would require time. In Halder's view, at most the German Army could undertake a strategic offensive-defensive operation to improve Germany's defensive capabilities in the West.[18]

Regardless of the OKH's views, Hitler believed that the Wehrmacht should take some action during the remaining days of 1939 if weather permitted. The Fuehrer thought that time was on the side of the Allies, and he was extremely fearful that they would launch a surprise invasion of Belgium in order to place air and ground forces in short striking range of Germany's industrial heart —the Ruhr. He therefore decided that a plan of operations should be drawn up which had as its objective the occupation of the southern Dutch provinces and the Flemish coast to forestall such a possibility and to improve the ability of the German air and submarine forces to strike at England. Accordingly, a directive based on Hitler's ideas was issued by the OKW on October 9, 1939. In addition, the directive ordered the German armed forces to stand ready at all times to meet any attempt by the Allies to invade Belgium ahead of the planned German attack.[19]

The OKW directive was not enthusiastically received at OKH headquarters. Brauchitsch and Halder doubted that the Allies would violate Belgian or Dutch neutrality to threaten the Ruhr, and they were uncertain as to whether the Army could be made ready either in equipment or training for a German offensive during the remaining days of 1939. If the German attack could be delayed until spring, 1940, the conversion of the four light divisions to full-fledged panzer divisions could be completed, and at the same time perhaps sufficient stocks of fuel and equipment could be accumulated. Weather conditions more suited to the blitzkrieg army might obtain by then as well, and it was therefore with some reluctance that the OKH undertook to plan a fall offensive.[20]

The OKH labors produced Plan I, *Fall Gelb* (Case Yellow), during October, 1939, calling for the employment of ninety-five divisions on the Western front. Forty-two divisions, including all of the panzer and motorized infantry divisions, were to be assigned to Army Group B under General Bock. This army group was to drive through the Liège Gap and overrun the Maastricht Appendix just to the north (Dutch territory extending south a few miles between Belgium and Germany which had so hindered German deployment in 1914), then occupy as much of Holland and Belgium as the Allied armies would permit. Army Group A under General Rundstedt, with twenty-three infantry divisions, would attack through the "Ardennes corner" of southern Belgium to threaten the Meuse defenses and to create a diversion that would draw Allied forces away from the main effort made by Bock's group. Army Group C under General Wilhelm Ritter von Leeb, with twenty infantry divisions, would tie down the French forces in the Maginot Line. Ten infantry divisions were to be kept in general reserve.[21]

One of the advantages of Plan I was that it placed the main effort where there were excellent roads and railways to support a major attack. The German railroads in the Rhineland area opposite Liège were developed in the pre-1914 period to support the concentrations of troops and supplies for the Schlieffen Plan and were capable of handling the rail transport needs for large numbers of divisions (thirty-four in 1914). This was an important consideration, since Bock's thirty-three infantry divisions would have to rely on railroad movement for assembly before the attack and on rail and horse-drawn logistics once it was begun. The 177,375 horses of these infantry divisions would require 3,902,250 pounds of fodder per day, or enough to fill 156 railroad cars.[22] Once the operation got underway, Belgium's excellent railroad network and hard-surfaced roads leading south and west would facilitate German supply transport and permit faster and easier movement by the combat forces if the armored spearheads could occupy them quickly. The condition of the roads would be especially important if Hitler ordered the offensive in rain or snow, since German wheeled transport could bog down on unsurfaced highways and might delay the motorized divisions in their capture of the enemy rail system so vital to the following infantry divisions.

The logistical situation of Army Group A was less desirable. There were fewer rail and road lines leading to the assembly area, and there were fewer still in the Ardennes. Nevertheless, along this front in 1914 the Germans had massed two armies (Third and Fourth) totaling twenty divisions, or a force almost equal to the twenty-three infantry and mountain divisions that Plan I assigned to Army Group A. Yet the 111,131 horses of Army Group A had a daily fodder requirement of 1,444,882 pounds, or enough to fill ninety-seven railroad cars.[23] Finding fodder in the forests of the Ardennes would be more difficult than in the plains of Belgium—a major objection to a winter campaign in any case—and the combat forces of Army Group A would be operating over a long and tenuous supply line. The sixty miles separating the assembly areas from the Meuse were equal to about five days' marching time for Rundstedt's infantry divisions, on the assumption that Belgian resistance in the Ardennes would be weak and that the French would not be able, as they had been in 1914, to send large forces over the Meuse to meet the German attack while still negotiating the difficult Ardennes country. But the German forces in this area were expected to play a more modest role than that assigned the German armies in 1914,[24] although an unexpected breakthrough over the Meuse could be exploited by OKH reserves.[25]

Despite all of its logistical advantages, however, Plan I lacked strategic surprise. Even before the outbreak of war, the Anglo-French staff talks in March, 1939, had resulted in a strategic appreciation that clearly anticipated both the motives and objectives of Plan I. The Allied appreciation held that, because of the defensive strength of the Maginot Line, the Germans might be impelled to seek quick success by turning the barrier through Belgium and Holland. By such a turning movement, the Germans might find

themselves well placed to attack northern France, while at the same
time obtaining control of the North Sea coast and putting air
forces within range of vital French and British objectives. With
the outbreak of war in September, 1939, the initial Allied deployment had been in anticipation of such a threat. Moreover, by November, 1939, the strength of the Allied left wing, which would
meet the brunt of such an attack, was being further increased as the
BEF continued its expansion.[26] Whatever the merits of Plan I, it
was not likely to catch the Allies off balance or greatly surprise
them.

The drawbacks of Plan I aroused criticism from General Erich
von Manstein, Chief of Staff of Army Group A from mid-October.
He was chiefly displeased because Plan I was too limited in its objective and was not intended to achieve a decisive success. In a series
of memoranda to the OKH during the fall of 1939, Manstein proposed that *any* German plan should aim at a quick and decisive
victory in the tradition of the Kesselschlacht doctrine and added
that to fritter away the offensive capacities of the Army on half
measures was inadmissible. The real chance, as Manstein saw it, consisted in launching a surprise attack through the Ardennes spearheaded by panzer divisions, an attack where the Allies were least
expecting a major blow and where the appearance of a concentrated
tank attack would come as a complete surprise. If the Allied northern wing containing most of the Allied mobile divisions could be
drawn onto the Belgian plain to meet a subsidiary attack there, a
breakthrough over the Meuse at Sedan could be directed toward the
lower Somme in order to cut off the enemy forces advancing into
Belgium. Manstein believed that this was the only way in which
the Germans might destroy the entire northern Allied wing preparatory to winning a final victory in France.[27]

Halder was skeptical of Manstein's ideas for several reasons.
First, the real intentions of the Allies were not yet known and there
was no assurance that the Allied northern wing would advance into
Belgium to meet an attack there. (Actually, the Allies had no such
plan until mid-November.) Secondly, a major German armored
advance through the Ardennes would pose serious logistical problems which would increase if a breakout should be directed all the
way to the Channel. Finally, the more limited OKH plan at least

avoided the risk of betting everything on a single line of action; a Schlieffen-like approach hardly recommended itself after the disaster of 1914 and the OKH preferred Moltke's "plan with branches." Brauchitsch and Halder intended to keep a large number of divisions in reserve which could be sent to the support of either army group if, unexpectedly, the opportunity for a total victory seemed in the offing, but they were unwilling to endorse a plan which inherently sought total victory at the risk of total defeat.[28] Despite the OKH satisfaction with Plan I, Hitler decided in November, quite independently, to switch Guderian's XIX Panzer Corps to Army Group A in hopes of exploiting in some way the reported weak Allied position around Sedan. Once Guderian joined Army Group A and became familiar with Manstein's ideas, he quickly backed Manstein's notion that pushing large numbers of tanks through such difficult country as. the Ardennes was feasible.[29] By then the idea of making a daring gamble for total victory with Army Group A was under discussion at several headquarters.

Meanwhile, Hitler had set a series of dates for the limited offensive planned under Plan I, each of which he cancelled because of adverse weather. These alerts became known to Allied intelligence each time shortly after they were issued. After mid-November the Allied High Command believed its northern wing strong enough to meet the expected German attack by advancing into Belgium and forming a defensive front behind either the Escaut River (Plan E) or the Dyle River (Plan D).[30] Consequently, German agents and aerial reconnaissance reported after each alert that the Allied left wing was apparently preparing for an advance into Belgium. Halder believed by the end of December that this Allied reaction could be counted on to meet any German attack on the Low Countries.[31] Still, Brauchitsch and Halder saw no reason for changing German dispositions.

Manstein continued to be dissatisfied with Plan I and the OKH arguments in its defense. He believed that a massive concentration of panzer and motorized infantry divisions must lead the attack through the Ardennes to insure breaching the Meuse barrier before the Allied High Command could detect the threat, and he wished from the outset to have three rather than two armies assigned to his group. Unless this was done, he wrote in a memoran-

dum to the OKH on January 12, a decisive thrust through the
Ardennes was not possible.[32] The OKH was reluctant to shift more
armor to the Ardennes, but agreed to hold map exercises in February
to test the contending theories.

Before the February map exercises could be held, still another
factor intruded. On January 17 a German aircraft carrying a staff
officer with papers relating to Plan I strayed into Belgian air space
and made a forced landing. Belgian authorities seized the papers
before they could be destroyed and promptly turned them over to
the Allies. Although only the bare outlines of Plan I were contained
in the seized documents, the OKH had to assume that they had
found their way to the Allies and that Plan I was compromised.
After this so-called Mechelen Incident, the need for the February
map exercises became more imperative than ever.[33]

The map exercises held at each of the army group headquarters
for a ten-day period in February gradually made clear that a concentration of forces while the army groups were already in motion
would lead to loss of time and much friction. The chance of exploiting a passing opportunity might be irretrievably lost. By the
end of the exercises the OKH was convinced that priority must be
given to either the front of Army Group A or Army Group B *before* assembly as the focal point of the main effort. Since all available intelligence indicated that any German advance into Belgium
and the Netherlands would be met by a counteroffensive from the
Allied northern wing pivoting on a weak hinge in the Ardennes, the
operational basis existed for a major stroke through the Ardennes
to sever connection between the Allied northern wing and the Maginot Line, to encircle the Allied forces moving into Belgium, and to
annihilate them in a giant Kesselschlacht.[34]

The final decision rested with Hitler, who was already swinging
in favor of a major drive through the Ardennes to seek a total
victory. Hitler held a dinner party on the last night of the map
maneuvers for several newly promoted corps commanders, among
them Manstein, who, as a result of a promotion, was about to be
transferred to command an infantry corps. Manstein did not let
this opportunity slip past without pressing his views on Hitler, who
immediately displayed his customary enthusiasm for a daring course.
But while this interview may have reinforced Hitler's attitude to-

ward the Ardennes plan, his interest in exploiting in some way the weak front along the Meuse and seeking a total rather than a limited victory had been rising for some time. More decisive were the map maneuvers, which convinced both Brauchitsch and Halder by the last day of the exercises (February 17) that the main effort must be made with Army Group A. On February 18 at a Fuehrer conference just following the exercises which had already converted the OKH to a total effort on the Ardennes front, Hitler definitely ruled in its favor. The most careful student of these events—Hans-Adolf Jacobsen—concludes that Hitler and the OKH made up their minds concerning the Ardennes drive almost simultaneously.[35] The German Army was committed to a daring gamble to bring about an early and decisive victory in the West.

The German Motorization Crisis

The OKH was not solely occupied with strategic questions during the winter months of 1939–1940. Halder's journal reveals during that time his growing concern with the Army's logistical situation. By early February, 1940, reports indicated that Germany was not producing enough motor transport to meet the Army's needs and that the Army was receiving an insufficient share of what was produced. Halder wrote in his journal on February 3 that, with a total production of 12,000 trucks per quarter, only 4,000 were being allocated to the Wehrmacht, including 2,500–2,600 trucks technically provided the Army. Actually, the Army was not receiving that many: deliveries were running to about 1,000 trucks per quarter or not even 1% of the Army's entire park. This meant, Halder wrote in his war journal (III, 54), that "we are not replacing normal losses through wear, let alone keeping anything to cover losses in operations and combat." The civilian economy had been raided earlier for 16,000 trucks, of which 3,200 had gone to supply shortages in the Army, 5,000 to replace trucks under repair, 5,000 more to equip newly activated units, and 2,800 for the Replacement and Training Army. No reserve remained.

The following day, February 4, Halder wrote "we have now about 120,000 trucks with shortages reported from the field of 2,668." Even including the trucks under repair, the Army was 5,000

trucks under its authorized strength. Halder commented that in
addition the vehicles in many units were quite old and in his opinion
the situation was so serious that the Army "cannot pull through
in any operation." Furthermore, he wrote, "if we allow . . . 2%
for the normal monthly loss (not counting combat casualties),
which is the normal rate, new production will cover only half that
loss. The consequence is a continuous drain on our truck strength,
impairing the operational efficiency of our forces."

Halder saw four possible remedies for the truck situation. The
first was an increase in truck production, but an increase would be
limited by rubber shortages, and not over four thousand trucks a
quarter for all three armed services could be expected. The second
alternative would be to change the Army's share of the current production, but this solution would require a ruling from the Fuehrer
and competition with the powerful Goering and his Luftwaffe. A
third alternative would be to dip into the reserves of the domestic
economy, and "there is no doubt that by dipping once (and only
that time)," Halder wrote, "we can supply the present shortage and
perhaps even set aside a small reserve." Still, Halder added, "this
backlog would be absorbed within seven months by the normal wear
of at least 2% a month (excluding combat losses). How fast it
would go *with* combat losses is beyond our power to estimate."
Moreover, Halder calculated, after deducting 5,000 trucks to supply
the current unit shortages, the Army would have only 11,000 left,
not counting new production. If the loss of 1,500 trucks a month
could be assumed, then Halder figured that even with new production the addition to the total park would be exhausted in about seven
months *if there was no operation!* (III, 57) In other words, even
under this alternative the Army would fall below minimal needs at
the current rate of loss just by standing still.

Halder favored a fourth alternative, although the most drastic
and one that would have to be executed concurrently with the
others to have effect. Halder proposed a sweeping "demotorization
program," which would entail a massive increase in the already
heavy German reliance on horse-drawn transport and "the pro-
curement of horses, vehicles and harnesses." In Halder's opinion,
this decision had to be made immediately in order "to make sure
that it would take effect in time to carry us on when the present *single*
[truck] addition to our park will have been exhausted." He pro-

posed that a special committee be appointed of representatives from the Army General Staff and the Chief of Army Equipment "to deal with details of the demotorization program and to determine its scope by exploring all the various possibilities in consultation with representative bodies of farming, small business, *etc.*" He concluded that *"the most important* thing, however, is to start at once with procuring [horse-drawn] vehicles, harness, *etc.,* without wasting a long time for computations and conferences." Such was the state of the "motorized, mechanized" German Army only three months before the French campaign!

Halder recognized that the shortages in motorization would have serious consequences for the future conduct of German ground operations. He wrote on February 4 that "at the present . . . level of motorization, the beginning of an operation with a distant objective is advisable only if a minimum truck reserve is available or the possibility of prompt replacement by horsedrawn vehicles is assured." (III, 58) Further, he wrote:

When operations have continued for a certain time (the length of which would vary with road conditions, supply and combat losses), it would be necessary to call a pause in operations in view of the impossibility [of obtaining] . . . replacement for all matériel losses. The pause after the Polish campaign lasted four weeks. We found that it was not long enough. After a new operation, the pause would have to be considerably extended, in proportion to the lessened operational value of our trucks.

Halder's analysis did not include the German situation in tanks and tracked vehicles of the artillery, but he recognized that "separate measures must be considered to deal with that situation." Still, Halder's journal entries leave no doubt that the blitzkrieg army was a force in transition, provided with only a thin cutting edge of armored and motorized forces, and not overly supplied with even horse-drawn equipment.

The Implementation of Plan II

Despite the Army's logistical handicaps in the spring of 1940, the OKH planners pressed forward with the implementation of Plan II, Case Yellow. The switch of the German center of gravity to the

Ardennes region required intensive work by the Army General Staff to solve the assembly and supply problems of a major thrust in that area. For instance, the assembly of the infantry divisions which would follow the armored spearheads through the Ardennes would involve so much rail traffic over an extended period of time that it might give away the real point of attack.[36] This problem was solved by moving the infantry divisions behind Army Group C, where they appeared to be reinforcements for the West Wall. Then special routes north by rail and road were laid out so that, as the panzer divisions broke into the Ardennes, the infantry divisions would move northward to the assembly areas vacated by the motorized forces, then pivot west to follow the spearheads. This solution also reduced the problem of echeloning in great depth and relieved the pressure on the railroads to the Ardennes during the build-up.[37]

The most important operational decision after February for the Germans was whether the armored spearheads should immediately exploit any bridgehead achieved on the west side of the Meuse or await reinforcements of artillery and infantry. Guderian, whose XIX Panzer Corps would be in the lead, preferred to attempt a crossing and exploitation without reinforcement by the following infantry divisions. He believed that the balanced panzer divisions with strong Luftwaffe support could breach the Meuse barrier unassisted, since they contained already the necessary assault infantry and combat engineers, and that no time should be wasted in pushing through the breach westward. Halder was highly skeptical about the ability of the panzer divisions to fight their way over the Meuse without assistance and especially doubtful about the wisdom of pushing far westward without waiting for the infantry divisions to catch up. At a March 15 conference, Hitler asked Guderian what he intended to do if his panzer corps secured a bridgehead over the Meuse before the infantry divisions came up. Guderian replied that, unless specifically instructed otherwise, he would continue to drive west. According to Guderian's account, Hitler nodded and said nothing more.[38] This decision was not actually left to Guderian. Another conference was held on March 16, and Halder recorded in his journal on March 17 that the "decision is reserved on further moves after the crossing of the Meuse," and that "the Fuehrer now approves the preparations made and is manifestly confident of success." (III, 125) On this evidence, it appears that Hitler had asked Guderian this "vital question" (as Guderian phrased it) simply to gauge whether he could expect to rein in or spur on his spearhead leader. The Fuehrer's nod is no evidence that he had granted Guderian *carte blanche* to carry on as he pleased.[39]

The concentration of forces under the new Plan II was again worked out under Halder's direction by the General Staff, and the final product reflected the OKH's fundamental understanding of the Ardennes strategy and the requirement for quick victory, the only kind that the Army's strained logistic situation was likely to permit. The *Schwerpunkt* (center of gravity) was shifted to the Ardennes, where forty-five divisions were assembled, including seven panzer divisions and three motorized infantry divisions. Instead of the three armies for which Manstein had asked, Halder and his staff had decided to concentrate five—three in line and two in reserve to be moved up when the constriction of the Ardennes was passed. These armies were (from north to south) the Fourth, with Hermann Hoth's panzer corps attached, the Twelfth Army, and the Sixteenth Army, with the Second and Ninth armies held in reserve. Excepting Hoth's panzer corps, all the panzer and motorized infantry divisions in Army Group A were organized into two corps (one under Guderian and one under Georg-Hans Reinhardt) and concentrated as a "panzer group"[40] under General Ewald von Kleist. Led by Panzer Group Kleist and Hoth's panzer corps, Army Group A was to advance on a front extending south from Monschau to Luxembourg, making a main effort to penetrate the southern Ardennes and to break the Meuse barrier around Sedan. If the Meuse could be crossed, the direction of Army Group A's attack would be toward Amiens and Abbeville to cut off the Allied northern wing, which presumably would have advanced into the Belgian plain to meet Army Group B's attack on Holland and northern Belgium.[41]

Plan II gave Army Group B a total of twenty-nine divisions, but only three panzer divisions and two motorized infantry divisions. Army Group B's forces were divided between the Eighteenth Army (opposite the Netherlands) and the Sixth Army (opposite Liège and the Maastricht Appendix). The mission of Army Group B was to advance on a front from Aachen north to Winterswijk and to overrun southern Holland and northern Belgium, thereby drawing the Allied northern wing northward to meet its attack.

The mission and strength of Army Group C behind the West Wall were unchanged by Plan II; its twenty infantry divisions (divided between the First and Seventh armies) were to make local attacks and feints to tie down the French divisions in the Maginot Line.

In addition to the forces concentrated in the army groups or in their local reserves, the OKH general reserve consisted of 41 infantry divisions, 1 motorized infantry division, and 1 motorized brigade. The total German strength in the West on May 10, 1940, was 136 divisions, of which only 16 were fully motorized.

The Norway-Denmark Affair

While planning went on for the German campaign in the West (code-name Case Yellow), Hitler decided to strike northward into Denmark and Norway. He had not intended to involve these neutral countries in the war [42] but a number of developments made their occupation imperative by the spring of 1940. In November, 1939, Russia attacked Finland. Hitler feared that under the pretext of aiding the Finns an Allied expeditionary force might violate Norwegian neutrality to turn Germany's northern flank. Secondly, Germany's main supply of iron ore came from Swedish fields of the far north and near the Norwegian frontier. When the Baltic Sea was frozen during the winter months, the iron ore bound for Germany was loaded on coastal craft at the Norwegian port of Narvik and then moved down the neutral Norwegian coast to German ports. An Allied occupation of Norway or even interdiction of the Norwegian water route might seriously injure Germany's war production. Finally, Admiral Raeder pressed for naval bases beyond the North Sea. German naval studies between the world wars had stressed the suitability of Norwegian ports for basing large surface units for forays into the Atlantic against Allied sea lanes. Although the collapse of Finland was imminent by February, 1940, and the danger of Allied occupation of Norway for that reason minimal then, Hitler's fear for the iron ore was reawakened on February 16

by the *Altmark* affair.[43] Preparations for the German occupation of
Norway and Denmark (the latter as a stepping stone) were speeded
up and two expeditionary forces organized. General Nicholas
von Falkenhorst's XXI Corps was redesignated as the XXI Group
and allotted five infantry and two mountain divisions for the
invasion of Norway, while General Leonhard Kaupisch's XXXI
Corps was assigned two infantry divisions and a motorized brigade
for the invasion of Denmark. Most of Falkenhorst's forces were to
be moved by sea aboard German warships, while the Luftwaffe provided air cover and made parachute drops and airborne landings on
the Norwegian airfields. The northern operation was given the
code-designation *Weseruebung* (Exercise Weser).[44]

From the OKH standpoint, the most important aspect of this
operation was that Hitler placed entire responsibility in the OKW.
The OKH took no hand in the planning, and, in fact, was unaware
that such an operation was being organized until Falkenhorst was
appointed the commander of the Norwegian expedition. Halder was
so surprised and annoyed by Hitler's deviousness that on February
21, 1940, he wrote in his journal: "Not a single word has passed
between the Fuehrer and [Brauchitsch] on this matter; this must
be put on record for the history of the war. I shall make a point of
noting down the first time the subject is broached. Nothing to
date." (III, 88–89)

Why Hitler deliberately excluded the OKH not only from the
planning stage in Exercise Weser but from any knowledge about it
is uncertain. Perhaps he wished to demonstrate his own military
flair without the hindrance and conservatism of the OKH, but in
any case Brauchitsch and Halder were relegated to the task of
merely supplying the forces for the operation. They took no part in
the execution of Weser either, an operation dominated by the OKW,
the Navy, and the Luftwaffe, and in fact may have wished Hitler's
private theater of war to fail so as to influence Hitler thereafter to
consult the OKH before all operations.[45] Actually, Kaupisch's troops
occupied Denmark without opposition, while the German air drops
and amphibious landings in Norway caught the Norwegians and
Allies by surprise. The key airfields were seized with little difficulty
and the Luftwaffe flew in squadrons to cover the amphibious operations. The Royal Navy struck back belatedly and without suf-

ficient air cover, and an Allied expeditionary force had to be with-drawn. Although the German Navy suffered heavy losses,[46] and the Germans experienced one major crisis in the affair, Hitler's private theater of war ended successfully and inflated the Fuehrer's not in-considerable ego to new heights. He showed a growing tendency to interfere with military operations from April, 1940, on.

Allied Preparations

While the Germans were using the winter of 1939–1940 to improve the condition of their military forces and to determine a proper strategy in the West, the Anglo-French armies struggled with their own problems. The French had called all their reservists to the colors in September, 1939, only to find that many were needed in vital war industries and had to be sent back to their jobs with a consequent disruption of organization and training. Maurice Gamelin, General in Chief of the Army,[47] was able to add only six-teen new divisions to his Northeast Command during the winter of 1939–1940,[48] but by early May three DLMs (light mechanized di-visions) and three DCs (infantry tank divisions) had been formed, and one DLM and another DC were in the process of organiza-tion.[49] But the French High Command was still clinging to prewar doctrine, and the warning of a far-sighted young tank general, Charles de Gaulle, went unheeded during the long "sitzkrieg." In a memorandum sent to the French High Command on January 26, 1940, de Gaulle warned that the internal-combustion engine would upset French military doctrine and circumvent fortifications. French war matériel, he argued, must be organized in the same way as the German. For effective counterattack, a concentrated armored strik-ing force was needed—such as he had urged on the government since 1934[50] in order to supplement the Nation in Arms. In his memorandum, de Gaulle pointed out that the French people should not suffer the illusion that the existing "sitzkrieg" was in harmony with the nature of modern warfare. He declared that the opposite was true and that the internal-combustion engine endowed any army properly equipped and organized with such force, speed, and range that sooner or later the war in which the Allies were engaged would be marked by surprises, breakthroughs, and pursuits on a scale and with a rapidity that would infinitely exceed even the most lightning events of the past.[51]

By May, 1940, the BEF had increased its strength to ten motorized infantry divisions,[52] but the BEF's armored component still consisted of several reconnaissance battalions of light tanks and one armored brigade. Although the British Army had moved to form an armored division in 1939,[53] shortages of equipment and uncertainties about organization delayed the day of its readiness. On May 10, 1940, the date of the beginning of the German offensive in the West, not over six hundred British tanks were in France and the "Armoured Division" was still resting in England.[54] Only one brigade was landed in time to see action in the battle of France, and that too late to affect the outcome in any appreciable way. In contrast to the halting improvements in the Allied armies, the Germans had used the time to form five more panzer divisions and to increase their total strength by thirty divisions of all types.

The French did not lack tanks by May, 1940, nor, for the most part, good ones. About three thousand modern machines were with the French armies of the Northeast Command,[55] compared to just 2,574 tanks in the ten panzer divisions.[56] Even if independent German tank battalions are added, the French had at least as many tanks of modern design as did the Germans. The French armored forces were composed of about eight hundred medium and heavy tanks, and about twenty-two hundred light tanks.[57] French armor and gunpower were on the average better than the German, but German tanks were on the average a bit faster and nearly all were radio-equipped.[58] Most authorities agree that in May, 1940, the German tank arm possessed no clear technical or quantitative superiority over the French.

The chief French armor problem lay not in inferior numbers of armored fighting vehicles nor for the most part in inferior tank design (although French tank development had tended, like the British, to overspecialization). The French Achilles' heel was still doctrine and organization. With fifty-six French tank battalions to only thirty-five German tank battalions,[59] the French High Command frittered away its battalion superiority by dealing out most units in "penny packets" among the infantry divisions. Even the few French armored and all-motorized divisions of varying kinds were not concentrated in groups as the Germans were combining their panzer and other motorized divisions, but were scattered over the whole front. The three DLMs were assigned to the Allied left wing armies preparatory to the planned advance into the Belgian plain, one DC was stationed with an army in the Maginot Line extension, one was in reserve, and only one was attached to the Ninth Army. The Ninth Army, with only 500 armored fighting vehicles, was to find itself opposed by 2,300 German tanks in the Ardennes during the May, 1940, blitz.

Despite Allied organizational and equipment deficiencies on the ground, by May, 1940, the greatest weakness of the Anglo-French forces remained their air defenses. The situation in the air had only slightly improved since the previous fall. On May 10, the RAF had a maximum of 400 operational aircraft in twenty-five squadrons on French airfields. Eight squadrons were equipped with an old, slow, and short-ranged bomber, six with an inferior light bomber, six with old British Army tactical aircraft, and only six squadrons possessed the excellent Hurricane fighter. After the battle began, six more Hurricane squadrons were rushed to France, but all of the even better Spitfire squadrons were kept behind radar protection in England. The French Air Force numbered not above fourteen hundred and fifty aircraft.[60] Counting RAF reinforcements sent to France after the battle began, perhaps two thousand Allied aircraft operated from French airfields during the first phase of the battle of France. Even more serious than the continuing Allied inferiority in numbers vis-à-vis the Luftwaffe,[61] the long lull had not produced any real improvement in the early warning systems around French airfields or in antiaircraft artillery defense of both air and ground forces. All the Allied airplanes within Luftwaffe range were open to surpise attack on their fields, and the Allies were almost certain to lose command of the air if the Luftwaffe were permitted to seize the initiative.

Blitzkrieg West (Phase I)

By early May, 1940, the last German preparations had been completed and the Wehrmacht awaited only a forecast of extended good weather. On Wednesday, May 8, reports became favorable enough

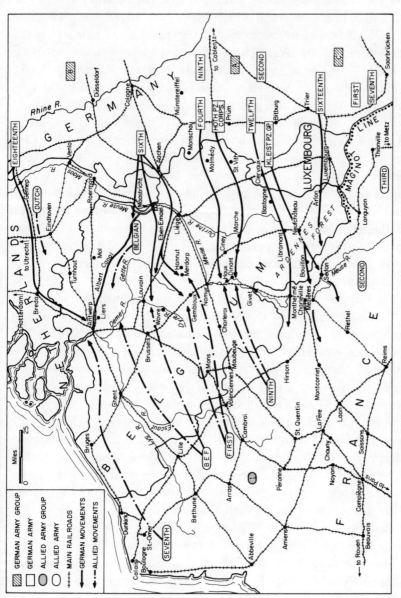

10. The Ardennes Breakthrough and the Western Front, 1940.

for Hitler to order the attack to begin at 5:35 A.M. on Friday,
May 10. On May 9, Halder and his staff departed from Zossen for
OKH field headquarters at Münstereiffel. At 10:15 P.M. that same
day, OKW headquarters, located a few miles away, confirmed the
orders to attack by sending the code-word "Danzig," and at dawn
on May 10 the campaign in the West got underway. (Halder, IV, 1)

The air fleets of Kesselring and Hugo Sperrle struck the first
blows by making sudden descents on most of the Dutch, Belgian,
and French airfields soon after dawn. Within a few hours nearly
the entire Belgian and Dutch air forces—numbering together perhaps a thousand planes—were wiped out, while the French Air
Force was severely damaged. Only the RAF fields in France escaped
serious injury, possibly because so many of them were far to the
west. The RAF had to carry the burden of air operations in France
for the next few weeks with forces heavily outnumbered and, except for its fighters, outperformed.[62] By the end of the second day
of the campaign, the Luftwaffe had achieved air superiority over
the battle area.[63]

The staggering air blows on May 10 were immediately followed
by German invasions of the Netherlands and Belgium. General von
Küchler's Eighteenth Army (one panzer division, one cavalry division, one motorized infantry division, and seven infantry divisions) advanced into the Netherlands at numerous points behind a
large-scale airborne attack which secured many vital causeways and
prevented the Dutch from flooding their dike system as a defensive
measure. The Luftwaffe's airborne operations surprised the partially
mobilized Dutch Army of ten divisions, which was speedily overcome in front and rear; at the end of five days it was compelled to
surrender. The Belgians were similarly surprised in their border
defenses when airborne operations permitted the capture of fortress
Eben Emael covering the approach across the Maastricht Appendix.[64] General von Reichenau's Sixth Army was allowed to turn
the defenses of Liège on the third day of the campaign.

The reports of the heavy German assaults on the Low Countries
immediately convinced the Allied High Command that the main
German attack, as in 1914, was coming through the Belgian plain.
It issued orders at 7:30 A.M. to the Northeast armies to implement
Plan D (Dyle),[65] under which the Allied northern wing was to

proceed into Belgium and take up positions alongside the retreating Belgian Army behind the Demer and Dyle rivers. The sixty miles from the French frontier to the "Dyle line" required a three-days' march, but once the Dyle line was reached a continuous Allied front might be formed from Antwerp up the Demer to its tributary, the Dyle, then up the Dyle to its source, then across the twenty-five-mile so-called Gembleaux Gap between the source of the Dyle and the banks of the Meuse, then up the Meuse through the Ardennes to the northern end of the Maginot Line. The Allied advance into Belgium was executed by General Gaston Billotte's Army Group One of General Alphonse Georges' Northeast Front. The Seventh Army on Army Group One's far left was to advance, independently of the other three mobile armies, via Antwerp, to assist the Dutch. The others in line—the BEF on the left, the French First Army in the center, and the French Ninth Army on the right (pivoting on the Ardennes)—would perform the actual wheeling movement to the Dyle, the Gembloux Gap, and the Meuse, while the largely immobile Second Army remained opposite the southern Ardennes and provided the link with the Maginot Line. The retreating Belgian Army was expected to take up a position on the left of the BEF between Louvain and Antwerp.[66]

The signal to execute Plan D on May 10 was given on the Allied assumption that the Belgians would contain the German drive at Liège for at least the three days required for the Allies to reach the Dyle, but the unexpected speed with which the German Sixth Army turned the Liège defenses forced the Belgians to evacuate their border positions a day ahead of schedule. This situation, in turn, compelled the Allied wheeling movement to drive to the Dyle before that barrier was overrun by the German advance and tended to rivet the Allied High Command's attention firmly on the Belgian plain.[67] The Allied High Command showed no concern over the Ninth Army's drive toward the Meuse since that army had the shortest arc of the wheeling movement and its junction with the mostly stationary Second Army on its right was covered by the "impenetrable" Ardennes. But the Ninth and Second armies, the weakest in Army Group One, were attempting to cover the longest front.

The Ninth Army's commander, General André Corap, had concentrated most of his nine divisions in a drive toward his army's

objective of Dinant on the Meuse in the northwest corner of the
Ardennes triangle. Only two cavalry divisions were ordered into the
central Ardennes to support the Belgian cavalry and to maintain
contact with the Second Army's left flank, which joined the right
flank of the Ninth Army at the southwest corner just north of
Sedan. The Second Army's commander, General Charles Huntziger,
also had only nine divisions at his disposal and, like Corap, was more
concerned about the open area—the southeast corner of the triangle
—of his front than the Ardennes. Hence, the Second Army advanced only two cavalry divisions into the forests. As a result of this
lack of concern for their vital junction point, the two army commanders allowed the forty miles of the front running through the
southern Ardennes to be covered by only four French cavalry divisions and some miscellaneous Belgian units.[68]

Allied weakness at the vital junction point in the Ardennes was
the result of a complete misjudgment by the Allied High Command
concerning German intentions and capabilities. The OKH had successfully misled the French as to the whereabouts of the main German concentration, and the French had completely misjudged the
ability of German armor to launch a major blow through the Ardennes without warning. Both facts were to be responsible for a
major Allied disaster.

The German advance through the Ardennes began the same day as
the more dramatic blows were being delivered in the Netherlands and
in northern Belgium. Still unnoticed by the Allied High Command,
Panzer Group Kleist quickly swept aside scattered Belgian resistance
in the Ardennes and pressed steadily toward the Meuse around
Sedan, while the German Fourth Army on its right was moving
rapidly ahead to the Meuse at Dinant. Although French reconnaissance planes reported seeing long lines of headlights moving westward through the Ardennes on the night of May 11–12, General
Billotte, Army Group One commander, failed to recognize the real
danger.[69]

Halder, meanwhile, was keeping a close surveillance of the logistical situation in the area of Army Group A, for here was the greatest
possibility that terrain and communications might create serious bottlenecks. Elaborate preparations for traffic control had been made
in advance, however, and the Quartermaster section reported every-

thing was running smoothly and "the supply situation good." By May 11, the German railroad troops had seized the Luxembourg and Alzette Valley railroads and had eighteen supply trains operating west of Bastogne. (Journal, IV, 4)

The following day, May 12, the intelligence section reported that the Allied northern wing was reacting as predicted, and that between twelve and fifteen Anglo-French divisions were approaching the Dyle and the Meuse around Dinant. Halder remarked that the Anglo-French air forces had shown a "surprising lack of activity," perhaps not realizing himself how badly shattered they had been during the first forty-eight hours of the campaign (IV, 5).

Thus from every standpoint the operation was so far proceeding exactly according to plan, with the Allied armies reacting precisely as predicted. By the evening of May 12 the OKH was convinced that the Allied High Command had mistaken the German drive into southern Holland and northern Belgium for the main effort, and that the real threat developing in the Ardennes had gone unappreciated. The next few days would be decisive.

On the evening of May 12, Guderian's panzer corps reached the French positions on the Meuse at Sedan.[70] Sixty yards across and unfordable, the river was defended on the French side by a complex of pillboxes and entrenchments with an average density of eight pillboxes and eight machine guns per mile, or one for every 200 yards of front. In the rear of this line were French batteries in open revetments, which were ready to lay down a heavy barrage on any force attempting to breach the Meuse barrier. But the French had few local reserves, few antiaircraft guns, and almost no antitank weapons for direct firing. A successful French defense at this point was heavily dependent on the artillery disposed in the open in the rear.[71]

The German appearance along the upper Meuse had at last wrenched the local French command out of its lethargy. General Huntziger, commander of the Second Army, on whose front the German tanks had appeared, at once ordered up reinforcements for his lines at Sedan but found that the best of his reserves were located too far in the rear to reach the area before the next day. Those nearer to the area were the inferior series "B" reserve divisions and were slow to move up. The X Corps commander, who was responsible for the defense of the Sedan sector, had only a single regiment in reserve, and it arrived too late to assist in resisting the German attack on May 13. Thus, as Kleist and Guderian made their dispositions during the night of May 12 for an assault the following day, the French were reacting far too slowly and with inadequate forces. Guderian's assault plan was referred to the OKH for approval, which it received, although Halder thought it was "rather complicated" (IV, 7). Actually, it worked as smoothly as a training exercise.

During the morning of May 13, the German forces made a few probing moves along the Meuse. These were instantly met with the expected heavy concentrations of French artillery fire. About noon Luftwaffe planes appeared in waves to attack the French artillery positions, and by early afternoon the artillery fire began to slacken. This permitted Guderian's tanks to roll forward to the river's edge and to open fire on the French pillboxes a short distance away on the opposite side. While the German tank shells continuously hammered the embrasures and forced the French infantry to suspend firing, German assault infantry brought up pneumatic boats and began to cross the river. Once across, they worked their way to the French pillboxes and knocked out each in turn with grenades and flamethrowers. With tactics similar to those used in 1918 to achieve breakthroughs on heavily fortified fronts, the Germans by late afternoon had cleared a few hundred yards of the French line, and work could begin on a pontoon bridge over which German armor would cross during the night.[72]

Further north the French were experiencing a second disaster. The Ninth Army's advance to the Meuse at Dinant proved too slow, and the German Fourth Army succeeded in breaching the Belgian defenses in a manner similar to the one just described. The Ninth Army thus came under heavy attack by the German armor along its front just as its right was being uncovered at Sedan. Its nine infantry divisions could not withstand such a German onslaught in the open, and its armored support was late in arriving and thrown in piecemeal. The entire French front in the Ardennes began to collapse.[73] Gamelin, the French General in Chief, at once ordered reinforcements from the Allied northern wing, now under heavy attack along the Dyle by Army Group B, but the lack of motorization delayed their arrival. As the hours passed, their overwhelming concentration in the Ardennes began to favor the Germans [74] and a yawning sixty-mile gap began to open in the Allied center.

Early on the morning of May 14 the French made their last attempt to save the Meuse line at Sedan by launching a tank counterattack in battalion strength. But Guderian had moved many of his tanks to the west side of the Meuse during the night, and the French attack was beaten off with heavy loss. The Germans were over the Meuse in strength a full twenty-four hours ahead of Halder's schedule and were ready to drive west.

However, a sudden hitch developed during the night of May 14, when Kleist and Guderian disagreed over whether the attack should proceed at once or await reinforcements. At length, Kleist relented and Guderian pushed his armor out toward Montcornet and Rethel along the Aisne during May 15–16.[75] The next day the Germans advanced toward Saint-Quentin and Péronne. Halder was elated by both this success and news that Reinhardt's corps had crossed the Meuse a short distance further north. On May 14, he wrote that Army Group A must "throw to the left wing everything not needed elsewhere in order to push on south of Brussels" and to cut off the enemy in central Belgium. Although he seems to have had no hand in Kleist's order to Guderian to halt for reinforcements, he planned to have Kleist's panzer group move forward in a "massive formation" in the general direction of the sea at Saint-Omer. He added in his journal that the preparation of the infantry to follow "has already been organized, partly by railroad . . . partly by foot marches" (IV, 13).

On May 17, Guderian's corps was halted for a second time, but Halder's journal indicates that he opposed this order and that it originated from Hitler. Earlier that day he had described the German drive in almost ecstatic terms: "Our breakthrough wedge is developing in a positively classic manner. West of the Meuse our attack is sweeping on, smashing tank counter-attacks in its path." There is no trace of doubt or hesitation in this entry. But the intelligence section had been giving him reports which indicated that Huntziger's Second Army on the left flank of the breach was at last assembling forces. Halder dismissed these French efforts to close the breach as too little and too late, but Hitler took them quite seriously. He called for a peeling off of the infantry divisions to bolster the southern side of the corridor extending west, a measure that Halder hotly opposed. Halder wrote in his journal that the continuation of the drive was "based on the condition that [Army Group A] does not tie up any of its strength on the southern flank, but keeps pushing westward in echelon formation." He saw no risk in this since he judged the French on the southern flank "too weak to attack at this time." (IV, 17) But Hitler would not be convinced, and at length the OKH agreed that three infantry corps would be halted and faced southward, much to Halder's annoyance. That evening he closed his journal entry for the day with some asperity:

Rather unpleasant day. The Fuehrer is terribly nervous. Frightened by his own success, he is afraid to take any chance and so would rather pull the reins on us. Puts forward the excuse that it is all because of his concern for the left flank! (IV, 17)

By the next day it was apparent that the French on the southern flank were attempting primarily to insure that no southern German drive would develop; the French forces there posed no major threat of a counterattack across German communications to the new positions Panzer Group Kleist was winning to the West.[76]

The situation was very different during the first few days on the Belgian plain, where the Allied northern wing had reached the Dyle and joined the Belgian Army against Bock's Army Group B. The French sent forward their mechanized cavalry corps to cover the withdrawal of the Belgians, and the first tank-to-tank battle of the war was fought around Merdorp, a village just west of Hannut, on May 12–13. The French tanks proved individually superior to those of the Germans, but were poorly handled and forced to withdraw. The German tanks then tried to take advantage of the temporary gap that opened between the Dyle and the Meuse, but were shattered by fierce French artillery barrages;[77] German assaults at Louvain and Wavre on May 14 and May 15 met with an equal lack of success.[78] With successes and failures on both sides in the Belgian plain, a near stalemate had been reached in central Belgium when the disaster in the Ardennes completely unhinged the Allied position.

By the morning of May 18 the Allied northern wing was rapidly retiring southward in an attempt to restore a strong continuous front against the advance of Army Group A, which threatened to sever its lines of communication with northern France. General Maxime Weygand replaced General Gamelin as General in Chief of the French forces at this critical moment and began to create a temporary defense line along the Aisne with troops from the Paris area. Halder, who was watching the intelligence reports carefully, could see "no concentrations foreshadowing a counter-drive" anywhere, as he wrote in his war journal. The situation convinced him that he had been right "in yesterday's conclusion that the operation must be continued in a southwestern direction . . . without the least delay" (IV, 18). As he saw it, the danger now was not an attack from the south but a re-establishment of a strong front between the northern and southern wings of the Allied forces, which, in turn, would convert Army Group A's enveloping movement into a fruitless frontal assault.

The Fuehrer, however, was more certain than ever that the German penetration was advancing into an Allied trap and that a stroke from the south might sever Kleist's communications at any moment. When Brauchitsch and Halder pointed out that there was no indication that forces powerful enough for such a task were present in the Allied southern wing, Hitler raged and screamed that they "were on the best way to ruin the whole campaign and . . . were leading up to a defeat." Halder wrote in an angry tone in his journal that Hitler would have no part in continuing the drive in either a southwestern or western direction and was now considering a return to his old plan for a northwestern drive! (IV, 18)

While Hitler and his military advisors were quarreling on the morning of May 18, the German advance in the areas of both army groups rolled on smoothly. At noon the OKH received word that elements of General von Bock's Army Group B had taken Antwerp, while the armored columns of Rundstedt's Army Group A had reached Cambrai and Saint-Quentin. Halder commented that it was becoming apparent that the Allied northern wing was desperately attempting to form a solid front "somewhere north of the French border" and extending south to the Maubeuge-Valenciennes area. The Allies were also trying to form a line still further south with elements from both northern and southern wings between Valenciennes and La Fère. Halder quickly decided that "we must punch through this new line before it has a chance to consolidate." Orders were issued

for Army Group A's armored spearheads to strike on the front between Cambrai and Saint-Quentin as soon as posible. The tanks were
in position by 6:00 P.M., and Halder personally went to see Hitler
for permission to launch the attack the following morning. Hitler, in
a sudden reversal of attitude, approved, but Halder could not refrain
from noting sarcastically, "so the right thing is being done after all,
but in an atmosphere of bad feeling and in a form calculated to give
the outside world the impression that it is a plan conceived by
OKW." (IV, 19)

Halder's determination to press on to a quick decision was partly
motivated by his realization that the rapid advance had placed an
enormous strain on the German logistical system. The last truck
reserves (including OKH general and local reserves) had been
thrown in the preceding day (IV, 15) and the pace of operations
would have to slow down unless a decisive victory could be achieved
rapidly. Supplies had so far kept up with the panzer and motorized
infantry divisions and the still more demanding infantry divisions,
but, as Army Group A's line of advance extended ever further west,
the strain on machines, men, and animals was certain to show. Railroad troops were working feverishly behind the advancing front to
repair damaged rail facilities and to keep the infantry divisions within efficient operating range of the railheads, but the speed with which
this could be done had its limits. From the logistical point of view,
the enemy had to be brought to battle as soon as possible and destroyed.

The German tank drive got underway at 7:00 A.M. on May 19 in
the vicinity of Arras. Halder calculated that it would strike the bulk
of the retiring northern Allied wing and would result in "a big battle
lasting several days in which we have the advantage of the initiative,
while the enemy has that of heavy concentration." But since he believed that all psychological factors were now working on behalf of
the Germans and they had "the benefit of a superior and tremendously
effective air force," he was "certain of success." Later that evening,
the OKH received reports of Allied counterattacks. Halder wrote
almost joyously, "Let them come! We are strong enough and have
sufficient depth." (IV, 19, 20)

The fighting around Arras reached its climax on May 21 when the
Allies made a ten-mile penetration of German lines in a desperate

effort to break through to the south, but were turned back by a stubborn German defense and counterattacks.[79] This failure convinced the BEF's commander—Lord John Gort—that all hope of regaining contact with the French armies in the south was lost. He began to maneuver his forces toward the coast at Dunkirk while the British Navy made preparations for an amphibious withdrawal. From May 23 on, the battle in Belgium was being fought only to save some part of the Allied armies in the German trap. On May 24 Halder noted in his journal that victory looked inevitable in the first phase (IV, 33).

Complete victory and capture of the entire Allied northern wing of armies now appeared to be in the German grasp. The panzer units which had reached Abbeville on the coast on May 20 had turned north and were seizing one port after another in the Allied rear. By the evening of May 23, Dunkirk, the last, was expected to fall within twenty-four hours. But a strange chain of circumstances was already set in motion that finally brought about the salvation of the BEF and a remnant of the French armies.

This chain of events began on May 23 when General von Brauchitsch decided against Halder's advice that the final phase of the encirclement battle should be directed from the headquarters of General von Bock, the commander of Army Group B. The decision was indeed a strange one. As the front constricted and the German armies crowded together, a need arose for even greater overall direction from OKH headquarters. Halder had noted during that morning:

The developments of the past few days show that [Army Group A] is indeed experiencing considerable difficulties in managing the unwieldy mass of 71 Divs. I have a good idea its staff has not been energetic and active enough. OKH must take the organization of liaison with the several armies in hand in order to insure execution of its orders up front. (IV, 31)

That evening, when Brauchitsch announced his decision to turn over conduct of the looming Kesselschlacht to Bock, Halder immediately criticized this decision as a serious error and an attempt to sidestep responsibility. Halder wrote in his journal that the Army Commander in Chief was adamant:

He keeps arguing that he has no choice but to coordinate the efforts of the various elements converging on the [Allied] pocket . . . under his command or under that of Bock. The first alternative, which I should think he would accept as the logical and manly one, he feels unsure about. But with that he foregoes the honor of victory. (IV, 33)

When the order was issued for Bock to direct the annihilation phase of the battle, Halder indicated his disapproval by pointedly refusing to countersign it.

The next day, May 24, Hitler saw Rundstedt at the latter's headquarters at Charleville, and at 4:00 P.M. the Fuehrer called Brauchitsch forward to Rundstedt's headquarters for a discussion. The Army Commander in Chief returned at 8:00 P.M. to OKH headquarters, where he informed Halder that Hitler himself had decided how the final battle was to be conducted. In shocked amazement, clearly evident in his journal, Halder wrote: "The left wing, consisting of [panzer and motorized forces], which has no enemy [front] before it, will . . . be stopped dead in its tracks upon the direct order of the Fuehrer! Finishing off the encircled enemy army is to be left to the Air Force!!" (IV, 35) The OKH issued the order at 8:20 P.M. When Guderian's headquarters near Calais received this message, they were "utterly speechless." [80]

This famous "halt order" of May 24 has confused historians ever since, and numerous and often conflicting explanations have been advanced as to why Hitler made this decision. Though no acceptable answer will probably ever be advanced, there is no doubt that Halder and the OKH were opposed to it. It is also clear that Halder believed then and later that Hitler made his decision so that the pro-Nazi Luftwaffe would have the final laurels.[81] At the same time, J. F. C. Fuller has pointed out that the low, boggy terrain around Dunkirk, cut by many drainage dikes, was most unsuited for the deployment of tanks, and that the whole area was one vast tank obstacle.[82] The day after the order was issued, this very argument was used by Hitler when Brauchitsch and Halder tried to persuade him to allow the armored forces to move in. Halder remained unconvinced and wrote in his journal after the conference of May 25 that "the political command has formed the fixed idea that the battle of decision must not be fought on Flemish soil, but rather in northern France." He added, "to camouflage this political move, the assertion is made that Flanders, crisscrossed by a multitude of waterways, is unsuited for tank warfare." (IV, 35) Whatever Hitler's real motive, he must have received his notions about tank terrain from somewhere besides the OKH, and that place was probably Rundstedt's headquarters. Major L. F. Ellis has pointed out that the Army Group A commander had, early on May 23, ordered his panzer divisions to halt (although the order was not obeyed), and after Hitler had talked with Rundstedt during the morning of May 24 he endorsed the measure. Both men agreed that the infantry divisions were more suitable to the terrain, and Hitler emphasized the importance of sparing the panzer forces for the second phase of the operation.[83] Still a third factor was Brauchitsch's virtual abdication of responsibility for the final phase of the battle on May 23. The OKW War Diary reveals that Hitler was irritated on learning at Rundstedt's headquarters that Brauchitsch had turned command of the Fourth Army over to Bock in preparation for the latter's assumption of responsibility for the final phase and had the order rescinded. The conference of May 24 at Rundstedt's headquarters apparently involved some strong disagreements, judging from Halder's diary entry, and Brauchitsch (from whom Halder had his information) had somehow received the impression that the decision had been made to permit the Luftwaffe to finish the job alone. When Brauchitsch returned to OKH headquarters, he apparently said nothing about the terrain's being unsuitable for tanks (at least Halder's journal does not mention it), and it is conceivable that Hitler was so angry with Brauchitsch for abdicating responsibility that he abruptly decided to halt ground operations and permit the eager Luftwaffe leadership to demonstrate what National Socialist spirit could do. The Fuehrer may well have calmed down sufficiently by the next day to attempt to justify his action on better grounds, and the supposedly marshy terrain became a good pretext. He may have alluded to political motives, and from those remarks Halder may have inferred these were the real reasons and the terrain merely an excuse. One thing does seem certain. There is no evidence whatever that Hitler desired the British to escape in order that gratitude might impel them to make peace. Beyond this, no certain conclusions can be drawn.[84]

The results of the "halt order" are, in any case, quite clear. By

May 26 the Allied armies had begun to occupy the area around Dunkirk in force,[85] and the senselessness of Hitler's order drove Brauchitsch and Halder close to the breaking point. In his journal Halder wrote:

All through the morning, [Brauchitsch] is very nervous. I can fully sympathize with him for these orders from the top just make no sense. In one area [Bock's group] they call for a head-on attack against a front retiring in orderly fashion and still possessing its striking power, and elsewhere they freeze the troops to the spot when the enemy rear could be cut into anytime you wanted to attack. (IV, 37)

Halder then added the curious notation: "Von Rundstedt, too, apparently could not stand it any longer and went up front to Hoth and Kleist . . . to get the lay of the land for the next moves of his armor." One cannot suppress a suspicion that Rundstedt realized by this time that Hitler's excuse was not valid, and that the BEF was about to get away as the result of overcaution.

The German tank spearheads stood motionless for nearly two days while the Allied forces consolidated their hold on Dunkirk. On May 26, as Halder reports, Hitler suddenly gave the panzer divisions permission to advance but the time wasted could not be redeemed. Moreover, ironically enough, rain during the previous twenty-four hours had made the ground soggy and unsuitable for tanks.

The battle of Dunkirk began on May 26 and was concluded for all practical purposes by June 1. As the German armies pushed ever closer to the beaches against the resistance of four Allied armies, a flotilla of craft ranging from motorboats to steamers evacuated as many troops to England as possible under the protection of the Royal Navy and Air Force. The crowded beaches and waters of Dunkirk offered the Luftwaffe a splendid target, and the evacuation might have ended in catastrophe if the RAF had not put on a remarkable display of fighter power from its bases in England. In this first real test between the RAF and the Luftwaffe on anything like equal terms, Goering's bombers were severely mauled.[86] This was the only bright star of victory in the dark firmament of defeat that closed over the Allies in May, 1940. Under RAF cover, the British in Operation Dynamo managed to evacuate 366,000 troops, nearly a third of them Belgian and French.

The German ring closed inexorably during the last days of May, and Halder recorded in his journal that resistance was fierce. On May 27, nevertheless, the Belgians gave up, and 500,000 troops laid down their arms. Since Bock had finally been entrusted with the task of directing the Dunkirk operation, Brauchitsch and Halder were almost onlookers at the closing scene. Brauchitsch was "rather restless for want of something to do" and could "hardly wait" until the detailed regrouping orders had been worked out by Halder and the General Staff. After a brief skirmish with Hitler, Halder's recommendations were finally accepted on May 28. So confident was the Chief of the General Staff that the second phase would take France out of the war altogether, and thereby bring Britain to terms as well, that he began to give some thought to the proper composition of the future peacetime army. (IV, 38–40)

The end of the first phase came on June 1, 1940. By that night Halder considered the evacuation of Dunkirk practically completed. Slight resistance by isolated and abandoned groups went on, but Halder wrote that "apart from this, the operation started on 10 May is now concluded" (IV, 45).

Phase II

The smashing German blows that led to Dunkirk had placed the French High Command in a desperate situation. Nearly all of the British ground forces had left the Continent and a badly battered and weakened French Army had to carry on almost alone. According to Halder's journal, the Allies had already lost 1,500,000 troops (including the entire Belgian and Dutch armies) and the Germans had seized enough equipment to outfit seventy divisions (IV, 46). The capture of so much equipment, especially motorized vehicles of all kinds, gave the Germans an enormous addition to their armament and motorized forces. Already a "scavenger army" since the occupations of Austria and Czechoslovakia, the German Army would become more so after the campaign in the West, making the 1940 blitzkrieg more than pay for itself. A heavy drain on the German Army's matériel did not occur again until the invasion of Russia. In contrast, during the first phase the French had lost thirty divisions and most of their tanks and motorized equipment. They no longer

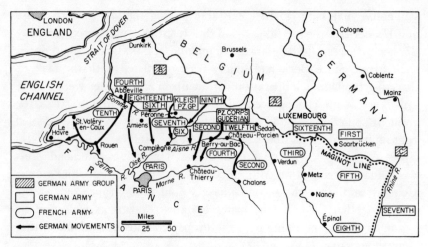

11. The Battles of the Somme and the Aisne, 1940.

had the vital support of nine British divisions, whose motorized transport had fallen into German hands, and their air forces were almost nonexistent.[87] Weygand unquestionably faced a far more critical situation than either Joffre before the Marne in 1914 or Foch in the spring of 1918.

While the Germans were occupied with the reduction of the Dunkirk pocket at the end of May, Weygand had hurriedly established a new defense line from the Somme River to the northern end of the Maginot Line. He had ordered troops from North Africa and the Italian frontier to increase his forces to forty-three infantry divisions, three DCs, and three DCLs. The six armored and semimotorized divisions were greatly depleted in strength and matériel. Weygand's force was supported by the remains of the French Air Force, about four hundred fighters and seventy bombers.[88] The only British ground forces left with the French Army was part of the British Armoured Division and the Fifty-first Highland Division.

Weygand faced the task of defending central and southern France with an army inferior in numbers and equipment and demoralized by defeat. The new front from the Channel to the Maginot Line was nearly two hundred and fifty miles long and with few natural barriers except rivers. The French system of linear defense had failed in the first phase, and Weygand was forced to improvise a defense in depth with officers and troops untrained and underequipped for its use. Yet in the little time that remained, Weygand and his staff did a remarkable job. As early as May 26, Weygand had issued to the French Army a new doctrine of defense in depth, which read in part that when a unit found the next in line had given way it must on no account retreat. It was to try to restore the line by counterattacks and, if the counterattacks failed, it was to form a perimeter defense and prevent a widening of the breach. All areas behind the principal line of resistance were to be organized in a checkerboard of centers of resistance to the greatest depth possible, with special attention given to the defense of highways and railways which were likely to become the principal axes of the German advance.[89] Under this directive, after Dunkirk the remaining French forces had been preparing a complex of field fortifications up to twenty miles in depth, making use of every village, even far to the rear, as a strong point. These measures, as the Russians later demonstrated, were sound for dealing with the blitzkrieg, but Weygand lacked the armored forces necessary for major counterattacks and the air cover to allow his forces to maneuver without interference from the Luftwaffe. The French High Command had learned its lessons too late to save France in 1940.

By the beginning of June, Dunkirk was no longer a major OKH concern, and Halder and his staff began to redeploy the German armies. German intelligence indicated that the French forces in the Weygand line were principally concentrated north of Paris to block any direct German drive on the French capital. Thus Brauchitsch and Halder decided to attempt another Kesselschlacht by concentrating Army Group B to the west along the Somme and Army Group A to the east along the Aisne. Bock's group would lead off the offensive by driving south across the Somme to the Seine, occupying the Atlantic coast ports, and then wheeling eastward to cut off the main enemy forces north of Paris. Rundstedt's drive across the Aisne would be the weaker of the two, since all the panzer divisions but those in Guderian's corps had been transferred to Bock's group, but if successful his divisions would advance toward the Marne between Verdun and Paris and wheel westward to complete the pincer operation. A third and final offensive was to be delivered by the previously quiescent Army Group C (Leeb) against the Maginot Line when

Rundstedt's drive had carried his forces into the rear of its defenses.[90]

At 5:00 A.M. on June 5 Army Group B opened its Somme offensive (Halder, IV, 52). The Luftwaffe, almost as strong as it had
been at the beginning of the May offensive,[91] assigned its Second Air
Fleet (Kesselring) to the support of Bock's army group. Kesselring's
fighters and bombers swamped the heavily outnumbered French Air
Force and easily gained control of the air. The Second Air Fleet then
carried out its usual duties of interdiction and close support. Nevertheless, the French resisted with great determination, especially
around Péronne, and Bock's troops did not completely break through
the Somme defenses until June 7. Halder recorded in his journal that
the Sixth and Eighteenth armies had met with stubborn resistance
throughout the two days of fighting (IV, 58).

After Army Group B's breakthrough over the Somme, Hoth's
panzer corps—attached to the Fourth Army—successfully pushed on
Rouen and the lower Seine, but further east, Reichenau's Sixth
Army, in its attempt to encircle the French forces along the central
front, met with heavy resistance. The Ninth Army was attacking
along the Aisne to close the encirclement from the front, but its
progress was so slow that the OKH decided to shift the German
center of gravity further east. It sent the XVI Panzer Corps to join
the German forces driving down the east side of the developing salient toward Château-Thierry (IV, 61). Halder realized that the
Ninth Army's bridgeheads over the Aisne east of Compiègne held
the key to the situation. The French Seventh Army, which was so
skillfully resisting Reichenau's advance, was falling back behind the
Oise river to protect its left flank. If the XVI Panzer Corps could
attack it from the east, its position before Paris would be compromised and its forces perhaps encircled and destroyed.

The following day, June 9, Army Group A launched its offensive
on the more eastern reaches of the Aisne, and this sudden new pressure on the front was too great for the French armies to withstand.
Although Rundstedt's chief of Staff, General Günther von Blumentritt, was impressed by the courage and tenacity of the French,[92]
from Berry-au-Bac to Château-Porcien their front was broken. The
flanks of the Compiègne salient were now fully exposed. The OKH
saw a decisive Kesselschlacht looming as it ordered the XIV Panzer

Corps to strike along the Oise on the west side of the salient, while the XVI Corps—now at Château-Thierry—struck from the east (Halder, IV, 64).

The battle of the Compiègne salient raged for twenty-four hours, but by the end of June 10 it was clear that the OKH pincer movement had failed. The French troops behind the Oise had beaten off every German assault, and an orderly retirement by the French Seventh Army on Paris was under way. A concentration of German effort in that direction would lead only to frontal attacks. Halder and Brauchitsch agreed that the main effort should again be shifted to the fronts east and west of Paris, and the XIV Panzer Corps was directed to move around the salient and join the drive further east (IV, 65).

At this critical moment, the French were beset by a new threat. Mussolini, observing that the Weygand line was broken, made his decision to intervene, and Italy entered the war against France. After June 10, French resistance, except on the Alpine front, became increasingly disorganized, and on June 12 Weygand informed a desperate Premier Paul Reynaud at temporary government headquarters at Tours that further resistance was useless. The next day the French government declared Paris to be an open city and began withdrawing all troops from its vicinity. The French decision not to defend Paris greatly relieved Halder, who had hesitated to allow a further drive south by Army Group B while powerful French forces remained intact around the capital. The OKH had planned to encircle Paris in anticipation of a siege which might have absorbed many troops and weakened the drives into southern France, but after June 13 both German army groups were ordered to launch the pursuit phase of the operation. On June 14, as Frenchmen stood along her streets and wept, for the second time in seventy years Paris felt the tread of German boots. Exultantly, Halder recorded in his journal: "A great day in the history of the German Army. German troops have been marching into Paris since 9:00 A.M." (IV, 76).

The end then came quickly. Outflanked, its defenses turned, the fortified area of Verdun fell on June 15. The next day German units reached the Loire in several places. Late on June 16, Halder learned that Paul Reynaud had resigned and that Marshal Pétain had become the new head of the French government. The following day the Pétain government requested armistice terms. Reflecting Halder's conviction that the war was over, the Army General Staff began to lay plans for demobilizing a large part of the German Army (IV, 80). By June 18 the OKH's only problem was the Italian failure to pierce the French Alpine defenses. The OKW directed the OKH to send forces to open them from the rear and permit the Italians to advance onto French soil. Disgusted by what was obviously a political move to benefit Italian prestige, Halder sourly commented on June 19 that "it is indeed an effort to keep calm in the face of such amateurish tinkering with the business of directing military operations." A day later he sarcastically referred to Hitler's orders regarding the Italian front as the meddling of the "Great Master." (IV, 85, 86)

On June 21, armistice negotiations got under way at Compiègne at the site and in the same railroad carriage where Marshal Foch had humbled the German representatives in 1918. On June 22, the French accepted Hitler's terms. Two days later Pétain's government came to terms with the Italians, and the last shots of the campaign in the West were fired at 1:35 A.M. on June 25 (IV, 92).

Conclusion

The high point in the fortunes of the German Army and of Nazi Germany seemed reached on June 22, 1940. Hitler's smashing victory in the West had made him master of Western Europe and seemed to demonstrate that his military machine was invincible on land. Doctrinally, the campaign in the West had fulfilled the promise of the Polish campaign on a scale for which not even the OKH had been prepared. Yet the Army had begun the campaign with serious logistic weaknesses and with many of its newer infantry divisions not fully trained.[93] Success had been due, of course, not only to a superior doctrine but also to a superior air force and glaring errors of organization and strategy on the part of the Allies. The speed with which the German motorized divisions had operated, their flexibility due to excellent internal organization, and their relative independence from the slower infantry divisions permitted the blitzkrieg army to outmaneuver its enemies, who had made the mistake of dispersing their armor and forming incompatible mixtures of motorized, horse-drawn, and armored units. The German armored spearheads were not so overwhelmingly irresistible as they appeared in May, 1940, but by striking with surprise and speed on a weak part of the enemy front they were able to achieve a breakthrough almost before the Allied High Command was aware of the threat. They were able to exploit that breakthrough in precisely the manner in which Guderian had originally conceived their strategic role, while the Luftwaffe played a vital supporting service by harassing Allied columns in motion and attacking unprotected artillery. Again, it was not that these forces inflicted so much physical damage as that their disrupting influence prevented the Allied infantry divisions from taking effective countermeasures to German encirclement.

While the OKH had every reason for self-congratulation at the close of the campaign in the West, the experience there also had some disturbing features for the Germans. French tactics during the second phase—although employed without sufficient numbers of weapons and troops and with inadequate training and air cover—had been difficult to overcome. Had the French possessed greater spaces in which to retreat and reinforcements to cancel their initial losses, the German drives southward might have been arrested. The Germans were also granted the advantage of mostly dry, clear weather, which aided both the German air arm and the wheeled transport of the ground forces, and Belgium and northern France were covered with a network of good roads and rails. In sum, the second test of German doctrine and organization was conducted under ideal conditions of weather, roads, rail, and range. The unspoken question remained unanswered as to how well the blitzkrieg army would perform under more adverse conditions.

Despite military victory in the West, in a sense the triumph of German arms had fatal consequences for Hitler's political policy. The Wehrmacht had removed from the field one powerful enemy, but a second had withdrawn its forces behind water ramparts. Whether Hitler realized it or not, his victory over France had transferred the focus of military operations to a plain where the Wehrmacht was bound to be less effective. Frustration at his inability to defeat Britain behind her water barrier would lead Hitler to turn East and this time against the largest of the land powers. Germany's military strength would be further tested by an Italian ally, ambitious in goals but incompetent in performance, whose ill-considered ventures would draw the German Army into the sands of North Africa on the insecurity of water-based communications. Against the British in their home island, against the Russians in their enormous land spaces, and against Anglo-American forces in North Africa across vulnerable sea lanes, the German Army's weaknesses were to be exposed and the process of overextension begun which would lead to ultimate disaster.

CHAPTER SIX

England: The Narrow Sea

Operation Sea Lion

The German victory in the West during May and June of 1940 had brought the Second World War to a crucial turning point. The Anglo-French powers had entered the war in September, 1939, to preserve the integrity of Poland, and in nine months the German armies had crushed the Poles, defeated the French, and forced the British to withdraw their forces from the continent of Europe. The Germans had also overrun Norway, Denmark, Belgium, and the Netherlands, leaving only part of Scandinavia, the Balkans, Iberia, and Soviet Russia outside of German-dominated Europe. The Balkan states were either pro-German or uneasy neutrals, Soviet Russia was a nominal German ally, and Franco's Spain leaned toward Germany. Great Britain was stripped of any coalition after the fall of France and could continue the war only by risking invasion and in the hope that eventually the United States or the Soviet Union would join her in an anti-Nazi alliance. Her armies shattered on the Continent, Britain possessed only her insularity, her fleet, and a heavily outnumbered air force. On June 22, 1940, the day of the French armistice, Halder wrote in his journal: "The near future will show whether Britain will do the reasonable thing in the light of our victories or will try to carry on the war singlehanded." He added grimly: "In the latter case, the war will lead to Britain's destruction, and may last a long time." [1]

Adolf Hitler shared the confidence of the Chief of the Army General Staff in final victory, and in addition the Fuehrer believed that the British would recognize the hopelessness of their position and would make peace in time. Hitler asked for nothing more essential than a free hand in the East. Britain had already lost her effective means of war on land for some time to come, and she would have to risk invasion to continue hostilities. As the Fuehrer expressed the matter to the Italian foreign minister on July 1, 1940, "How could military thinkers among the English still believe in victory when they see before them . . . [a hostile] front extending from Narvik to the Gironde." [2]

Yet the days passed with no approach by the British government for peace terms. Finally, on June 30, Halder visited the German Foreign Ministry and Secretary Baron Ernst von Weizsaecker. The State Secretary told Halder that despite Hitler's confidence, no real prospects for peace with Britain existed. In his opinion, the situation would require "one more demonstration" of Germany's military power before Britain would come to terms and leave Germany "a free hand in the East." (Halder, Journal, IV, 98) Halder left the Foreign Ministry convinced that the war with Britain would continue and that plans for its prosecution must be drawn up without further delay.

The next day, July 1, Halder met with his old friend, Admiral Otto Schniewind, Chief of the Naval Staff, to obtain the Navy's view of the practicability of a cross-Channel invasion of England in the summer of 1940. Unlike the Army, which had scarcely given any thought to such an operation until then, as early as May the Navy had brought up the question to Hitler. The Fuehrer had been too preoccupied with the campaign in the West to show much interest, and the Navy allowed the matter to drop. [3] The Navy, nevertheless, was the most informed service on the subject, and it was heartening to Halder to learn that Schniewind considered such an operation very difficult but not altogether impossible. [4] The two officers agreed that the primary requisite was the Luftwaffe's control of the air over England and the English Channel in order to prevent the Royal Navy and Air Force from interfering with the movement of German troops by sea to English shores (Halder, IV, 98, 99).

The day following the Halder-Schniewind discussion, the OKW issued a directive to the three armed services to study and prepare reports on the possibilities for an invasion of England.[5] Hitler had not made up his mind to attempt an invasion, but the stubbornness of the British was beginning to vex. On July 11, the Luftwaffe General Staff sent a report to Halder indicating that the Royal Air Force could be destroyed within two weeks after the start of unlimited air operations (Halder, IV, 104). This assessment was important for Halder's calculations. An invasion was clearly not possible for a weak naval power like Germany unless the Luftwaffe could at least control the air over the English Channel and the landing beaches. Halder would have been appalled had he then been aware of the serious errors upon which the Luftwaffe report was based.[6]

Halder attended a conference with Hitler on July 13 at which the reports from the three services were submitted. From the moment the conference at the Berghof opened, Halder detected that the Fuehrer was still puzzled by British unwillingness to make peace. The only reason he could see, Hitler told his generals, was that Britain was convinced that eventually the Soviet Union or the United States would join her in a coalition against Germany. This attitude forced Hitler to continue the war against Britain, although it went "against his grain." He had resigned himself nevertheless to the fact that Britain could be brought to terms only by "main force," and therefore he approved the preliminary reports as a basis for practical preparations. (Halder, IV, 116)

Based on the assessments presented to Hitler on July 13, the OKW issued a directive to the three services on July 19[7] to prepare a plan for the invasion of England under the code name Operation *Seelöwe* (Sea Lion). Halder found that the general outlines of the operation contained in the directive conformed to his recommendations made at the Berghof, and therefore the Army General Staff could press on with preparations.

July 19 was also a date memorable for the Fuehrer's official tribute to his victorious generals at the Kroll Opera House in Berlin. Halder flew from OKH field headquarters, then at Fontainebleau, to the

German capital for the occasion, and that night he sat among the
large assembly of beribboned generals and admirals while the
Fuehrer himself was master of ceremonies. (IV, 121) While re-
serving to himself chief credit for victory in the West, Hitler
handed out decorations and promotions on an unprecedented scale.
A dozen generals were promoted to the rank of Field Marshal,
while Goering was given the ancient and recreated rank of *Reichs-
marschall*.[8] Brauchitsch was among those promoted to the rank of
Field Marshal, and Halder was promoted to the rank of *Generaloberst* (Colonel General).[9] He was also awarded the *Ritterkreuz*
(Knight's Cross of the Iron Cross) with diamonds, one of Germany's highest military decorations. Hitler used the occasion to
make a speech in which he extended the olive branch once more to
Britain, although by this time he must have known that no response
would be forthcoming.

The festivities and congratulations over, Halder soon returned to
OKH headquarters at Fontainebleau, where he and his staff quickly
settled down to work. The invasion plan called for the employment
of forty infantry and mountain divisions, with an initial assault
wave of thirteen divisions to be landed from Ramsgate to Lyme Bay

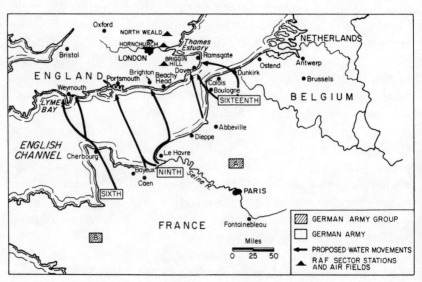

12. OKH Invasion Plan for England, July, 1940.

(a straight-line distance of nearly two hundred miles on the map). The total sea transportation required was estimated at 1,722 barges, 471 tugs, 1,161 motorboats, and 155 transports. The whole was to be assembled between Dunkirk and Cherbourg.[10]

The problems of amphibious assault were almost wholly new to the Army General Staff in the summer of 1940. As officers of a Central European land power, the German generals had concentrated on the problems of land war appropriate to Central and Western Europe. German military doctrine was not concerned with seaborne operations, and as a result the German Army was unprepared mentally, organizationally, and in equipment for such an enterprise as Sea Lion. Halder and his staff were compelled to make many decisions on sheer guesswork and to improvise techniques and equipment at almost every turn. Moreover, Army radio intelligence was faulty, and the British were successful in misleading the Germans into believing that thirty-nine serviceable divisions were awaiting them in the British Isles.[11] Actually, the British never had more than twenty-two divisions in condition to fight during the summer of 1940, and only eleven of these were wholly mobile.[12] Thus the Germans prepared an operation far beyond their capacity to carry out, against an enemy half as numerous as expected.

The German Naval Staff was also unfamiliar with the problems of amphibious assault, but possessed a better grasp of the difficulties involved in large-scale sea transportation. The Naval Staff during July came to the realization that the Army's plans were simply beyond German naval capacity to execute. The number of barges could be provided only by stripping part of the German inland waterway system, a system which played a vital role in Germany's internal economy.[13] At the same time, the wide-front landing approach, however desirable from the Army's viewpoint, could not be adequately protected by German surface units, and to rely entirely on the Luftwaffe would place the entire operation at the mercy of the weather. The Naval Staff concluded late in July that the landings would have to be restricted to a narrow front and the size of the landing forces reduced or the time greatly lengthened for their movement.

The OKH received the Naval Staff memorandum on July 28 and was greatly discouraged by its contents. Halder wrote in his journal that if the Navy's proposals were the best it could do, "all previous statements of the Navy are so much rubbish and we can throw away the whole plan of invasion" (IV, 135). The OKH decided to send Colonel von Greiffenberg, Chief of the Operations section, to Berlin for a conference with the Naval Staff.

Greiffenberg returned to Fontainebleau on July 30 with bad news. The Naval Staff had informed him that the invasion could not take place before September 15 because of the lack of landing craft, and the Navy could not undertake to guarantee protection of the German convoys against the British Home Fleet under the Army's wide-front plan. The German Navy had lost most of its destroyers in Norwegian waters, and only a single heavy cruiser— *Admiral Hipper*—two light cruisers, and four destroyers were available for the support of Sea Lion. The Navy's four major ships [14]— *Scharnhorst, Gneisenau, Lützow,* and *Admiral Scheer*—were laid up for repairs and refitting. After hearing Greiffenberg's report, Brauchitsch and Halder agreed that the Navy would not have the means for a successful invasion of England before the fall of 1940 and, in that case, the entire operation should be postponed until the spring of 1941 (Halder, IV, 140).

Brauchitsch and Halder next considered the proper course to follow in the meanwhile. They thought that the interval might be used to shift forces to North Africa, where the Italians were about to launch attacks on British-held Egypt and Somaliland, or perhaps capture Gibraltar from the land side through Spain. On one point they were in firm agreement:

The question whether, if a decision cannot be forced against Britain, we should . . . turn . . . against Russia, must be answered that we should keep on friendly terms. . . . Russia's aspirations to the Straits and in the direction of the Persian Gulf need not bother us. [Concerning the Balkans], we could keep out of each other's way. (IV, 141)

The following day Halder departed from Fontainebleau for the Berghof for a military conference on Sea Lion. The Commander in Chief of the German Navy, Admiral Erich Raeder, was first to report, and he immediately urged postponement of Sea Lion until the spring of 1941 (IV, 142). Raeder was acutely aware that the

British Home Fleet could muster ten battleships and three battle-cruisers,[15] a force which would suffice to outmatch any surface attack the Germans could bring to bear. On the other hand, if the invasion were delayed the Luftwaffe could spend the interval in attacks that would whittle down the British Home Fleet, while the German Navy concentrated on building up its surface naval strength.

Hitler agreed that Raeder had strong arguments for postponing Sea Lion, but pointed out that each day's delay gave the British that much more time in which to repair the deficiencies in their ground forces and prepare against invasion. Moreover, if the Luftwaffe could crush the Royal Air Force, it might then be able to neutralize the Home Fleet long enough for an invasion to be carried out. Therefore, it was his decision to launch the aerial phase of Sea Lion and, if the Germans received the impression that the British were crumbling under the air assault, to proceed with the invasion. If not, he would postpone Sea Lion until the spring of 1941. All preparations were to be continued, and Hitler set the date of September 15 for the cross-Channel move. The attack would be executed under the Army plan for a wide-front landing. (Halder, IV, 143)

Hitler then addressed himself to the question of Germany's course should Sea Lion be postponed. In that event, he declared to his listeners, "our action must be directed to eliminate all factors" which encouraged England "to hope for a change in the situation." It seemed evident to Hitler that *"Britain's hope lies in Russia and the United States.* If Russia drops out of the picture, America, too, is lost for Britain, because the elimination of Russia would tremendously increase *Japan's power* in the Far East." In the Fuehrer's view, "Russia is the Far Eastern sword of Britain and the United States pointed at Japan." But Japan, Hitler reminded his listeners, had her own program of expansion, which she was likely to attempt to carry through before the end of the war. The fall of France and the Netherlands had opened their rich colonies in the Far East to attack, and Japan was eager to seize the opportunity. She was restrained by the United States and by a powerful Russia on her flank. But if Russia were smashed, Hitler went on, this would release Japan to challenge the United States in the Pacific and divert the latter's power and resources away from the aid of

Britain. Thus indirectly, *"with Russia smashed, Britain's last hope would be shattered.* Germany would then be the master of Europe and the Balkans."* In Hitlerian logic,[16] "Russia's destruction must therefore be made a part of this struggle," perhaps as early as the spring of 1941 (IV, 144).

Hitler's views on Russia did not come as a surprise to Halder. At the Berghof conference of July 19, Hitler had expressed the opinion that Britain's failure to come to terms was based on a faith in eventual Russian intervention, and on July 21 the Fuehrer had asked Brauchitsch to study the possibilities of a campaign in Russia. Upon being informed of Hitler's request, Halder instructed Greiffenberg to create a special study-staff, and subsequently General Erich Marcks, Chief of Staff of the Eighteenth Army, was chosen for the task. Consequently, as soon as Halder had returned to Fontaine-bleau after the July 31 Berghof conference, he ordered General Marcks to report to him at once concerning the progress of his studies. The report does not concern this chapter and will be treated later at the appropriate place, but it may be pointed out that planning for the campaign in Russia was underway by August, 1940. (IV, 117, 128, 146)

On August 4, the issue of the width of the landing front came up again (IV, 149), and Halder became greatly irritated at the OKW's failure to resolve the matter. At the same time, the Luftwaffe General Staff was having its own doubts, chiefly because of the limited range of its fighters.[17] The Navy's reservations are already known, and only the Army retained its original confidence. Halder wrote in his journal on August 6:

We have the paradoxical situation where the Navy is full of misgivings, the Air Force is very reluctant to tackle a mission which at the outset is exclusively its own, and OKW, which for once has a real combined forces operation to direct, just plays dead. The only driving force in the whole situation comes from us, but alone we would not be able to swing it either. (IV, 152)

In an attempt to resolve the landing-front issue, representatives from the Army General Staff and the Naval Staff met on August 7, but to no avail. The Army Staff officers argued that the Navy's narrow front landing would be easy for the British to contain and offered only "back-breaking obstacles to any advance." Matters were made worse by the new Naval Staff prediction that forty-two days would be required to ferry over all the landing forces, a period of time "utterly prohibitive," in the Army's view, to the success of Operation Sea Lion. Nothing was settled by this conference, and not until August 18 did the OKW finally take a hand. It ruled out the landings west of Beachy Head (limiting the invasion front to about fifty miles) and reduced the initial landing forces to nine divisions. (IV, 153, 164) This action only served to raise the Army's doubts.

Operation Eagle Attack

The fate of Sea Lion was, however, not to be settled on English beaches but in English skies. The Luftwaffe launched Operation *Adlerangriff* (Eagle Attack) on August 12 in a massive effort to shatter the Royal Air Force on the ground, as the German Air Force had earlier shattered the air fleets of Poland, Norway, the Netherlands, Belgium, and France. This time the Luftwaffe was pitted against the modern RAF Fighter Command equipped with a thousand interceptor fighters, a radar early warning system, Fighter Control, and well-defended airfields.[18] The RAF was braced for an attack, and the early warning system gave adequate notice as the first German raiders swept over the Channel. Guided by Fighter Control, swarms of Hurricanes and Spitfires rose from their airfields and climbed to the prescribed altitude. The Luftwaffe soon found itself dealing with a powerful opponent already airborne.[19]

The British air defense system proved to be very different from any the Luftwaffe had met before. Because of it, British fighters were difficult to surprise on the ground, and once in the air pilots and machines were fully the equal of the Luftwaffe's. The tremendous firepower of the Hurricanes and Spitfires sealed a German bomber's fate once the British fighters broke through the Luftwaffe's fighter cover, while radar and Fighter Control allowed tremendous flexibility in RAF concentrations and deployments. For the first time, really, the Luftwaffe had to fight for air superiority, and very soon the odds began to go against it. On August 15, 1940, on just the third day of the campaign, the Luftwaffe suffered its worst defeat of the summer, when it lost 76 aircraft to the RAF's 34.[20] During the month of August, the RAF lost 222 fighters, but only 35 of those were destroyed by the Luftwaffe on the ground. As early as August 23 the German losses were 403 destroyed and 127 damaged.[21]

Nor was the British air effort restricted to defensive operations by the Fighter Command. At every opportunity during August and September the RAF Bomber Command struck at Sea Lion shipping concentrated along the coast of France and by the end of September had sunk or seriously damaged twenty-one German transports (12% of those assembled), 214 barges (20%), and five tugs.[22] These raids greatly hampered the Germans, who were short on ships to begin with, in their preparations for Sea Lion.

The first week in September marked the climax for Operation Eagle Attack. In a week of blitzes, beginning on September 1, the Luftwaffe made its supreme bid for aerial superiority. By sheer weight of numbers the German formations broke through to the RAF airfields around Biggin Hill and temporarily put them out of operation. The next day it was Hornchurch's turn, and on September 3 the main German blow fell on the North Weald sector station, a central link in the British air defense system. On September 4 the German bombers struck the Vickers aircraft industry, and on the following day they concentrated on the Biggin Hill airfields again. On September 6, in the final sorties of the campaign, the Germans heavily bombed the Hawker aircraft plant.[23]

The week of blitzes severely strained Fighter Command, which suffered attrition in aircraft and in crews. Yet German losses were even greater than the British, and the Luftwaffe's objective—annihilation of the RAF—was never approached. In the period August 24–September 6, the Luftwaffe lost 378 aircraft and suffered damage to 115 more. The RAF losses in that period were about half as many as Germans', but by September 7 the total number of Fighter Command aircraft available for operations was almost back at its peak, with 746 operational machines. The pilot strength of Fighter Command was 1,381 on that date, or 207 pilots below the number authorized (1,588). Clearly, the strain imposed on the RAF had been in trained crews rather than in aircraft, but in neither category were the British depleted.[24]

Still, the best opportunity for Sea Lion from the viewpoint of air operations was in this period. The fierce German attacks had imposed a severe strain on British air defenses, forcing part of the RAF air-base organization to move beyond the maximum range of the German fighters.[25] While total air victory was beyond the Luftwaffe's reach, local air superiority over parts of the British coast might have been possible through concentration and effective fighter operation. Then why did not Hitler launch the invasion?

The truth is, regardless of the success or failure of air operations, the planned amphibious operation had been breaking down almost from the beginning. On August 16, Halder made a tour of the embarkation ports from Ostend to Dieppe. He observed that "practically nothing [had] been done in the harbors," and although "most of the waterfront installations [were] intact," he found in most instances that "the approaches [were] . . . entirely blocked" (Journal, IV, 162). The vessels sunk or scuttled during the previous campaign in the key harbors prevented rapid concentration of new shipping, and a week after Halder's tour the Naval Staff reported that it would not be ready for loading until September 15 at the earliest. Halder was convinced by this time that the entire operation had very little chance of execution (IV, 171).

The picture changed momentarily on August 26 when the Germans thought they detected an improvement in the air situation, and Brauchitsch told Halder that Hitler's interest in Sea Lion was increasing. But the Fuehrer's renewed enthusiasm was short-lived. The next day, in a conference with Brauchitsch, the Fuehrer talked vaguely about North Africa as a theater of operations against the British. When this new turn in Hitler's mind was revealed to Halder, he was irritated at Hitler's lack of determination and indecisiveness. He remarked in his journal concerning North Africa: "And the Army is supposed to have everything nice and ready without ever getting any straightforward instructions" (IV, 175). Thus, the most opportune period for Sea Lion slipped away day by day as the Army High Command, hampered by the lack of preparation and the Fuehrer's indecision, watched the aerial situation grow more and more discouraging.

By September 7, the air war had reached a crux. In the fortnight before that date, the Germans had lost 378 aircraft to the

RAF's 277 (IV, 186), and obviously such a rate of attrition could
not go on much longer without a decision. In a last desperate effort,
the Luftwaffe turned against the City of London. Hitler specified
that its new mission was to be "the complete destruction of London's
docks, industries, and supplies by means of continuous air attacks
and so hasten the decision." He told Raeder that his final decision
on Sea Lion would depend upon the outcome of the new air
strategy.[26]

The decisive air battle raged over London between September 7
and September 15, 1940. The German assault against the vital
communication and political hub of the British Isles brought on
furious air engagements as both sides brought their whole strength
to bear. The fate of Sea Lion was in the balance. Within a week,
Halder realized that the Luftwaffe was suffering disastrous losses.
He wrote in his journal on September 14 that German victory reports were not giving an "entirely reliable picture" of the struggle
over Britain (IV, 194—probably one of the epic understatements
of 1940), and the next day saw a clear turn of the tide. On September 15 the RAF destroyed fifty-six raiders over London and
in effect broke the back of the flagging Luftwaffe.[27] The same day
the OKW issued orders to postpone the execution of Sea Lion
until October.[28] Although Hitler would not admit it, any hope of
invading England in 1940 had been dashed.

Immediately after the big day over London, rain and clouds
closed the British skies to further large-scale air operations for over
a week. Rested and somewhat rehabilitated during this lull, the Luftwaffe took to the skies again when the weather cleared on September 23. Within three days the Luftwaffe realized that the renewal
of its air assault had been a mistake. By September 26, a third of
Germany's fighter strength was out of action and over three hundred
bombers had been downed since mid-August (Halder, IV, 209).
The Luftwaffe made its final daylight appearance over Great Britain
in major force the following day.[29]

For a time Hitler seems to have been unwilling to accept defeat,
and on September 28 the OKW reset the deadline for Sea Lion.
Halder, probably worn from tension and frustration, commented
that "this chronic state of indecision is intolerable" (IV, 209). In
reality, by the end of September Hitler had no option. The Luft-

waffe was in no condition to cover an invasion with only three hundred serviceable single-engined fighters, less than half the number in the RAF Fighter Command at the end of September.[30]

The failure of German air operations was finally brought home to the OKH when on October 7 a report from the Luftwaffe General Staff admitted that the battle of Britain had so depleted the German Air Force in planes and crews that they could not be repaired before the spring of 1941. In Halder's opinion, even after the Luftwaffe's recuperation, Germany would need "four times that number" to compel the British to come to terms (IV, 224). In the three months from August through October, the RAF destroyed or disabled about half of the Luftwaffe's first-line forces committed to battle, a punishment of the highest order.[31]

On October 12, the OKW issued orders postponing Operation Sea Lion until the spring of 1941 (Halder, IV, 224); eventually, it was discarded altogether. Already Hitler's mind was turning toward the East for that final victory which had evaded him in the West.

Conclusion

The battle of Britain shattered forever the aura of invincibility which the Wehrmacht had acquired during its triumphant march from the plains of Poland to the English Channel. The struggle in the skies over England during the late summer of 1940 established the fact that some types of Luftwaffe fighters proved highly vulnerable to a modern fighter-arm and air-defense system, while others were too short-ranged to give the German bombers the needed escort to penetrate far into the British hinterland. Stripped of its weapons of surprise and accessibility, the Luftwaffe was totally incapable of either preparing the way for invasion or independently forcing an insular power such as Great Britain to terms.

But the failure to invade England was not entirely the failure of the Luftwaffe to gain aerial supremacy. The lack of an amphibious doctrine, equipment, and organization hampered the Army's ground preparations, and, as we have seen, the Naval Staff recognized soon after the first discussions with the Army General Staff that the operation would be quite difficult and a severe strain on German resources. As the weeks passed, it became apparent that German sea power was not up to such a task, and the Army alone continued to believe in the probability of success. The lack of a joint amphibious doctrine and experience led to much interservice quarreling over the width of the landing area and the timing of the operation. These matters themselves did not raise insuperable obstacles, but they are indications of the lack of a joint-service outlook so necessary for the success of any joint-service operation.

The abortive attempt to mount an amphibious assault also indicates that the German Army was the real strength of the Wehrmacht and that neither the Luftwaffe nor the Kriegsmarine was capable of supporting a large-scale overseas amphibious operation, the German success in Norway notwithstanding. The German Navy suffered prohibitive losses during the Norwegian invasion and its aftermath, while German aerial invasion had been successful chiefly as the result of surprise and the weakness of the local forces. Neither the Navy nor the Air Force was able to carry out a similar operation on a much vaster scale against the kind of power the British could muster for the defense of their home island. The English Channel— that narrow sea—was sufficient to balk the Wehrmacht by being a Maginot Line whose flank could not be turned.

Another significant factor demonstrated in the abortive effort against England was that, with the campaign in the West, the Germans had overrun nearly all of the areas in Europe in which German doctrine and organization had been designed to operate. Operation Sea Lion, the first major venture beyond the boundary which encompasses Europe from Poland to the Channel, had proved impossible largely because it presented problems to the Wehrmacht with which it was not prepared to deal. Only the Balkan states remained in the German Army's zone of operational effectiveness. On every side of Western and Central Europe, but one, stretch bodies of water: the Baltic, the North Sea, the English Channel, the Bay of Biscay, and the Mediterranean. In the East, the very immensity of European Russia was itself a barrier. Nevertheless, Hitler believed he had to risk committing the Wehrmacht to one or more theaters of war for which its doctrine was not designed and its organization was unsuited in order to retain the initiative. The future would test the versatility, as well as the resources, of the blitzkrieg army.

CHAPTER SEVEN

The Balkans: An Interlude

The Search for a New Strategy

With all prospects for an early invasion of England ended in October, 1940,[1] the Nazi dictator had to reconsider the directions in which Germany's energies ought to be applied in order to bring about final victory. By October the situation had become considerably more complicated than in the previous July, when the plans for Operation Sea Lion were first formulated. In September the Italians had launched an invasion of British-occupied Egypt from their bases in Libya and by October were making little headway. The Germans were already beginning to question whether the Italians would be able to drive forward without at least a minimum of German help, and, as British reinforcements arrived in Egypt, they feared that even German forces sent to North Africa would be hard pressed to keep Libya out of British hands. The poor Italian showing against Egypt, as earlier against France, made clear that Germany's Italian ally might prove to be more of a liability than an asset. Still, in October the British remained on the defensive in Egypt, and the Italian situation in North Africa was not yet critical.

Besides the question of the Mediterranean, Hitler's declaration of July 31 concerning Russia[2] had caused the Army General Staff to busy itself with plans for an operation against the Soviet Union. Halder was personally opposed to broadening the war to include the

Russians, and he continued to think that—next to an invasion of the British Isles—the Mediterranean was the proper focal point for German efforts to compel Britain to come to terms. As mentioned earlier, both Brauchitsch and Halder had opposed an attack on Russia from the time that Hitler had first mentioned the possibility. By concentrating on the Mediterranean instead, they believed, the Wehrmacht "could deliver the British a decisive blow . . . shoulder them away from [the Mid-East], help the Italians in building their Mediterranean Empire, and, with the help of Russia, consolidate the Reich." Even if the British did not seek terms after their defeat in the Middle East, Halder believed that Germany could confidently face war with Britain for years if necessary. (Halder, Journal, IV, 141)

In the fall of 1940, with good campaigning weather in Russia over for the year, Hitler also turned his thoughts to the Mediterranean. During a conference held three days after the postponement of Operation Sea Lion, the Fuehrer declared that temporarily the German war effort was to be directed against the British position in the Middle East, with special attention to the possibilities of taking Gibraltar and giving aid to the Italians in North Africa. (Halder, IV, 232–33)

As a good staff officer, Halder was far ahead of the Fuehrer in planning the Gibraltar project. He had already sent a secret scouting mission under Lieutenant Colonel Mikosch to survey the situation. Mikosch returned to Halder's headquarters in Berlin on October 16 with the optimistic report that Gibraltar could be assaulted with about two regiments. Commenting on the colonel's report, Halder wrote:

He underestimates the defense capabilities and forgets that the enemy facing us has no place to withdraw. Nor has he taken into account that British naval forces might also be on the scene. . . . Should the British decide to hold . . . we would find it necessary to secure the entire peninsula right down to its southern tip, or else it might become another Alcazar.[3] . . . The command in the field will have to prepare for an operation at a much slower pace. (IV, 236)

Thus planning for Operation Felix, the code-name for the Gibraltar enterprise, got underway.

Halder quickly discovered that the chief problem in sending aid
to the Italians was logistical. A preliminary survey of the Italian
supply system indicated "total confusion." Halder believed that the
first step in extending aid to North Africa must be an effective reorganization of supply so that German reinforcements could be
dispatched on a "unified basis." He reckoned that using Italian
supply procedures it would take two months to ship one German
motorized division to North Africa. Still, the Italians were not expected to take Mersa Matruh before the end of the year; no British
counterstroke had yet endangered the Italian position in North
Africa. The movement of German reinforcements at the end of the
year could be "staged as a 'sneak' through the British blockade."
(IV, 241)

While Operation Felix and aid to the Italians were being worked
out, Halder gave considerable thought as to the various ways in
which German entry into the Mediterranean war could be carried
out most effectively. He saw clearly that aid to the Italians in North
Africa would be a stopgap measure at first, for the Axis powers did
not have command of the sea. Reinforcements would arrive slowly,
and only gradually could a powerful military force be created. But
the British forces in Egypt were still weaker, and with the help of
a panzer division or two the Italians might be able to drive the
British across the Nile. If this proved practicable, even if further
ground movement was impossible, German air forces from air bases
in Egypt might be able to deny the British "their vital bases in the
Eastern Mediterranean." (IV, 249)

Yet the lack of sea power led Halder to believe that Axis operations in North Africa could only be conducted on a risky basis with
a highly vulnerable line of supply open to British naval attack. Any
operation in the Mediterranean likely to produce favorable and decisive results, he believed, must be conducted in such a manner as to
maximize German land power and minimize British naval power.
The only way this could be done was by a German drive "through
Anatolia and Syria executed concurrently with the drive in Egypt."
In brief, he contemplated a gigantic pincer movement along the
Mediterranean coasts of Anatolia and Syria with a point of conversion at Suez. The vast flanking movement would of course "raise
complex questions of high policy which . . . [could] be answered
only by the supreme command [i.e., Hitler]." (IV, 249)

The period of relative calm that followed the postponement of Operation Sea Lion and the halt of the Italian offensive in North Africa did not last long. On October 28, against the wishes of Hitler, Mussolini launched an Italian invasion of Greece from Italian-controlled Albania. This sudden turn of events caught the Army High Command off guard, and there was considerable speculation at OKH headquarters as to what it would mean. "In any event," Halder commented, "the immediate effect is a completely new picture of the situation in the Eastern Mediterranean and the Balkans, which sooner or later cannot fail to affect also Bulgaria" (IV, 250).

Hitler's irritation at Mussolini's unilateral decision to attack Greece inclined the Fuehrer to leave the Italians to their own devices (V, 4), even though it became quickly apparent that Mussolini's armies were making no better progress in Greece than in North Africa. He hurriedly changed his mind, however, when a few days after the invasion began the British occupied the islands of Crete and Lemnos off the Greek coast. With Lemnos in their possession, the British had an advanced base from which to invade the Balkans or even perhaps bomb the vital Rumanian oil fields around Ploesti, Germany's main oil supply. In a military conference held on November 4, Hitler ordered the transfer of antiaircraft guns and fighters to protect the Rumanian oil fields, accelerated preparations to take Gibraltar, and ordered plans for an invasion of Greece from German bases in Rumania and Bulgaria. Since Hitler thought that Franco's Spain was willing to enter the war as a German ally at any time, he believed that the necessary political steps for Operation Felix could be completed shortly.[4] Halder's proposed flanking movement through Anatolia and Syria was also brought up at this conference and rejected, but Hitler did agree that preparations for Sea Lion should be maintained. Halder took this opportunity to stress the improvement achieved in these preparations (V, 7), apparently in the hope that Hitler would not abandon the invasion plan for England altogether.

After the November 4 conference, Halder was as occupied in planning for Operation Felix and the assault on Greece (code-name Marita) as with the preparations for the attack on Russia (Operation Barbarossa). The Italian situation in the Mediterranean continued to deteriorate and, on November 11, a British aircraft carrier raid on Taranto sank or disabled three out of four of Mussolini's battleships.[5] On November 12, the OKW issued the official directive for the several operations. This Directive Number Eighteen, received by Halder's headquarters two days later, declared that political steps were being taken to bring about an early Spanish entry into the war and that the aim of the German intervention in the Iberian peninsula was to drive the English out of the western Mediterranean. For this purpose Gibraltar was to be taken and the straits of Gibraltar closed, and the British were to be prevented from gaining a foothold at another point in the Iberian peninsula or in the Atlantic islands. The directive also gave the objectives for Operation Marita. The OKH was to make preparations for occupying the Greek mainland north of the Aegean Sea, entering through Bulgaria, in order to provide the Luftwaffe with bases from which it might strike British targets in the eastern Mediterranean, especially the British air bases from which the RAF might threaten the Rumanian oil area. In order to execute these tasks, the OKH was to plan on the use of an army group of about ten divisions.[6] In addition to these preparations for Felix and Marita, Halder was to keep one panzer division ready to move to Libya at the proper time (V, 21).

By November 18, the German build-up in Rumania was taking place at a rapid rate, and the considerable shift of German strength into the Balkan area caused Halder to believe that Hitler and the OKW had pushed the Russian operation into the background. About a week later, Halder wrote: "The matter seems to be developing further, *i.e.* in the direction of a possible German attack on Turkey. . . . We must not lose sight of the fact . . . that our chances [of success] against Russia diminish if we commit forces against Turkey." (V, 21, 34)

On November 25 the Army General Staff submitted its plan for Operation Marita to Halder. The Chief of Staff was not entirely pleased with the plan since he believed that Hitler would demand "stronger security" against Greece. "It is based on the assumption," Halder wrote in his journal, "that we detrain in Rumania and group for operations after that. . . . Start of the offensive on 11 February. (Bear in mind Eastern Operation!)." On the same day, Halder received reports that fifteen transports were standing by in Venice, Trieste, and Genoa for amphibious phases of Operation Felix. This shipping was to assemble at Genoa by mid-December. (V, 36)

Halder became increasingly concerned about the wisdom of diverting so much German strength to the Balkans, where the objectives of the OKW seemed rather vague. He wrote on November 25:

Taken as a whole this day shows again the vast amount of unnecessary work imposed on the General Staff in consequence of the failure of the OKW to furnish any positive leadership. No directives have been forthcoming on what they really want in Bulgaria, but there is endless talk about troop strength, even about individual units.

Any way we look at this Bulgarian business, it is nothing that would really hurt Britain. But that after all is the only thing that should count.

In this connection it is heartening to see that the Fuehrer is again taking an interest in [Sea Lion]. That is the surest way to hit England. But then again, the Spanish question does not seem to be getting anywhere [i.e., Hitler's negotiations with Franco]. Neither Bulgaria nor Spain are to let themselves be dragged into the war. They know they would have to pay the piper even after German victories. (V, 37)

The danger which Halder imagined he saw in Marita continued to prey on his mind. On November 27 he began to think of the operation as a possible error in strategy in view of the scheduled Russian offensive for the coming spring. Writing of the possible effects of both Felix and Marita, he commented: "The diversion of strength to these operations would compel us to give up [Sea Lion] and to confine ourselves to reaching the first objectives in the Russian offensive." He realized that the Balkans would provide an excellent base for the southern prong of an encirclement maneuver against the Russian forces in western Russia, but he also had misgivings about the application of the traditional German doctrine in the immense Russian spaces. (V, 43)

A few days later, Halder's apprehensions were raised still further when Hitler called Brauchitsch and Halder to a conference. Hitler had decided that Operation Felix was to be launched as soon as possible and no later than January 10, 1941. "The decision to do Felix is final," wrote Halder afterwards. Preparations for Marita were to be hastened so that German forces could "march into enemy territory early in March." However, the decision as to whether Marita would be actually carried out was left open. Probably with a heavy heart, Halder heard his Fuehrer declare that Operation Sea Lion could be left out of the Army High Command's further calculations. (V, 55)

In early December, the British in North Africa launched a general offensive against the Italian positions at Sidi Barrani. Within a few days the entire Italian army was in full flight through Cyrenaica. Almost simultaneously, the Greeks struck the Italians in Albania and sent them reeling back (V, 60). With the Italian position crumbling in both theaters, Franco informed Hitler that Spain had no intention of entering the war. These events produced a main shift in German strategy.

During the afternoon of December 8 (the day after the British offensive in North Africa had begun), Halder visited Field Marshal Wilhelm Keitel, Chief of the OKW, and outlined the new plan of operations which he had in mind. Since it was no longer possible to use Spain as a base of operations against Gibraltar, he proposed that German forces should move quickly across the western Mediterranean and occupy French North Africa. From ports in this area, the Germans could then launch a surprise assault on the Mediterranean side of the Gibraltar fortress. Since it was unlikely that Marshal Pétain would sanction such a move, the plan (to be given the code-name Operation Attila) involved the occupation of Vichy France and capture of the French fleet interned at Toulon. (V, 61)

That evening Halder, at his headquarters on the Bendlerstrasse, received a phone call from Keitel. Keitel informed Halder that Hitler had approved Halder's proposal and that preparations were to begin at once. The units assigned to Felix were to be diverted to Attila.

On December 9, the Operation sections of the Army General Staff reported that Attila would require ten days of preparation. Halder then met the Fuehrer for lunch and went over the operation with him, and Hitler approved Halder's plans as a basis for preparation. Taking advantage of the relaxed mealtime atmosphere, Halder also turned the Fuehrer's attention to overall direction of the Mediterranean operations, stressing two crucial points: (1) the necessity of continuing the attack on the British Isles by every means; and (2) the threat posed by the build-up of British strength in the Mediterranean east of Malta in view of the demonstrated Italian weakness and "the possibility of a British front in the Balkans." Halder indirectly brought up Sea Lion and pointed to Gibraltar as the means of closing Britain's direct route to the eastern Mediterranean. Hitler would not commit himself fully, but told him that the OKW would advise the Italians "to limit themselves to defensive operations in Libya" in order not to draw more British strength to North Africa. (V, 62)

For the next ten days Halder was busy with planning Attila and other operational matters (the OKW directive for Operation Barbarossa was issued in this period), and he paid little attention to the Italian struggle in Libya. On December 31, the military attaché in Rome telegraphed Halder that General Archibald Wavell's offensive in North Africa had virtually wiped out the Italian Tenth Army and that its remnants were fleeing Cyrenaica. It was now obvious that the Italian forces were in danger of collapsing in both North Africa and Greece. (V, 79)

After the Christmas lull, on January 8–9, 1941, Hitler held a military conference at the Berghof to stress the importance of getting aid to the battered Italians before Libya was overrun by the British. He visualized this aid as a stopgap measure, for he did not believe that enough Axis strength could be concentrated in North Africa for an offensive towards Alexandria and Suez before the winter of 1942. Preparations for Attila were to be continued in the event that the French became troublesome and had to be crushed completely. The French fleet interned at Toulon was not to be allowed to escape to the British under any circumstances, although the new events in Africa made it clear that there was little immediate chance that Attila could be put into action. Hitler also announced that negotiations were under way to obtain Bulgaria as a base from which the German armies in Rumania might launch Operation Marita against Greece; the troops for this operation were to be ready to strike no later than March 26.[7]

Toward the end of January, 1941, Hitler called Brauchitsch and Halder to the Reich Chancellery for another conference. At this time Halder recommended that Marita be launched as early as February 15 in order to leave plenty of good campaigning weather to complete Operation Barbarossa. Yet the conference turned out to be a discouraging one for Halder. The more Hitler talked about the Russian campaign, the more obscure became his aims. The "purpose is not clear," Halder wrote later. "We do not hit the British that way. . . . Risk in the West must not be under-estimated." Then he added, "It is possible that Italy might collapse . . . and we get a Southern front in Spain, Italy and Greece. If we are tied up in Russia, a bad situation will be made worse." (V, 98)

But Halder had little time to reflect on these long-range problems. By the beginning of February, he was fully occupied in planning for a German expeditionary force to North Africa. A delegation of German officers sent to investigate matters there reported on February 1 in favor of sending at least one German motorized division. When Halder informed Hitler on February 3 that one motorized unit with supporting elements was ready for shipping, the Fuehrer selected one of his leading armor experts, General Erwin Rommel, as commander of the new *Deutsches Afrika Korps,* and Rommel reported to Halder for final instructions on February 7. Halder briefed Rommel on the situation and stressed that his main task would be to see that Italian Marshal Rodolfo Graziani did not retreat to Tripoli "without a fight." The German intervention in North Africa was given the code-name Operation *Sonnenblume* (Sunflower). Rommel's main unit, the Fifth Light Division, was to be transported to North Africa in order to be ready for action by the end of March. (V, 102–106)

For the next two weeks Halder watched anxiously as the German convoys ran the British blockade without incident. When the second convoy arrived safely on February 15 at Tripoli, he began to turn his attention elsewhere. (V, 116)

On February 17, predictions of bad weather in the Balkans led the Army High Command to push back the starting date for Marita to March 2 (V, 118). Meanwhile, the German Foreign Office was engaged in negotiations with the Yugoslav government. On the same day that Marita was postponed, Hasso von Etzdorf of the German Foreign Office informed Halder that the negotiations with the Yugoslavs were proceeding satisfactorily (V, 117); it was unlikely that Yugoslavia would be a foe in the Balkan operation. In that event, it would not be necessary for Halder to include Yugoslavia in his calculations, and he seems to have given Yugoslavia little further thought.

On the basis of a political agreement signed on March 1, the Bulgarian government permitted the German Twelfth Army under Field Marshal von List to occupy Bulgaria on the following day (VI, 11). The entry of German forces into Bulgaria thoroughly alarmed both the Greek and British high commands. Earlier in the year, in the fear that the Germans were planning an intervention in Greece, the British and Greek high commands had held joint conferences at Athens. At that time the British advised their Greek counterparts that if the Germans somehow achieved the use of Bulgaria as a base, the exposed salient in Thrace would be indefensible. The Greeks agreed with the British view, but they were hesitant to abandon the entire area. If the Yugoslavs intended to fight the Germans, the Greeks intended to hold western Thrace, which was protected by the Metaxas line fortifications. If the Yugoslavs allowed the Germans free transit to Greece, the Greek High Command intended to pull its eastern divisions back to the Vermion mountains at the head of Thessaly and behind the Aliakmon river, and to establish a new line from Mount Olympus north along the Vermion range to the Albanian front. The British were to ascertain the intentions of the Yugoslavs through negotiations.[8]

In some manner, liaison between the Greek and British governments faltered after January, leaving the British with the impression that the Greeks had already withdrawn to the Vermion position and the Greeks with the impression that they would not withdraw until they heard from the British. When List's Twelfth Army occupied Bulgaria, the British inquired of the Greek Commander in Chief, General Alexander Papagos, whether the Greeks were ready in the Vermion position where British reinforcements were to join them. Papagos had to reply that the Greeks were still in western Thrace and that it would take twenty days to redeploy to the Mount Olympus line. Since he estimated that the Germans could strike within fifteen days of their occupation of Bulgaria, Papagos could not risk the chance of beginning a withdrawal from the Metaxas line that might be caught in mid-course by a German attack.[9] The net result was that three Greek divisions remained exposed in the Metaxas line, while the British moved their expeditionary forces no further north than the Vermion position. This faulty deployment played a considerable role in the outcome in Greece.

Meanwhile, the German march into Bulgaria had provoked a strong diplomatic note from Moscow, which declared in part that the Soviet Union found it regrettable that the Third Reich had chosen a course "infringing on Russian security interests." Moreover, the German move had met with an "unfriendly reception" from the Yugoslav government, with whom the Germans were still negotiating. Halder decided not to move the panzer forces to the Greek frontier until these uncertainties were resolved. (Halder, VI, 13, 14)

By March 8, German intelligence had informed Halder that in case of a German attack on Thrace down the Vardar or Struma valleys (via Yugoslavia and Bulgaria), the Anglo-Greek forces would attempt to hold a defensive position "with the right wing based on Mt. Olympus, and the left wing extending over Mt. Grammosi" on the Greek-Albanian border (*i.e.,* the Vermion position, at least according to the interpretation put on the strange Anglo-Greek deployment by the OKH). This intelligence also accurately informed Halder that the British were preparing to support Greece with no more than two or three divisions. (VI, 19)

On March 17, Hitler held another conference on Marita. At this time Hitler decided to overrun Greece completely, including even the islands off the Greek coast.[10] Since this operation would be more extensive and might require some time for accomplishment, the forces allocated to Marita were to be "written off" from the build-up for Barbarossa (Halder, VI, 27).

Three days later, on March 20, General Rommel returned to Berlin to report on the situation in North Africa. Rommel believed that the British gave every indication of going over to the defensive there for the time being. Halder therefore agreed to a limited offensive[11] by the new German Afrika Korps (VI, 32), doubtless with the idea of holding back British reinforcements from Greece.

With the strategy in North Africa settled, Halder returned his attention to the Balkans. Here at last matters were coming to a head. On March 25, Prince Regent Paul of Yugoslavia signed a political agreement with Hitler (VI, 34), and the way was open for the Germans to invade Greece on April 1.

Within forty-eight hours the careful German calculations went completely awry. During the night of March 26–27, a *coup d'état* at Belgrade overthrew the government of Prince Regent Paul, established young King Peter on the throne, and repudiated the political agreement with Germany.

The events at Belgrade were not fully clear to Berlin until nearly noon on March 26, when Brauchitsch and Halder were called hastily to the Reich Chancellery. As Halder related the incident years later at Nuremberg:

We didn't know what it was all about. Hitler received us with the words: "I have decided to annihilate Yugoslavia." And the second question [sic] which was put to me was, "How long do you think you will need to get the troops moving?" The whole subject was a completely new one to us.[12]

The Army High Command was caught completely off guard. The signing of the political agreement on March 25 had removed Yugoslavia from their minds. Halder continued his testimony at Nuremberg:

The German Army was then in a state of regrouping . . . [for] a possible campaign in the East. The majority of the divisions were not in a state of readiness to be used at once. . . . [The] necessary forces . . . had to be gathered from half of Europe. I recall that part of them were called in from the Biscay area and another part from the North Sea area . . . and all took place without any preparation at all.[13]

Faced by one of the greatest crises of his career, Halder set to work with Brauchitsch on the afternoon of March 27 to design a plan of operations against the Yugoslavs. Brauchitsch and Halder quickly drew up a plan (code-name Operation Twenty-Five) which called for three major thrusts. List's operation against Greece would go on as before, except that part of his panzer forces would strike from Bulgaria into southern Yugoslavia to capture the vital rail-junction at Skoplje, thereby severing the main communication link between Greece and Yugoslavia and preventing co-ordinated Yugoslav-Greek resistance. Another part of his armored divisions—Panzer Group Kleist—would swing north, via Nish, toward Belgrade. The Second Army, still to be formed in Austria under General Maximilian von

Weichs, would invade Yugoslavia to seize the Croat capital at Zagreb and then drive south between the Sava and Drava rivers toward Belgrade. The end result of these moves was to be a German vise that would crush the Yugoslav forces between its northern and southern jaws. (Halder, VI, 37)

The speed with which the plan was implemented was almost as phenomenal as the rapidity with which it was drawn up. Orders were flashed to units all over Europe that same evening and on the night of March 27 put into motion a vast military movement that had not been in Halder's wildest dreams as little as twelve hours before. By the next day German units in half of Europe were on the march, as Halder met with Hitler again to request permission to negotiate with the Hungarian General Staff for assembly grounds and the use of railways adjacent to Yugoslavia. When Hitler readily agreed to such negotiations, Halder dispatched his new First Deputy,[14] General Friedrich Paulus, to Vienna to brief List, Weichs, and the Hungarians on the manner in which Operation Twenty-Five would be carried out. (Halder, VI, 38)

On March 29, Paulus telephoned Halder from Vienna to report that co-ordination among List, Weichs, and the Hungarians was proceeding satisfactorily, and the OKH decided that Operation Marita should be launched in co-ordination with Operation Twenty-Five. Halder approved List's request to postpone Marita until April 5 (VI, 41), and the next day Paulus returned from the Austrian capital as Brauchitsch and Halder put the finishing touches to their operational plans for the Balkans. The Second Army was assigned three panzer corps, three infantry corps, and a mountain corps, for a total of sixteen divisions. The Twelfth Army was assigned one panzer group, a panzer corps, one independent panzer division, and two infantry corps, for a total of sixteen divisions.[15]

On March 31, much to Halder's surprise, Rommel's Afrika Korps in Libya launched an offensive at Agedabia; no major operations in North Africa had been authorized until Rommel had been fully reinforced, but Halder was too deeply immersed in the final details of planning the Balkan operations to pay much attention. Rommel's attack met with success, and by April 3 his mixed German and Italian forces had broken the British hold on Agedabia and were pushing the battered British on to Tobruk. His success had been so unexpected that Hitler felt compelled to advise him to proceed cautiously, lest he advance into a British trap. (Halder, VI, 47)

With good news pouring in from North Africa, Halder decided to recommend that Operation Twenty-Five and Operation Marita be launched simultaneously on April 6. Hitler quickly approved this recommendation. (VI, 48)

Blitzkrieg South

Early on the morning of April 6, the blitzkrieg army struck in the Balkans. List's Twelfth Army suddenly lunged forward into southern Yugoslavia, while the Luftwaffe made massive attacks on Belgrade and key Yugoslav airfields. Caught by the suddenness of the onslaught, the Yugoslavs made little resistance on the first day, and the German motorized forces moved forward rapidly. (VI, 55)

The next day another part of the Twelfth Army invaded eastern Thrace, but the Greek holding forces fought tenaciously. Progress on this front was so slow that the Luftwaffe's Chief of Staff, Hans Jeschonneck, could not resist a "dig" at the expense of the OKH. In a vexed tone, Halder wrote on that day:

Jeschonneck calls up, and hints sort of vaguely . . . that [Goering] has dropped remarks to the Fuehrer on "unsatisfactory" progress of XVIII Corps. This damned back-biting is starting again. Fortunately, in this case, the Fuehrer already had the news that meanwhile the XVIII Corps has broken through the mountains after hard fighting. (VI, 59)

Actually, List's forces were performing splendidly. By April 8 his armor had occupied Skoplje, thereby cutting the main transportation artery between Greece and Yugoslavia, while further south the Second Panzer Division had broken through the Yugoslav defenses, wheeled south towards Greece, and was advancing toward Salonika in order to trap the Greek forces in Thrace (VI, 59).

By April 8 matters were going so well that Brauchitsch considered diverting the German forces at Skoplje westward to link up with the Italians on the Albanian front. Instead, Halder induced him to direct these forces toward the strategic Monastir Gap, thereby setting off a second flanking movement that would ultimately strike the Vermion

13. The Invasion of Yugoslavia and Greece, 1941.

position unexpectedly from the northwest rather than northeast and which would cut across the rear of the Greek forces in Albania.

Later that same day, Brauchitsch and Halder sped by train to Breslau, where they discussed the situation with List. List urged that Ewald von Kleist's First Panzer Group, now moving on Belgrade, detach one panzer division in order to strengthen the drive against the Greeks. Brauchitsch and Halder declined on the grounds that they expected a decisive battle in Yugoslavia around Nish, which would probably decide the whole campaign. (VI, 59–60)

Brauchitsch and Halder moved their headquarters to the Maria Theresa Academy in Vienna the following day. By this time their decision not to divert strength to the Greek drive had begun to justify itself. The German armored forces succeeded in capturing Salonika with little difficulty, forcing the local Greek commander to capitulate. (VI, 60)

About noon on April 9, reports that were coming into German headquarters indicated that Yugoslav resistance on the Nish front was collapsing. At once the Army High Command ordered the Fifth Panzer Division to press on toward Belgrade.

At this point, however, Brauchitsch began to have second thoughts about joining units of the Twelfth Army with the Italians on the Albanian front, largely because of pressure from Hitler, who probably wanted to bolster Italian prestige. Sensing that this move would divert German forces from the drive to turn the Vermion line, Halder hotly opposed it. "To me this seems wrong," he wrote ". . . for it delays [XL Panzer] Corps with the trivial business of joining up with the Italians when perhaps there is still a chance to push ahead." He added: "Probably this step, which I denounced when talking with [Brauchitsch] in the forenoon, is motivated by political considerations on top level." (VI, 61)

On April 10, General Weichs's Second Army entered the campaign by invading Yugoslavia from Austria and Hungary. This new blow from the north was the breaking point for the already hard-pressed Yugoslavs. Complete disintegration began to follow. Almost unopposed, elements of the Second Army swept into the Croat capital of Zagreb. (VI, 63)

During the night of April 10–11, Hitler called OKH headquarters to express his fear that the OKH plans would allow many Yugoslavs to escape to the western mountains, where they might carry on resistance. Colonel Adolf Heusinger, Chief of the Operations section, took the call and apparently was able to contain what Halder later characterized as an "outbreak of the jitters." Halder was, however, already irritated by Hitler's previous interference with the operation and expressed resentment to Brauchitsch over the incident. Later that day, he released his feelings in his journal:

This timorous shying away from every risk while continuously clamoring for victories, may be acceptable politically but from the military standpoint it is intolerable. We have our job cut out in the south, against Greece. Every unnecessary step in another direction is a sin against success. (VI, 64)

Despite irritating interference from Hitler, Halder had reason for satisfaction with the way German operations were going. A day later Yugoslav resistance in the north had completely collapsed (VI, 65), and on April 13 Belgrade fell to the triumphant German armies.

With Operation Twenty-Five virtually completed, Halder turned his attention to the Twelfth Army's operations against the Greeks. The Greek forces had begun a withdrawal to the Vermion position, where the British were setting up their lines to hold Thessaly and the rear of the Greek forces in Albania. By this time List had eliminated the Thrace salient altogether (capturing five generals and 20,000 troops) and was preparing to launch a drive from Salonika towards Mount Olympus (VI, 66). At the same time, the German Ninth Panzer Division was already through the Monastir Gap and was pressing toward the Vermion position via Ptolomais (VI, 69). This latter situation so endangered the communications of the Greek divisions in Albania that they had no choice but to withdraw as rapidly as possible. About the only hope left for the Anglo-Greek forces was to fight a holding action on the Vermion line.

From April 14 to April 18, the Anglo-Greek forces fought heroically on the line in northern Thessaly, but by the latter date German forces had forced a general withdrawal into the plain of Thessaly. Since it became obvious that the British would seek a secondary defense line behind which they might hold until they could evacuate, Halder thought it probable that the Anglo-Greek forces would establish their left on the Pindus Mountains and their right at Thermopylae. Large numbers of Greek forces were also west of the Pindus. "Here the retreating enemy," Halder wrote, "cannot help being crowded together and forced into a bottleneck, where our massed Air Force will have opportunity for effective action." (VI, 75)

The next day List, in his eagerness not to lose contact with the retreating foe, proposed to the Army High Command that at least one mountain division should be moved toward Thermopylae in order to hurry the German build-up for assault on the pass. Halder vetoed this measure on the grounds that movement of the semimotorized division through the plain of Thessaly would be too slow. Slowness in building up infantry divisions was unavoidable, although the delay permitted the British additional time to fortify historic Thermopylae Pass (VI, 76).

The following day, April 20, was Hitler's birthday, and the General Staff held a special luncheon in celebration. The military situation provided them with an agreeable background for festivities, since by this date it was evident that the British were preparing to evacuate Greece. Already German motorized units were well south of Larissa (VI, 77).

On April 21, Halder and Heusinger flew to List's headquarters at Salonika. They arrived in the midst of surrender negotiations between the commander of the Greek Epirus Army and List. Matters were practically concluded when Hitler dispatched an order to List to await Italian representatives who would take part in the surrender ceremonies. Rather caustically, Halder commented:

This was to give the Italians an opening for appearing as partners in conclusion of capitulation. Such a political maneuver makes [List] . . . look foolish in the eyes of the Greek Army. (VI, 78)

On April 22 Halder flew back to the temporary headquarters at Vienna and rejoined Brauchitsch. Apparently he was still vexed at Hitler over the Greek surrender affair. When he learned that Hitler had ordered an air-drop on Corinth to trap elements of the British forces before they could cross to the Peloponnesos, the signal to be given by Hitler himself, Halder remarked smugly, "That [*i.e.,* Hitler's signal] of course, implies the risk of missing the critical moment." (VI, 79–80)

The following day Brauchitsch and Halder switched their head-quarters back to Berlin as the Greeks formally laid down their arms. However, large bodies of British troops were still fighting stub-bornly near their embarkation ports, where British ships were slowly evacuating them.

During the next two days, April 24 and 25, British forces at the Thermopylae Pass put up a splendid resistance to the German forces driving on Athens, but on the latter date the pass was assaulted suc-cessfully and the last Allied defense line in Greece was breached (VI, 84). The Germans rushed forward quickly and on April 26 Thebes fell (VI, 85). Athens was now doomed, and on April 27 the Germans proudly raised the Nazi banner over the Acropolis. British evacuation from the Piraeus and the Peloponnesos now went into high gear. (VI, 87)

On May 2 the last British soldier boarded his ship, and the battle of Greece was over. Behind the British was a Balkan area totally overrun by Hitler's legions. Perhaps still worse, although 43,000 British troops had escaped, some 12,000 British soldiers were left be-hind either dead or as prisoners.[16]

Conclusion

The blitzkrieg army had scored another in a long string of suc-cesses. The Balkan campaign removed any immediate danger of British air attacks on the Rumanian oil fields from bases in the Greek islands or mainland, while inflicting a severe defeat on the first Brit-ish attempt since Dunkirk to return to the European continent. The Balkan victory helped to wipe away the stain left by the abortive Sea Lion attempt of the previous summer and to establish a secure flank for the German Army in the attack on Russia. In all of this the OKH had had the satisfaction of seeing its plans succeed to an overwhelm-ing extent.

The speed and outstanding success of the Balkan campaign was the direct result of German aerial and armored superiority over the Greeks and Yugoslavs, while striking once more with the benefit of surprise. The Yugoslav Army never fully mobilized and was crushed before effective resistance could be organized. Both the Yugoslavs and Greeks lacked modern antitank weapons and air cover, while the

Germans struck from bases in close proximity to their objectives. Only the British had equipment modern enough to make an effective defense against this southern blitzkrieg, but the failure of the Greek Army to redeploy from Thrace in time and the small size of the British force undermined any chance of a successful stand in the Vermion position. The mountainous terrain might have favored the defense of the Balkans and did create some logistical difficulties for the Germans, but the failure of the Allies to secure the approaches from the Monastir Gap compromised the Vermion position and permitted German panzer and motorized infantry divisions to sever the lines of communication with the Greek forces in Albania simply by advancing down the valleys. Once the Anglo-Greek forces began their withdrawal into the plain of Thessaly, they benefitted from German delays caused by infantry divisions having to march over difficult roads and mountainous terrain. By that time, however, the OKH's flanking movement by panzer and motorized forces had so effectively destroyed the Greek Army that the Anglo-Greek forces lacked the means for a counterattack; only escape by the British was assured. The distances involved in the Balkan campaign were not great, and the farthest German advance was only 250 miles from its starting point. Difficult terrain, poor roads, and limited railways were sufficiently offset by faulty deployment and inferiority in armor and airpower on the part of the Allies, combined with the advantage of surprise held by the Germans to give the blitzkrieg army another cheap and relatively easy victory.

CHAPTER EIGHT

North Africa: To Aid an Ally

Rommel's First Offensive

Though events in the Balkans and Greece had come to a satisfactory conclusion for Halder and the OKH by the end of April, 1941, this was far from the case with German operations in North Africa. In this theater a great rift had developed between the OKH and its commander in the field, Erwin Rommel.

When the decision had been made to send German aid to the battered Italians in North Africa in January, 1941, Hitler had made clear that few German forces could be committed because the Italians themselves needed the available ports for unloading supplies; he no longer considered it possible for the Axis powers to reopen the offensive against Egypt with any hope for success.[1] When in early February preparation of the first of two motorized divisions to compose the Afrika Korps was completed,[2] Rommel reported to OKH headquarters for instructions. Halder stressed that his mission was to stiffen the Italian determination to hold the Libyan port of Tripoli. He also told Rommel to set up a staff, to inform the OKH as to his ideas for defending Cyrenaica before taking the plane to Rome, again from Rome before leaving for North Africa, and finally to report from Italian headquarters in North Africa.[3]

Rommel's own later account of his OKH briefing goes into greater detail. German aid was being sent to the Italians on the understand-

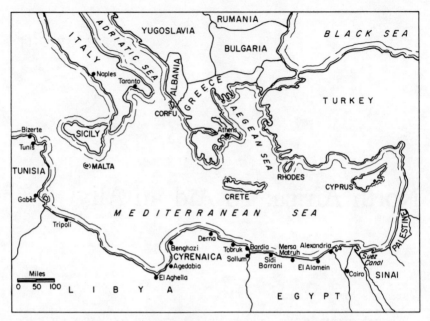

14. General Map of the Mediterranean Theater of War, 1941.

ing that they would attempt to make a stand on the edge of the Gulf
of Sirte (Sidra) at the base of the Cyrenaican bulge around Ras el
Ali, a wide place in the sandy track about twenty-five miles west of El
Agheila. This position, if it could be held, would allow Luftwaffe
units supporting the Axis forces in North Africa sufficient room to
develop airfields in Cyrenaica and was an important change from the
Italian plan of making a final stand at Tripoli. While Rommel was
to use his influence to stiffen the Italian will to resist, his forces were
to be subordinated to Marshal Rudolfo Graziani, the Italian commander in chief in North Africa.[4]

By the time Rommel had reached North Africa, Graziani had
been replaced by General Italo Gariboldi, to whom Rommel reported
on February 12. Rommel was not greatly impressed by the Italian
leadership and he privately resolved to take command at the front
into his own hands as soon as possible, although this was expressly
contrary to his OKH instructions. He believed that this decision was
justified by the seriousness of the situation and the lack of energy
shown by the Italian command.[5]

The rest of February was taken up with the convoying of elements of the Fifth Light Division to North Africa, a process still going on when Halder sent instructions on March 10 reminding Rommel not to court action with the British before the complete arrival of the Fifth Light Division and Italian reinforcements. Back in Germany, Halder was already sketching the courses open to Axis powers in North Africa after the Afrika Korps assembled. Halder wrote on March 12 that apart from remaining completely on the defensive, two courses of action were open to Rommel and the Italians. The first was a major Axis offensive to drive the British back to the Egyptian frontier and to capture Tobruk. The second course was to combine several minor offensives along the coast around Agedabia during the spring and summer and then perhaps to make a major drive on Tobruk during the fall. The first course would require the doubling of supply-column battalions already shipped to Libya by the Germans. The second course would not strain the supply elements already available, though Halder recognized its drawbacks as a loss of time and lessened striking power. (War Journal, VI, 20)

After considering the problem for a week, Halder proposed at a Fuehrer conference on March 17 that Rommel attempt nothing more ambitious than a forward shift of the defensive front, with a view to passing over to the offensive whenever a favorable balance of strength with the British could be obtained. With other operational tasks impending, Halder felt that to send forces to the Afrika Korps greater than those already planned would be unwise. Hitler agreed and the defensive strategy for North Africa was reaffirmed. (VI, 29) [6]

Three days later Rommel returned from his reconnaissance trip and reported to OKH headquarters. He was convinced that the British too were thinking in terms of defense only. British armored units were located as far west as Benghazi, but the British were treating the areas around Agedabia and El Agheila as no-man's land. To Halder, this British deployment seemed to indicate an intention to offer a serious defense of Cyrenaica only in the Jebel el Akhdar area around Benghazi, an area conducive to health and affording favorable tactical conditions. Before an Axis drive on Tobruk could be launched, the British would have to be driven out of this mountainous region. But Halder did not believe that the Afrika Korps was strong enough to attack the British in the Benghazi area successfully and that at most the no-man's land around Agedabia could be occupied with the possibility of making an offensive toward Tobruk the next fall. (VI, 32)

But Rommel had not come to hear such conclusions. When Brauchitsch told him that there was no question of striking a decisive blow in North Africa in the near future and that he might strike at Agedabia and perhaps Benghazi only after the Fifteenth Panzer Division arrived at the end of May, Rommel argued that the Germans would have to seize the whole of Cyrenaica, as the Benghazi area could not be held by itself. Unhappy with the efforts of Brauchitsch and Halder to limit the size and mission of the Afrika Korps—efforts which in Rommel's view left the future of North Africa to chance—Rommel returned to his North Africa headquarters in a very disgruntled state of mind.[7]

In retrospect, something can be said for the views of the OKH and those of Rommel. The commander of the Afrika Korps was probably right in a tactical sense in wishing to strike the British in Cyrenaica at once. The British forces in the Cyrenaica Command were actually far under the four-to-eight divisions which Halder supposed. Following the crushing defeat of the Italians at Sidi Barrani in December and the surrender of virtually all their forces east of Tripoli in February, the British Defence Committee in London decided that Cyrenaica was to be held as a secure flank for Egypt with the minimum forces necessary and that all extra land forces were to be returned to Egypt in preparation for a move to Greece. Therefore, General Archibald Wavell, the British Commander in Chief, Middle East, redivided his forces in time to begin sending units to Greece on March 5. Selected for the transfer to Greece over the month of March were the New Zealand Division, the Polish Brigade Group, and the Sixth and Seventh Australian divisions. By the end of that month, only the Seventh Australian and the Second British Armoured Division (minus one brigade) were left in the Cyrenaica Command.[8]

There was a second side to the question, however. In order for Rommel to undertake a large-scale offensive to retake all of Cyrenaica, the Afrika Korps had to have a well-developed base of supplies in North Africa. It was this factor which played heavily in Halder's calculations. The building up of such a base would take time, and for that reason Halder had not believed it feasible to undertake major operations before the fall of 1941. (War Journal, VI, 32)

Halder's reasoning is better understood when the route of supply from Italy to the Axis base at Tripoli is studied. The normal route of the Axis convoys at this time was around the western coast of Sicily, across the Mediterranean to the eastern Tunisian coastline, and then, hugging the Tunisian coastal waters, down to Tripoli. This circuitous route was about four hundred miles in length and was necessary because the British-controlled island of Malta lay on the direct route from Sicily to Tripoli. Even by the indirect route, the Axis convoys faced air, surface, and submarine attacks by the Malta-based British forces over much of the trip.[9]

The British on Malta were just beginning to attack Axis shipping to North Africa in early 1941. The Axis convoys usually numbered about four vessels each, one convoy being dispatched every two or three days. These convoys attempted to slip across the Mediterranean unobserved by the sea and air searches of the British. The British were slowly becoming more efficient in detecting these convoys and in attacking them, although at first their successes were minor. In February, the month when the movement of the Afrika Korps began, the British sank only 6,027 tons of shipping enroute to North Africa, or about 1.5% of the supplies dispatched to Rommel; in April, the figures rose to 10,194 tons or 9%; in May, the British sent 47,507 tons or 8% of the dispatched supplies to the bottom. During this period, the Afrika Korps consumed on a monthly basis about 70,000 tons (including the needs of the Italian forces) in order to stay fully effective. In February, the Axis convoys carried 79,183 tons of supplies to Africa; in March, 95,753 tons; in April, 81,445 tons; in May, a month of crisis, a drop to 69,331 tons; and in June, in a notable rally, about 125,076 tons.[10] The factor to be noticed here is that in one out of five months the normal needs of the Afrika Korps and its allies could not be met; three months permitted only modest stockpiling above immediate needs; and only in the month of June was there any generous stockpiling in North Africa. Halder correctly anticipated that stockpiling would be slow and difficult, and for that reason he and the Army High Command were correct in opposing a major offensive operation in North Africa prior to the fall of 1941.

After Rommel returned to his headquarters in North Africa in
March, he gave instructions for an attack on the British outpost at
El Agheila to prevent further periodic British forays on German
truck convoys to the nearby German outpost at the Marada Oasis.
This minor operation took place on March 24, and after a brief fight
the small British garrison withdrew to the defile at Mersa el Brega.
The heights of Mersa el Brega controlled the approach to Agedabia,
but until now the British had not bothered to fortify them. However,
after the withdrawal from El Agheila, the British prudently began
to wire and to mine the defile, a relatively minor tactical precaution
which was to change the face of the North African campaign. Rommel's orders were to make a minor offensive at the end of May to
seize the area around Agedabia, but if he waited until then the Mersa
el Brega defile would be more difficult to secure and the capture of
Agedabia more costly. Rommel therefore decided to attack Mersa el
Brega with what elements of the Fifth Light Division had already
arrived by March 31.[11]

The battle for Mersa el Brega lasted a day, and at its close the
British were forced to withdraw. Rommel learned of this success the
following day, April 1, when at the same time Luftwaffe reconnaissance aircraft detected a general British withdrawal northward.
Probably sensing the British weakness at this moment, Rommel decided to overstep his orders. He wrote later that it was a chance he
could not resist, and he gave orders for Agedabia to be attacked

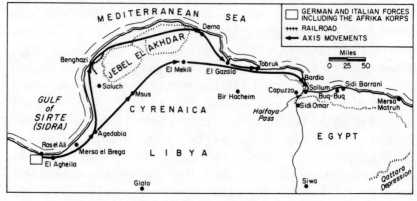

15. Rommel's First Offensive in North Africa, 1941.

and taken, in spite of the fact that his instructions were not to under-take any such operation before the end of May. The attack on Age-dabia was successful and on April 3 Rommel shifted his headquarters there. By this time it was evident that the British were in full retreat, which was all the encouragement Rommel needed. Hurling both the Army High Command's orders and Halder's strategy to the winds, Rommel decided to make a bid to seize the whole of Cyrenaica at one stroke.[12]

The unexpected capture of Agedabia far ahead of schedule awoke Halder and the Army High Command at last to the fact that Rom-mel was acting rather independently of orders. This recognition caused Hitler himself to send a dispatch to the Afrika Korps, which Halder summarized in his war journal:

Fuehrer order to Afrika Korps. Recognition of accomplishments and reminder not to be reckless, as Air Force units are being withdrawn, and arrival of the Fifteenth Panzer Div. will be delayed; moreover, the Italians now need all their strength against Yugoslavia and so have noth-ing left for North Africa. Under these circumstances there is danger of English counter-attack on [flanks]. Further advance authorized only when sure that British armd. elements have been taken out of area. (VI, 47)

This message arrived at Rommel's headquarters just when the leader of the Afrika Korps found himself in a warm dispute with General Gariboldi, the Italian Commander in Chief, over whether the offensive should be continued. Gariboldi was objecting on logistical grounds and the lack of authority from Rome. When the message from Berlin arrived, however, Rommel claimed that it gave him complete freedom of action, and settled the argument exactly as he wanted it.[13] Needless to say, the message said nothing of the kind, and doubtless Halder would have been highly incensed had he known of its interpretation. But Rommel was a master innovator of orders as well as tactics, and the Axis advance continued.

After April 3, Rommel was given virtually a free hand as Halder became almost totally immersed in the Balkan operation. On April 6, the German invasion of the Balkans began, and two days later Brauchitsch and Halder left Berlin by train to direct operations there close at hand. On April 9, the two set up a temporary general headquarters at Vienna, where it is likely that Halder received only sketchy accounts of the events in North Africa. In any case, the Chief of the General Staff had his hands full with the rapidly changing situation in the Balkans and hardly would have had time to check on Rommel even if information had been available. Consequently, for the first two weeks in April, Rommel was to all intents and purposes an independent commander, and he made the most of it. On April 5, his forces swept over Benghazi; on April 9, El Mekili fell into his hands along with Lieutenant General P. Neame, V.C., the British leader of the Cyrenaica Command; and on April 14 the Afrika Korps bypassed Tobruk and requested permission to drive straight through to Suez. (Halder, VI, 69)

Rommel's request to drive on Suez on April 14 brought Halder's attention back to the North African theater. Belgrade had fallen the day before, and the Yugoslav phase of the Balkan operation was virtually finished. Before turning his entire attention to Greece, Halder made a long-distance telephone call from Vienna to General Alfred Jodl, the OKW operations chief. The two planners agreed that "to hold Suez, we have neither the troops nor the supply facilities." Earlier, Hitler had dropped his cautious attitude toward North Africa and, carried away by Rommel's successes, had become enthusiastic about sending him more forces to exploit the German gains. It was all that Brauchitsch and Halder could do to convince the Fuehrer that no extra troops were available with other operational tasks impending and that even if troops were available there was no shipping space. Brauchitsch pointed out that without the strongest air support it seemed unwise to enter upon operations with ambitious objectives, and the nearer Rommel came to Egypt the more British resistance would stiffen. Faced with these arguments, Hitler finally abandoned the idea and sent Rommel word that the prime objective now was to build up a "front of ample width in the Sollum area [on the Egyptian border]. . . . Apart from this, only raids." (Halder, VI, 68, 70)

With or without Hitler's permission, it is quite likely that Rommel's advance would have come to a halt. The Afrika Korps had advanced about five hundred miles across the desert in two weeks' time. Before a major offensive against Suez could be undertaken, supply lines had to be established, troops brought up, and fuel moved for-

ward for the tanks; the logistical situation which Halder had foreseen would have made a continuation of the offensive inadvisable.

Rommel's swift advance had also bypassed the British fortress of
Tobruk; and the British garrison there, only seventy miles from the
Egyptian border, remained a threat to Rommel's rear, which had to
be eliminated before any new forward movement.[14] Under the circumstances, Rommel had no choice but to divide his meager forces,
placing part of them in a siege operation around Tobruk and the
remainder in the area of Sollum and Bardia along the Egyptian
frontier. While this action could not be avoided, the division of forces
made Rommel vulnerable to any major British attack from Egypt.

As early as April 15, Brauchitsch became particularly concerned
over Rommel's exposed position. Even though Brauchitsch and Halder were now in the midst of the Greek operation, Halder recorded
that Brauchitsch spent much of the day casting about for ways to
speed the build-up of a supply base in Africa for Rommel. When
Brauchitsch even proposed using German submarines to guard the
Axis convoys to North Africa and airborne troops as reinforcements,
Halder coolly opposed both proposals. "I think both methods are
wrong," he wrote. "The airborne [division] is non-motorized and
therefore useless, once it is landed in Africa. . . . I think it would
be a mistake to withdraw any of our submarines stationed round
England and . . . Freetown." [15] Halder's views on the submarines
were supported by the Naval Liaison Officer at Army High Command headquarters later that same day (VI, 70, 71). The earlier
experience of the nonmotorized divisions of the Italians gave weight
to Halder's argument against sending nonmotorized German troops
to North Africa. As usual, Halder had his way with the Army Commander in Chief, and the proposals were dropped.

Actually, there was little that the Army High Command could do
for Rommel at the moment in a situation which the "Desert Fox"
had brought upon himself. With a note of smugness, Halder wrote
on April 15 that his earlier predictions concerning a premature offensive were coming true:

[Rommel] has to use the two Italian Divs. to tighten the line of encirclement [around Tobruk]. Moreover, he is being attacked on the land side
from Egypt. Now at last he is constrained to state that his forces are

not sufficiently strong to allow him to take full advantage of the "unique opportunities" afforded by the overall situation. That is the impression we have had for quite some time over here. (VI, 71)

Halder then returned his attention to the Greek situation.

In the meantime, the British were recovering from their initial defeat. Wavell decided to give priority to the defense of Egypt early in April and cancelled the transfer of the Seventh Australian Division to Greece. By the time Rommel had reached the Egyptian frontier, Wavell had reconstituted the almost-destroyed Western Desert Force with the Seventh Australian Division, elements of the Sixth British Division, a mobile force under Brigadier General W. H. E. Gott, and elements of the Cyrenaica Command which had escaped capture or destruction. Most importantly, Wavell had decided to hold Tobruk, under the command of Major General L. J. Morshead, and its garrison was increased to four brigades by bringing troops across the Mediterranean. The command of the Western Desert Force was placed in the hands of Lieutenant General Sir Noel Beresford-Peirse.[16]

Even so, the strength of the Western Force was not very great, and it was especially weak in armor. Most of the force began to dig in along the Egyptian border, but Gott's Mobile Force was directed to take the initiative while Egypt's defenses were being strengthened. Gott's forces consisted only of one brigade group at Halfaya Pass and four small mobile columns supplied with a few armored cars and light tanks. The best he could do was to gain time and to apply pressure wherever he could.[17] It was fortunate for Rommel that at the moment this was all the British could do.

Such was the case when on April 23 the Greek surrender terminated German operations in the Balkans. Halder at once became eager to return to Zossen, where steps might be taken to retrieve the North African situation. The campaign there was worrying him. Rommel had not sent the Army High Command a single "clear-cut report all these days," but Halder had "a feeling things [were] in a mess." Reports from officers in the African theater indicated that Rommel was "in no way up to his operational task." No one seemed to have a clear picture of Rommel's troops or their striking power, and it was certain only that they were "widely dispersed" and that their striking efficiency had considerably deteriorated. In these circumstances, Halder decided to intervene directly. Momentarily, the Chief of the General Staff considered going himself to North Africa but dropped this idea because he believed Brauchitsch would oppose it. Nevertheless, in Halder's opinion, someone from the General Staff was needed to go to North Africa "with enough personal influence to head off this soldier gone stark mad." (Journal, VI, 81)

The following day Halder reached OKH headquarters at Zossen, about an hour by train from Berlin. He was met by the First Deputy of the General Staff, General Paulus, whom in the meanwhile Halder had chosen for the mission to Africa. The Chief of the General Staff told Paulus to get a clear picture of the situation and to make an estimate of the possibilities for defensive operations if Sollum were lost.[18] Above all, Paulus was to make Rommel understand that [German] resources for sending aid to him [were] very slender" and to find out Rommel's intentions in the light of "present circumstances." (VI, 83)

That same day, April 24, it seemed that a crisis had been reached in North Africa. Gott's Mobile Force launched a small but spirited attack along the Egyptian frontier near Capuzzo, which caused the local German commander to make an exaggerated report of British activities and caused Rommel to conclude that his forces at Bardia and Capuzzo were in danger of being cut off. If this happened the investment of Tobruk would have to be abandoned.[19] Gott's forces were driven off the next day, but not before the threat from Egypt was firmly impressed on Halder's mind.

With the renewal of British activity along the frontier, it became even more imperative for Rommel to capture Tobruk, an operation which Rommel was planning for April 30. He sent his plan of attack to Halder, but the Chief of the General Staff was not pleased by it. Halder wrote in his Journal on April 28: "[Rommel] will concentrate all German forces for this [attack], leaving defensive operations around Sollum to the Italians. In my opinion this is all wrong." (VI, 88) Halder's confidence in Rommel was steadily waning.

In the meantime, Paulus had arrived in North Africa and at once suspended the attack on Tobruk until he could study Rommel's dispositions. After a discussion with General Gariboldi, who in this instance supported Rommel, Paulus sanctioned the attack, radioing

Halder that he recommended two lines of action, depending on whether Rommel could capture Tobruk. If Tobruk fell, Paulus proposed that the Afrika Korps take up defensive positions along the Siwa-Sollum-Bardia line near the Egyptian border. If Tobruk did not fall, Paulus wished to establish a line of defense to the rear about El Gazala. In the event of a defeat at Sollum and the raising of the siege of Tobruk, the Axis forces would have the El Gazala position to fall back on. Halder, who had great confidence in Paulus, concurred with his deputy's proposals, adding that under no circumstances would Rommel be permitted to advance into Egypt further than Siwa-Sollum even if Tobruk fell. Halder suggested that Italian troops might be used to man El Gazala in the rear while the Germans took over at both Sollum and Tobruk. (VI, 92, 93)

Rommel began his attack on April 30 and continued his assaults until May 3. At that point, Paulus despaired of success and instructed Rommel not to resume the attack unless it offered chances of a quick success without further major expenditures of German forces. Further, Paulus radioed Halder that he had instructed Rommel that the latter's main mission now was to defend Cyrenaica against British attacks from Egypt. "To this end," Halder wrote in his journal, "[Rommel] was to reinforce the line Gialo-Sollum with mobile forces forthwith, regroup and dispose his troops in depth around Tobruk, and prepare a defense line along the eastern edge of the Djebel [El Akhdar] (El Gazala and southward)" (VI, 95). All these actions were in accordance with Halder's ideas, and he and Brauchitsch quickly confirmed Paulus's orders to Rommel and then began to make preparations to send to Libya two "heavy battalions" and five "independent battalions" with replacements to bolster the Afrika Korps (VI, 96). The situation now depended upon the speed with which Halder could rush supplies and troops to Rommel before the British could launch a counteroffensive.

Malta and Crete

The supply situation of the Axis forces in North Africa was by this time becoming serious. A member of Paulus's staff returned to Germany and reported to Halder on May 5 that coastal shipping for

Rommel could proceed no further from Tripoli than Benghazi except "in dribbles." British control of Malta made a direct sea route from Sicily to Benghazi out of the question, and, with Rommel's limited land transportation already overburdened, this problem had become even more important. Halder concluded from the officer's report that "as long as the British have Malta, Rommel cannot stage an offensive to the East." (VI, 99)

The Malta problem was underlined the following day, May 6, when Halder received a memorandum from the Italians asking for the French port of Tunis.[20] Without that port, the Italians doubted that they could supply enough forces to hold Libya, "let alone prepare an offensive" against Suez. Halder commented that "it becomes increasingly evident that without Malta we'll never have a safe supply route to North Africa. But the Italians hold that Malta cannot be attacked and so want us to mount a drive on Suez via Turkey." (VI, 101)

Actually, Halder would have had little chance of getting permission for an invasion of Malta had he urged it. Against the advice of his advisors in the OKW, who wished to attack Malta,[21] Hitler decided that the German airborne forces should attack Crete instead. This decision seems to have been motivated by the influence of Goering and Luftwaffe General Kurt Student, Chief of the German Airborne Forces. Hitler agreed with the Luftwaffe chiefs that from bases in Crete there were far-reaching possibilities for decisive air action in the eastern Mediterranean, and, in any case, Crete could not be allowed to remain in British hands because of the danger of air attacks on the Rumanian oil fields only four hours' flying time away.[22] On April 25 the OKW issued Directive Number Twenty-Eight for the invasion of Crete, then dubbed Operation *Merkur* (Mercury). The directive gave command of this operation to the Luftwaffe, which was to employ the airborne forces and the air forces stationed in the Mediterranean area. The Army was to assemble in Greece suitable reinforcements for the airborne troops, including a mixed armored detachment, which were to be moved by sea with the assistance of the Italian Navy.[23] The execution of this airborne and amphibious operation was set for May 17, but because of the difficult roads and limited railways in Greece the necessary force concentrations and supply arrangements could not be completed until May 19.[24] Accordingly, a new date of May 20 was set for Operation Mercury.

In the meanwhile, the British were taking decisive steps., While their provisions for the defense of Crete [25] proved too little and too late, British leadership was reacting to the threat from Rommel. Under the express orders of Prime Minister Winston Churchill, a British convoy braved the dangerous central Mediterranean route and attacks by the Axis air forces in Sicily to deliver about two hundred tanks to Alexandria on May 12. The arrival of this armor completely changed the balance of power in North Africa, and General Wavell prepared to launch a major offensive on June 15 in order to relieve Tobruk.[26]

The day before the armored reinforcement for Wavell reached Alexandria, General Paulus had returned to Germany and painted a gloomy picture for the Chief of the General Staff of Rommel's prospects. Halder concluded that "by overstepping his orders, Rommel has brought about a situation, for which our present supply capabilities are insufficient." Then he added, "Rommel cannot cope with the situation." At once Halder set about to reorganize the German command in North Africa. On May 12, Halder had a conference with Brauchitsch during which the subject was broached of a new headquarters in North Africa whose chief would be entitled "Commander of German Troops in North Africa." Several generals were mentioned in Halder's notes (Journal, VI, 111). Presumably, Rommel's Afrika Korps would have been subordinated to this headquarters.

The idea was then presented to the OKW, and on May 14 Halder wrote that the organization in North Africa was to be revised by attaching a German chief of staff to Gariboldi's headquarters. For some reason this plan fell through, and on May 19 the OKW proposed that a second chief of staff be appointed to Rommel's headquarters to handle the rear services for him. Halder's comment on this proposal was to the point. "Idiotic!" he wrote. Halder's deputy, Paulus, then took up the matter with General Jodl of the OKW. It was soon evident that Hitler himself was protecting Rommel's command functions. Paulus informed Halder afterwards that "all the Fuehrer cares about is that Rommel should not be hampered by any superior headquarters put over him. Jodl will send us another plan." (VI, 116, 124)

The wrangle between the OKH and the OKW over the command in North Africa was finally settled by the appointment of Colonel Alfred Gause to act as the German Liaison Officer at Italian headquarters in Libya. Actually, Gause and his staff were to introduce some system in handling Rommel's supply problems and to lay the groundwork for the introduction of larger German forces to North Africa. Rommel was less than cordial to the Gause group after it arrived at his headquarters, when he learned (according to Rommel's account) that Gause had received explicit instructions not to place himself under Rommel's command. But after Rommel told him categorically that all German troops in North Africa were his responsibility, Gause accepted his authority.[27] According to F. W. von Mellenthin, who served on the Gause staff, the group soon established good relations with the "Desert Fox" and vitally assisted Rommel's further successes in North Africa.[28]

On May 20 the invasion of Crete was launched.[29] This operation was at the time touted as a highly successful airborne invasion, but in terms of cost it was in fact little less than a catastrophe for both the German airborne forces and German strategy in the Mediterranean. The difficult landing terrain and the stubborn British resistance put out of action six and a half battalions of the nine in the Seventh Air (Parachute) Division; fifty officers and 1,000 men of one assault regiment were killed. Of the 600 transport aircraft (mostly JU-52s) used in Operation Mercury, 170 were either shot down or seriously damaged. (Halder, Journal, VI, 137). The amphibious phase was a complete fiasco. The British fleet based at Alexandria intervened effectively to sink a number of vessels crowded with German troops and forced the Italian Navy to abandon its mission of moving German reinforcements to Crete by sea.[30] Although the Germans finally secured Crete after heavy fighting, and the Luftwaffe's domination of the air between Greece and Crete forced the withdrawal of the British fleet from the area, the casualties among the airborne units and the loss of transport aircraft made a similar aerial invasion of Malta impossible for many months to come. Like Norway earlier for the Navy, Crete proved to be a largely empty victory for the Luftwaffe.

The battle for Crete was not over until nearly the first of June, and by then the British had reinforced Malta and stepped up their relentless war against the Axis convoys bound for Rommel's forces in North Africa.[31] Moreover, even before Operation Mercury had been launched, the Wehrmacht's redeployment for the invasion of Russia was in full swing, and only the X Air Corps, the Italians, and weak German ground forces remained in the Balkans, Italy, and North Africa.[32] The X Air Corps had furiously bombed Malta throughout May to knock out its military and naval facilities, but by the beginning of June both Malta's air defenses and striking forces were stronger than they had been at the beginning of the Luftwaffe's attacks. During the month of May, as we have seen, British air, surface, and submarine raiders made a record sinking of Axis shipping bound for North Africa.[33] Although by a concentration of effort the X Air Corps successfully convoyed the sea passage of the Fifteenth Panzer Division to North Africa in the same period, protection of routine supply could not be guaranteed with the air forces available.

Operation Battle-Axe

The Afrika Korps' situation remained tense throughout the month of May as its ranks slowly increased and its supply dumps were only gradually replenished. But no British offensive materialized during this awkward period, and early in June the last elements of the Fifteenth Panzer Division[34] arrived safely (Halder, Journal, VI, 150–51). With 150 more tanks, the Afrika Korps was redeployed on Halder's orders to meet a British attack from Egypt, and was at last relatively secure.

The long-feared British offensive from Egypt finally came on June 15, when Wavell[35] launched the greatest desert battle up to that time. The British offensive (code-name Battle-Axe) hurled nearly two hundred tanks at the German defensive positions around Sollum and Halfaya Pass in a struggle that lasted three days. During this engagement, Rommel demonstrated his brilliant flair for desert tactics, while the British command showed that it had not yet mastered the techniques of armored warfare.[36] When the battle came to a close on June 18, the British had been badly worsted.

They had failed to penetrate Rommel's defenses, and the German counterattacks had thrown them back with severe loss. The British lost eighty-seven tanks to Rommel's twenty-five, and about one thousand casualties to half that number in the Afrika Korps.[37] The battle of Sollum guaranteed Cyrenaica from further British attacks until the winter of 1941.

The battle of Sollum inaugurated a long stalemate in the desert war just as the focus of world struggle was about to shift elsewhere. Halder and the General Staff were putting the final touches to the plans for Operation Barbarossa when the smoke and dust lifted from the Sollum battlefield. On June 22, 1941, within a week of the battle, the climactic German campaign of the Second World War began as the German armies advanced into Russia.

Conclusion

The events of the first five months of the North African campaign found Halder in the unenviable position of being between a superior given to rash projects and an inferior unwilling to obey orders. At the onset of the North African commitment, Halder had laid down a careful strategy to prevent the whole of Cyrenaica from falling into British hands, while at the same time conserving German military strength for the more important struggle looming with Russia. The unwillingness of Rommel to accept this strategy led to a far deeper German involvement in North Africa than the OKH had anticipated or could support, and only with the greatest difficulty did Halder prevent Hitler from losing strategic perspective altogether.

Halder's attitude toward the strategy for North Africa was influenced by his clear understanding of the German Army's logistical weaknesses in overseas operations and desert warfare. Far more than Rommel and far sooner too, Halder appreciated the fact that African operations with long-term effect could not be performed without creating first a well-developed supply base. The Chief of the General Staff recognized that in order to do this a careful conservation of forces would be necessary at first in order to permit the handicapped Italian Navy to make such a build-up possible. The Italian experience between February and June justified Halder's caution.

Rommel's independent actions won temporary tactical successes at the price of complicating the Axis' logistical situation in North Africa and by weakening in the long run the Afrika Korps' ability to meet a British counterstroke. Realizing that Rommel's rash actions had precipitated a crisis in North Africa that only prompt action could redeem, Halder did not hesitate to intervene to enforce a regrouping of Rommel's forces to meet an attack from Egypt, and to rush all the properly equipped troops and supplies that available shipping space could carry to the Afrika Korps. Halder's action on the logistical problems, combined with Rommel's undeniable tactical brilliance, led to the successful repulse of the major British offensive in June, 1941. Without Halder's intervention, it is doubtful whether Rommel would have redeployed his forces in time or would have had the necessary strength to meet Wavell's thrust.

Halder's role in the North African campaign between March and June, 1941, is all the more commendable from a military point of view because much of the time the Chief of the General Staff was preoccupied with the Balkan operations and the planning for the attack on Russia. Despite these distractions and the unexpectedness of the crisis in North Africa, Halder showed powers of decision and a grasp of logistical factors which effectively headed off the impractical schemes of Hitler and Rommel. As during the earlier Polish and French campaigns, Halder had once again revealed himself as the driving force of the General Staff and the keenest judge of the logistical limits of the Wehrmacht.

Finally, the fate of North Africa and of the Mediterranean as a whole was perhaps sealed by Hitler's decision to attack Crete instead of Malta in the final weeks before the invasion of Russia. Had Malta been removed as a deterrent to Rommel's sea communications with Sicily, the defense of Libya and perhaps even its preparation as a springboard for attack against Suez would have been guaranteed. After the beginning of Operation Barbarossa, the Luftwaffe never again had the opportunity of concentrating its forces in the Mediterranean—a concentration vital both for the capture of Malta and the use of Crete to support and supply Rommel's drive into Egypt. Thus perhaps fully two years before the Axis cause met with final defeat on the Mediterranean's southern rim, the destruction of Rommel's forces was assured.

CHAPTER NINE

Russia: Climax of the Blitzkrieg

Preparations

The train of events which led to the fatal attack on Russia may be said to have begun on July 21, 1940, when Hitler informed Brauchitsch that he desired studies made by the Army High Command concerning the possibilities of a campaign against the Soviet Union in the spring of 1941. Brauchitsch informed Halder the following day and entrusted the latter with the task of setting the study into motion. Halder and the OKH General Staff were then deeply involved in the planning for the invasion of England, but Halder at once ordered the creation of a special staff to examine the Russian question and to reach conclusions as soon as possible.[1]

On July 29, a week after the OKH had begun work on the Russian project, Colonel Walter Warlimont's National Defense section in the OKW assigned Lieutenant Colonel Bernhard von Lossberg the task of making a similar independent study. Lossberg soon discovered that the OKW lacked the necessary data and had to use that provided the OKH. The result was that the OKW never carried out a wholly independent study of the proposed attack on Russia, and Lossberg's final report was based on the same assumptions and data as those of the Army. Thus the opportunity to test the Army's planning factors was allowed to pass and the OKW's views generally reflected those of the OKH General Staff until June, 1941.[2]

While the special OKH study staff was being created under the direction of General Erich Marcks, Halder was briefed on July 26 by Lieutenant Colonel Eberhardt Kinzel, Chief of the Foreign Armies' East section of the OKH Intelligence division. Kinzel pointed out that apparently Russian deployment had its center of gravity in European Russia and that very large forces were located quite close to the German frontiers and to the frontiers of the pro-German Balkan states. The principal Russian concentration appeared to be in the Ukraine, with lesser concentrations in eastern Poland, White Russia, and in the Baltic states. This deployment led Halder to consider the possibility of a German drive from Poland directly to Moscow and then a wheeling movement south to trap the main Russian forces against the Black Sea (Journal, IV, 132). He deferred his final decision until General Marcks could complete his study.

In the meanwhile, Hitler called a general military conference on July 31 to discuss the probabilities that Operation Sea Lion, the plan of invasion against England, would be launched. During the course of this conference, Hitler announced for the first time his decision to attack Soviet Russia in the spring of 1941 if the British could not be brought to terms before then. The Fuehrer explained that his objective in such a campaign would be the conquest of eastern Poland, the Baltic states, White Russia, and the Ukraine, and the establishment of a defense line in Russia from Archangel to the Volga to screen European from Asiatic Russia. By destroying the Russian armies and occupying Russia up to the Volga, Germany might dash British hopes that the Soviet Union would eventually challenge German domination of Western Europe and at the same time open new routes to undermine the British position in the Middle East. The Fuehrer believed that if Germany struck a surprise blow in the spring of 1941 the Russians could be beaten before the onset of winter. (Halder, Journal, IV, 145)

On August 1, after Halder's return to OKH headquarters, General Marcks presented his report. Marcks proposed that the Russian campaign be carried out in two phases. In the first phase the Germans would seek to encircle and destroy the main Russian armies close to the frontier, before they could withdraw into the depths of Russia. After the main Russian armies had been wiped out, the second or pursuit phase could be launched in an attempt to occupy the most valuable industrial areas of European Russia. These were deemed to be Leningrad in the north, Moscow in the center, and the Donets Basin of the Ukraine in the south. Once these areas were secured, and German air bases established along the Volga to neutralize Russian industry in the Urals, Marcks believed the Russians would be incapable of effectively continuing the war.[3]

Halder approved the general conception of Marcks's plan but stressed that the surviving remnants of the Soviet armies must be relentlessly followed and destroyed. As they were most likely to make a final stand before the Russian capital, Halder thought that the main effort in the pursuit phase should be directed toward Moscow, with only subsidiary and flanking drives toward Leningrad and the Donets Basin. Marcks was ordered to revise his plan along these lines and to report again with an estimate of the forces necessary to carry out the operation. (Journal, IV, 146)

Marcks made another report on August 5 with a plan to divide the German army in the East into three army groups and to launch two of these north and one south of the Pripet Marshes, which divided the theater naturally into two sectors. The central group would be the most powerful. In the first phase these groups would encircle and destroy the Russian armies along the frontier. In the second phase, they would undertake pursuit toward Leningrad, Moscow, and the Donets Basin, keeping the center of gravity in the central army group moving on Moscow. After Moscow had been taken and its defenders destroyed, the central army group could wheel north or south if necessary to assist the other groups before a general advance was begun to the Volga. The assumption of the revised plan was that the capture of Moscow, the nerve center of Soviet military, political, and economic power, would lead to the final disintegration of Russian resistance.[4]

By November, 1940, the OKH was ready to carry out map maneuvers to test the plan's operational and logistic capabilities. The results of these exercises made it clear that the main Russian armies would have to be destroyed west of the Dvina-Dnieper line in order to stay within the most effective striking range of the German Army. Beyond the Dvina-Dnieper line the great distances involved and poor road and rail communications would make the logistic support of large forces against strong resistance very difficult.[5]

During November the OKH and OKW also carried out economic studies of Soviet industry and concluded that 75% of the total was still located in European Russia, mostly in the Donets Basin, around Moscow, and at Leningrad. In addition, General Thomas's OKW Economics section reported that in a short campaign German expenditures of machines and fuel would probably be balanced by captures from the enemy, but that in a campaign of longer duration it would be necessary to take over the production of captured Russian industry and foodstuffs for their own use and that the vital Caucasus oil fields should be seized if possible.[6] It is possible that the reports on Soviet industry inclined Hitler toward an economic view of the campaign rather than a purely military one and to believe that if the Donets Basin (36% of Soviet industry) could be seized in the south and Leningrad in the north (16%) it would be unnecessary to seize Moscow very soon. Ideological factors may also have impelled him toward Leningrad, for Moscow, by German reckoning, contained 28% of Soviet industry.[7]

Brauchitsch and Halder were ready by December 5 to brief the Fuehrer on their conception of the proposed campaign against Russia. Hitler agreed that in the first phase his forces should aim at destruction of the Soviet armies near the western frontier, but he insisted that the capture of Leningrad and the Donets Basin must precede the German advance on Moscow. Although Halder pointed out that by capturing the railway hub of European Russia the Germans could effectively destroy the north-south co-ordination of Russian resistance, Hitler maintained that the battle of the frontiers would have already decided the fate of the existing Soviet armies and that the key industrial areas must be seized in the pursuit phase to prevent them from equipping new Russian armies for the field. (Journal, V, 56).[8]

On December 18, the OKW issued a general directive to the armed services for the forthcoming Russian campaign (Barbarossa). The overall plan was described as follows. During the initial phase the bulk of the Russian Army stationed in western Russia was to be destroyed in a series of daring operations spearheaded by panzer forces. These frontier encirclements were to insure that no major Russian units escaped into the interior of Russia. During the next phase a rapid pursuit was to be carried out to reach a geographical

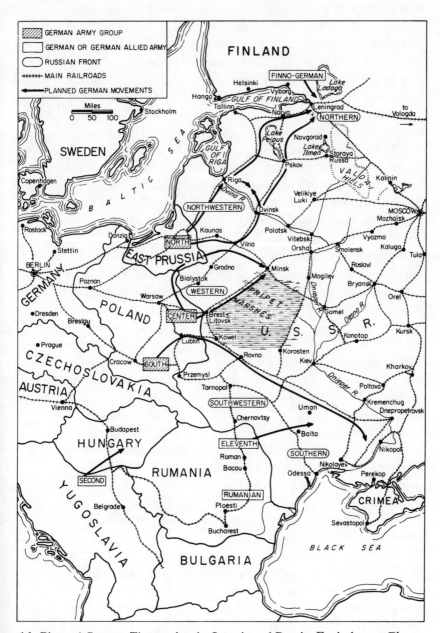

16. Planned German Thrusts for the Invasion of Russia. Encirclement Phase.

line which would place the Russian air forces beyond range of attacking German territory. The ultimate objective of the operation was to screen European Russia from Asiatic Russia as far north as Archangel, and to permit the Luftwaffe, if necessary, to attack targets in the Urals, which by then would be the last industrial region remaining in Russian hands.[9] The directive described the objectives to be captured in a manner that suggests that Hitler was trying to compromise his views with those of the OKH. Leningrad's capture was to be co-ordinated with the battles of encirclement in the first phase, and once the battles north and south of the Pripet Marshes had been brought to a successful conclusion the pursuit phase was to be launched toward Moscow and the Donets Basin.[10] No date was set for the attack in the directive, but all preparations were to be completed by May 15.

The logic behind the Barbarossa directive was based on Germany's imperative need to achieve a quick victory in the East and to avoid a lengthy struggle of attrition. Germany did not possess the industry or the manpower for a prolonged contest, nor were her army and its doctrine suited for a war of long duration. Some authorities have criticized German planning on the grounds that it attempted to do too much in too brief a period of time, but, given Germany's industrial capacities and the short striking range of its armed forces, Hitler could have hardly chosen any other course, militarily speaking.[11]

More fundamental is the question of whether the attack should have been launched in 1941, a question that involved Germany's intelligence estimate of conditions inside Soviet Russia. German assumptions were based on the reports of the OKW intelligence division, the Abwehr, for military matters, and on those of the foreign intelligence service of the Gestapo for political matters. The Abwehr found it very difficult to obtain reliable information on Soviet Russia except in the areas adjoining German territory, while the Gestapo obviously underestimated the political strength of the Soviet regime. Clearly in nearly all respects—industrially, militarily, and politically—Germany's leaders underestimated the power of the Soviet Union.[12] This was a major factor in Hitler's defeat in the East.

German intelligence indicated that the Red Army was about two

hundred divisions strong. The Germans believed that 154 were infantry divisions and 25 were cavalry divisions; 37 armored brigades
made up the balance. By Halder's reckoning, this force was the
equivalent of 213 divisions (Journal, VI, 160). Not all of this
force was concentrated in European Russia, but the great majority
of the Soviet divisions were believed to be located near the western
frontiers. The Marcks plan assumed that 55 infantry divisions, 9
cavalry divisions, and 10 armored brigades were located at the
frontier and that a total of 96 infantry divisions, 23 cavalry divisions, and 28 armored brigades would be thrown into the fight
against Germany in a short time. The mass of the remaining mobilized forces was believed to be in the Far East, protecting Siberia
from Japanese encroachment, and, even if freed for action in the
West, could not arrive in time to stave off Russian defeat. The
Marcks plan estimated that, to insure complete success, the German
forces in the East must number 110 infantry divisions, 24 panzer
divisions, 12 motorized infantry divisions, and 1 cavalry division.[13]

The quality of the Red Army was an unknown factor prior to
June 22, 1941, but the Germans correctly believed that much Soviet
equipment was obsolete.[14] The Russians had more modern tank and
plane types in production, but the German attack came before Soviet
industry produced them in quantity. The early battles were thus
fought by the Russians under conditions of technical inferiority.
During the fall of 1941 the Russian tank arm was partly rejuvenated
by quantity deliveries of the T-34, perhaps the best medium tank
produced by any country during the entire war, and thereafter the
Germans no longer enjoyed a technical superiority in tanks.[15] The
Soviet Air Force had numerous but mostly obsolete tactical aircraft,
poorly protected on frontier airfields from the Luftwaffe's speciality
—surprise air assault at the beginning of hostilities.[16]

In the period of the outbreak of war between Nazi Germany and
Soviet Russia, Soviet military doctrine was heavily oriented toward
the offensive. The aim of this doctrine was to crush the aggressor's
attack at the start by vigorous counteroffensives.[17] The Germans
believed that the Soviet High Command (after June 24, 1941,
designated as the Stavka[18]) had therefore disposed its forces quite
close to the German frontier in a manner reminiscent of the Polish
deployment in 1939. In so doing, the OKH hoped that the Soviets

had unconsciously played into their hands, since the Army High Command feared above all else a successful Soviet retreat into the interior of Russia.

The old Russian frontier before 1939 had been protected by a series of fortifications called the "Stalin Line." After the partition of Poland and annexation of the Baltic states, the revised frontier was far west of these permanent fortifications. Beginning in 1940, the Stalin Line was gradually dismantled and work begun on a new line further west between Memel and Przymsyl. By June, 1941, this new line was, in reality, only a series of still incomplete strong points, and the Germans knew that the Russians had no well-fortified line anywhere in European Russia. The Russian forces in the northern Ukraine, in eastern Poland, in White Russia, and in the Baltic states were especially vulnerable to sudden attack and encirclement.[19]

The Russians had shifted back and forth between 1937 and 1940 in their views of the proper organization and deployment of their armor and motorized forces. Like the Germans, they faced the problem of having to combine an essentially modern cutting edge with an old-fashioned blade. But like the French and Poles earlier, they made the mistake of relying on indirect artillery fire to halt the German panzers, even though such tactics had failed badly for the Poles and the French in the 1939 and 1940 campaigns. The Red Army's chief weakness was, however, the same as the German Army's—insufficient motor transport.[20] The Russian rifle division depended even more heavily than its German counterpart—the infantry division—on rail and horse-drawn transport for strategic movement.[21] Until the "Winter War" with Finland (November, 1939–March, 1940), the Soviet High Command had interpreted the lessons of the Spanish Civil War in a manner that recommended an organization similar to the French in 1940. But the "Winter War" revealed many shortcomings in doctrine, leadership, and matériel, and after its conclusion the Red Army began a reform in organization and equipment which was intended to reach completion by the summer of 1942. The reorganization called for each field army to be composed of two rifle corps (each composed of two or three rifle divisions) and one mechanized corps. The mechanized corps was to consist of two tank divisions and one motorized rifle division.[22] In addition, one or more cavalry divisions might be attached to each field army. Thus by June, 1941, the Red Army was moving slowly toward a better organization than the French in 1940, although still inferior to the German organization of 1941.[23]

The chief advantages that the Red Army enjoyed in 1941 were tremendous areas in which to maneuver and retreat, a large and hardy population, and a powerful industrial base. So long as the Red Army's first-line units remained largely intact, the industrial centers remained in Russian hands, and the political leadership did not falter, the Soviet Union could endure enormous punishment and still continue to be an effective opponent. The German plan of campaign against Russia was essentially a gamble that the Russian first-line forces could be destroyed near the frontiers and that their destruction would lead to a rapid collapse of the Soviet political system and quick occupation of the key industrial centers in European Russia. The magnitude of Russia's population was not in itself sufficient to defeat the Wehrmacht. Without armor and air support, great masses of infantry and horse-drawn artillery would have little effectiveness.[24] In at least this respect the German assessment in the spring of 1941 was correct—the campaign in the East would probably be won or lost in the first few weeks of the struggle.

During January, 1941, General von Brauchitsch briefed the staffs of the army groups which would carry out Operation Barbarossa, emphasizing that the success of the campaign depended on the encirclement and annihilation of the main Russian forces west of the Dvina-Dnieper line—approximately two hundred miles behind the border, except in the area south of Kiev. Pointing out that Russian deployment favored German tactics of encirclement, Brauchitsch was confident that the Soviet High Command would fight in the border area rather than retire to the interior. General Halder was less confident, for he recognized that a successful withdrawal would largely wreck the foundations of the German strategy in the East. German strategy assumed that the Russians would adopt a linear defense at the frontier and attempt to contain all German breakthroughs. Failing this, the Russians would attempt to withdraw behind the Dvina-Dnieper line. The OKH repeatedly stressed to its field commanders the necessity of permitting no large organized Russian

forces to escape intact east of that line and laid down the requirement that to all practical purposes the Red Army must cease to
exist before the pursuit phase could be carried out.[25]

While these briefings were continuing in January, Halder became
convinced that the German forces called for in the Marcks plan
would not be available by the summer of 1941. That plan had pre-
supposed a German striking force of not less than twenty-four full-
strength panzer divisions and twelve motorized infantry divisions.
By the beginning of February, Halder reluctantly concluded that
these numbers were beyond German production capacities. German
tank production during the last half of 1940 and in the opening
months of 1941 averaged only 200 machines per month,[26] and in
order to create even nineteen panzer divisions the authorized tank
strength of each panzer division had to be reduced from three or four
battalions to two or three. The Army General Staff hoped that the
reduction in the number of tanks in each panzer division would be
offset by the replacement of most of the Mark I and Mark II tanks
with the more powerful Mark III, rearmed with a 50-mm-gun, and
Mark IV models. Nevertheless, whereas in May, 1940, each panzer
division had two hundred and forty to three hundred and twenty
tanks, in May, 1941, each panzer division had only one hundred and
fifty to two hundred tanks.[27]

The tank issue came up at the February 4 Fuehrer conference,
when Halder pointed out to Hitler that at best the Germans could
have in the East by the summer of 1941 only about three thousand
tanks, while the Russians were reputed to have ten thousand. Hitler
replied that the Russian figures were exaggerated and their tanks of
obsolete design. When Halder also raised the objection that the truck
shortage was so severe that fragile French equipment had to be used
in eighty-eight infantry divisions, one panzer division, and in three
motorized infantry divisions, Hitler answered that the only hard
fighting would be at the very beginning. He declared that after the
initial Russian defeats at the frontier the Germans would be able
to move into the vast Russian spaces without opposition.[28]

The assembly of the German forces in the East for Barbarossa
began in February, 1941, and was carried out in three phases and on
a gradual basis until May in order not to alert the Russians.[29] Since
October the eastern division of the German railroad service had been

rebuilding and expanding the Polish rail system to handle the enormous traffic involved. Preparations were also under way for the rapid repair of the Russian railroads and their conversion to narrow gauge tracks as the German armies advanced. The shortages in motorized equipment and the size of the German forces being assembled for Barbarossa made the German railroads and animal-drawn supply wagons even more important than in past campaigns. Indeed, for the infantry divisions especially, the advance of the railheads behind the German front would be of critical importance. Hans Pottgiesser, an authority on the German rail service in the East during World War II, has written that no theater of war as much as the East so impressively demonstrated the validity of Moltke's rule that supply difficulties will result if military operations are removed further than sixty kilometers from the railhead.[30]

By early June, 1941, the OKH had assembled 75% of the entire German Army for the attack on Russia, a force totaling 3,300,000 men. The German ground forces were organized into 102 infantry divisions, 19 panzer divisions, 14 motorized infantry divisions (including 3½ SS divisions), 4 light divisions (of a type abolished in 1940 and reintroduced in 1941), 2 mountain divisions, and 1 cavalry division. The German Army entered the Russian campaign with 142 combat divisions against a Red Army estimated to total 213 divisions.[31]

During this time the OKH was also busy preparing Germany's allies to participate. In October and November, 1940, German missions were sent to Rumania to train and organize dictator General Jan Antonescu's forces. This action followed Antonescu's adherence to the Tripartite Pact among Germany, Italy, and Japan. The Rumanian Army had only twelve battleworthy divisions, but the Germans were anxious to offset their undoubted inferiority in numbers in every way possible and to obtain the use of Rumanian bases for the attack on southern Russia.[32] Rumania's government was anxious to reacquire Bessarabia, which the Soviets had extorted in 1940 while the Germans had been preoccupied in the West. Finland was also ready to participate in the attack in order to recover her territories lost in the "Winter War" of 1939–1940 and offered her sixteen divisions to a joint Finno-German force under the command of General Waldemar Erfurth, formerly a deputy chief of the OKH General Staff.[33] The main mission of the Finno-German force was to attack Leningrad on both sides of Lake Ladoga and to join the northern German army group striking from Poland and East Prussia.[34]

By May, 1941, the German truck situation had somewhat improved, although it proved impossible to provide every unit with its authorized strength in motor vehicles (Halder, Journal, VI, 103). Since the infantry divisions would depend heavily on horse-drawn transport for the movement of supplies beyond the railheads, the OKH assembled a total of 625,000 horses for that purpose. The OKH also assembled in the East 600,000 motor vehicles, 3,350 tanks, and over 7,000 artillery pieces.[35]

The final German plan called for the three army groups—Army Group North, Army Group Center, and Army Group South—to launch the invasion from German-occupied Poland, East Prussia, and northern Rumania. The Rumanians and Finns would attack along their frontiers sometime later. Army Group North under Field Marshal von Leeb, with the Eighteenth Army (eight infantry divisions) under General von Küchler, the Sixteenth Army (twelve infantry divisions) under General Ernst Busch, and the Fourth Panzer Group (six panzer and motorized infantry divisions) under General Erich Hoeppner, would attempt to encircle and annihilate the Russian forces in the Baltic states west of the Dvina and to capture Leningrad. Army Group Center under Field Marshal von Bock, with the Ninth Army (nine infantry divisions) under General Adolf Strauss, the Fourth Army (sixteen infantry divisions) under Field Marshal von Kluge, the Third Panzer Group (seven panzer and motorized infantry divisions) under General Hoth, and the Second Panzer Group (nine panzer and motorized infantry divisions) under General Guderian, would attempt to encircle the Russian forces between the frontier and Minsk on the Moscow highway. Army Group South under Field Marshal von Rundstedt, with the Sixth Army (six infantry divisions) under Field Marshal von Reichenau, the Seventeenth Army (thirteen infantry divisions) under General von Stülpnagel, the Eleventh Army (seven infantry divisions) under General Eugen Schobert, and the First Panzer Group (nine panzer and motorized infantry divisions) under Field Marshal von Kleist, would attempt to encircle and annihilate the Russian forces in the

Ukraine west of the Dnieper. With the exception of Army Group South, the planned encirclements were to take place within about two hundred miles of the German frontiers, well within the striking radius of the blitzkrieg army. The original OKH plan called for the assembly of the Twelfth Army on the southern flank of the entire front to attack from Moldavia and to allow Army Group South to carry out a double envelopment of the enemy in the Ukraine, but Hitler decided in March, 1941, that the obstacle of the Dniester should be outflanked from the north by a turning movement of Rundstedt's Sixth Army and Panzer Group Kleist.[36] Because of the limitations of road and rail facilities in Rumania and the inferior quality of the Rumanian troops, the Germans counted on little help from that quarter. As a consequence, Rundstedt's army group carried out its envelopment primarily with its left wing by a drive via Kiev to the great bend of the lower Dnieper—a distance of 400 miles from its Polish bases and from a direction that allowed the enemy maximum opportunity to wheel about and block the thrust.[37] Moreover, in June, 1941, Rundstedt's army group encountered the most powerful Russian concentration under the most skillful of the Russian commanders.

The mission assigned to the Luftwaffe was to launch surprise attacks against Russian airfields near the frontier at the outset of hostilities and to destroy the bulk of the enemy air forces on the ground. Once command of the air was obtained, the Luftwaffe would carry out its customary duties of interdiction of the battlefield and close support of the Army. No special effort was made to prepare the Luftwaffe for long-range operations or winter conditions. A basic assumption of the German war plan was that European Russia would be occupied before the onset of winter and before significant Russian reinforcements from the Far East and Central Asia could arrive. If enemy resistance east of the Urals continued after 1941, the Luftwaffe bases to be established along the Volga would permit attacks to be directed against the Soviet arms industry in that region. In the campaign in European Russia the Luftwaffe was to give special attention to the role of interdiction to help prevent large-scale, orderly Russian retirement from the frontier areas. Since only 3% of Russian roads were hard-surfaced and most were really sandy tracks, the Red Army's strategic movements would be heavily dependent on the railroads.[38] The Luftwaffe was to give special attention to the role of rail interdiction within a 250-mile radius of the frontier.[39]

Given its missions and the OKH-OKW assumptions, the Luftwaffe General Staff decided to support the three army groups with an air fleet apiece. The Finno-German force would be assisted by German air units stationed in Finland and Norway. Army Group North was to be supported by the First Air Fleet (General Alfred Keller), Army Group Center by the Second Air Fleet (Field Marshal Albert Kesselring), and Army Group South by the Fourth Air Fleet (General Alexander Loehr). The total number of airplanes in these fleets and in the Norway-Finland areas came to 2,150. Although this total is a far smaller number than that used against France and England, the area of deployment in Russia was vastly larger. But given the Luftwaffe's responsibilities in the West and in the Mediterranean by the spring of 1941, a larger concentration of force was not possible.[40]

Although undertaking an enormous responsibility with limited forces, the Luftwaffe High Command had some reasons for optimism. The Red Air Force reputedly numbered about 9,000 combat aircraft, but 2,000 of these were in the Far East and Central Asia. Of the remaining 7,000 combat planes in European Russia, only 2,000 were modern and nearly all were located on relatively few airfields near the western frontiers. Since they were poorly defended on the ground and were without early warning systems, the Luftwaffe might hope to eliminate Soviet air power in European Russia in the same manner in which it had destroyed the Polish, Norwegian, Dutch, Belgian, and French air forces.[41] Once the German ground forces overran the Soviet European air bases and seized the aircraft production plants, a significant revival of Soviet air power west of the Urals was not possible. Similarly, the Luftwaffe leaders reasoned that, as in the past, they could combine interdiction and close-support operations successfully for a limited time during which the decisive battles of encirclement on the ground would take place. They failed to foresee the recuperative powers of both the Soviet Air Force and the Russian railroad system once the Luftwaffe shifted its main effort to close-support operations with the Army.[42]

The Russians

Thus far we have examined German plans, intentions, strength, and disposition of forces. But what of Russian plans, strengths, and deployments, and how closely did they correspond to estimates by German intelligence? Since the publication of the official Soviet history and the increasing number of Russian military memoirs, authorities on the Russo-German war have a clearer picture of the state of the Russian Army on June 22, 1941. The condition of the Red Army's tank and air forces and the fact that the Red Army was in the process of transformation to more modern lines have been mentioned. On the day the German attack began the Russian order of battle was approximately as follows.

Under the direction of the Soviet High Command, the frontier area was divided between five military districts, each corresponding to the geographical limits of an army group (or "front," in Russian parlance). The Leningrad District under M. M. Popov was to mobilize as the Northern Front (*i.e.,* Northern Army Group), and was primarily concerned with the threat from Finland. The Northern Front mustered three field armies and one mechanized corps, a total of perhaps twenty rifle divisions, two tank divisions, one motorized rifle division, and two cavalry divisions. The Baltic District under F. I. Kuznetsov was assigned three field armies and one mechanized corps. Mobilized as the Northwestern Front, the Baltic District boasted perhaps eighteen rifle divisions, two tank divisions, one motorized rifle division and two cavalry divisions. The most important Western District under D. G. Pavlov included eastern Poland and was the most vulnerable to attack. Designated as the Western Front upon mobilization, it was assigned four field armies (one in reserve) and six mechanized corps, or a total of twenty-four rifle divisions, twelve tank divisions, six motorized rifle divisions, and three cavalry divisions. Three more field armies in skeleton form were being assembled in the rear of the Western District around Vitebsk. The Kiev District encompassed the western Ukraine and fell under the command of the ablest of the front commanders at the beginning of the war, General M. P. Kirponos. Mobilized as the Southwestern Front, this district was intended to deploy four field armies and six mechanized corps, with perhaps a total of twenty-four rifle divisions, twelve tank divisions, six motorized rifle divisions, and six cavalry divisions. Finally, the Odessa District (Southern Front) was to mobilize one field army of perhaps six rifle divisions, two tank divisions, one motorized rifle division, and one cavalry division.[43]

On paper the Russian frontier forces appear impressive—perhaps a total of ninety-two rifle divisions, thirty-seven tank divisions, fifteen motorized rifle divisions, and fourteen cavalry divisions—a grand total of 148 divisions. In reality, the Red Army's effective strength along Russia's western frontier was much less. Many units were under strength and underequipped, and some were scattered from twenty to 300 miles behind the frontier they were supposed to protect.[44] None were in tactical deployments on June 22. Many of the mechanized corps were at less than half their authorized strength in tanks, and all the mechanized corps were short of their full complement of the new KV and T-34 tanks. Obsolescent tanks were still the most numerous in tank divisions and were scattered about among the motorized rifle and rifle divisions.

On the Eve

On June 9, Halder made a final, personal inspection of the German and Rumanian assembly areas and on that date a trace of foreboding enters his journal. He wrote:

The imposing vastness of the spaces in which our troops are now assembling cannot fail but strike a deep impression. By its very nature [the expanse of the East] puts an end to the doctrine of "Tuchfuehlung" [i.e., continuous lines or fronts]. The Division as a self-contained operational unit becomes the dominant factor. All the work of decades, which was undertaken to train the division commanders for independent leadership, must pay dividends here. (VI, 147–48)

No theater of operations the German Army had yet encountered offered such vast possibilities for maneuver-war and none threatened to impose greater strains for the logistics of the blitzkrieg army. The initial German and Rumanian front was 995 miles wide and, as the

German and allied forces pushed east, this front would expand to 1,490 miles. The Finno-German front would extend another 620 miles.[45] The straight-line distance from Warsaw to the Volga is 900 miles. Perhaps Halder sensed that the impending operation was altogether too much like Schlieffen's plan, which had gambled everything on quick victory. Yet a year earlier such a bold strategy had brought victory over France.

The final selection of June 22 for the beginning of Operation Barbarossa—the anniversary of Napoleon's attack on Russia in 1812—was mainly due to the spring weather in 1941. The unusually heavy spring rains so soaked the ground and raised the level of the rivers in European Russia that an earlier date would have been inadvisable on that account alone.[46] No evidence exists to support Winston Churchill's claim that the Balkan campaign imposed a fatal delay on the German attack, although two panzer divisions were not back from Greece in time for the first assault, and Weichs's Second Army had to join Army Group Center after operations had begun. Mistakes during the course of the Russian campaign lost more time than the Balkan operation consumed, and, in any case, factors other than time were at the root of German defeat in 1941.

With final preparations underway, OKH field headquarters was shifted to East Prussia near Angerburg (now Polish Wegorzewo). Hitler's OKW field headquarters was forty miles away near Rastenburg (now Polish Ketrzyn) in the so-called "Wolf's Lair." [47]

Blitzkrieg East

The greatest land war ever fought began precisely at 3:30 A.M. on June 22, 1941. Shortly before dawn thousands of German guns opened intense artillery bombardments of Russian troop cantonments across the frontier. At the first sign of light, hundreds of Luftwaffe planes rose from their airfields and headed east toward the Russian airfields. They arrived to find Soviet aircraft lined up wing tip to wing tip along the edges of the runways, perfect targets for German fighters and bombers. The Soviet High Command had neglected even the most elementary measures of protection, such as dispersal of fighter units located on airfields close to the frontier, the transfer of bomber units to the interior, and the provision of

antiaircraft artillery defenses around the airfields.[48] By early afternoon Luftwaffe headquarters could inform the OKH that 800 Soviet aircraft had been destroyed, most of them on the ground, in the
first sorties.[49] The Luftwaffe had lost just ten aircraft. The Red
Army was similarly surprised and unprepared. As the German
armies moved forward, Russian resistance was initially weak and
disorganized, and the Germans easily succeeded in piercing the incomplete Soviet frontier defenses (Halder, Journal, VI, 162).

After the momentary confusion of the first twenty-four hours, the
Red Army began to react vigorously. On June 24 Halder recorded
in his journal that "the enemy is making a stand almost everywhere
in the border area." He commented that the German troops hardly
grasped this fact because resistance was still disorganized and relatively ineffective. Relieved by the Russian determination to fight
rather than retreat, Halder added "there are no signs of an operational withdrawal of the enemy" anywhere. He felt even more confident when large stockpiles of supplies were reported captured near
the border. Halder took these supplies caches "to be the logistical
basis of the plan" to fight in place. On June 24 the Luftwaffe claimed
that 2,000 Russian aircraft had been destroyed in the preceding
forty-eight hours and that organized aerial resistance was not to be
expected thereafter in the frontier area. (VI, 162, 168)

On the ground, the northern and central German army groups
made rapid progress in the next few days, and only in the Ukraine
were results less than satisfactory. Here General Kirponos' forces
were putting up a determined defense with considerable skill and with
superior numbers (forty-eight Russian divisions to forty-three German divisions). In addition, the poor roads were hampering German
deployment. Halder commented on June 26: "The enemy on this
front has energetic leadership. He is continuously throwing new
forces against the tank wedge, attacking frontally . . . and [on
both] flanks" (VI, 173).

Along the front of Army Group Center, Guderian and Hoth's
armored groups had broken through the Russian lines in two places
and were moving to converge at Minsk in the rear of the Russian
forces caught between them. Hoth's Panzer Group reached Minsk on
June 26, and a day later Guderian's did the same to spring the Kesselschlacht trap. German infantry divisions made forced marches to

seal the encirclement and to release the panzer groups for new tasks. Thirty-two Russian rifle divisions and eight tank divisions were caught in the Minsk pocket, and their frantic efforts to escape were repelled by the terrible fire of the infantry divisions. When the enemy finally surrendered, the Germans captured 290,000 prisoners, 2,500 tanks, and 1,400 guns. Hitler desired to hold the armor at Minsk until the last Russian resistance was wiped out, but, with Bock's tacit approval and to Halder's secret satisfaction, Guderian turned his panzer group east once more and drove toward Smolensk, where the enemy was assembling new forces (VI, 182, 215).

The German infantry divisions were performing magnificently despite poor roads and growing fatigue, but the march to Minsk had seriously depleted their sources of strength. Forced marches on hot and dusty roads permitted little respite, but they were necessary if the infantry was to keep up with the armored spearheads. At the end of every long march the troops faced the savage resistance and counterattacks of a trapped foe.[50] The animals drawing supplies and guns reduced the speed of advance to such an extent that infantry commanders were frequently compelled to order their men forward without normal fire support and protection against tanks. The relatively few self-propelled guns assigned to the infantry gave excellent service, both as assault weapons and as protection against enemy tanks,[51] and the Luftwaffe's Flak units often filled critical gaps in the line,[52] but the infantry suffered heavy casualties from the lack of enough artillery support. Still more serious, despite the greatest exertions, many infantry divisions arrived too late to prevent large bodies of Russian troops and tanks from escaping through gaps in the encirclement.[53] Although Minsk ended in a great German victory, the battle failed to realize German hopes for a decisive engagement of the central Russian army group. The OKH was also alarmed by growing evidence that large Soviet forces located far behind the frontier had not been caught up in the first encirclement.

Hoeppner's panzer group had made a pivoting movement northward to trap Kuznetsov's forces in the Baltic states, but most of the Soviet northwestern army group had realized the danger of the German turning movement in time to retreat to temporary safety behind the Dvina. The German infantry divisions pressed forward resolutely behind the armored spearheads, but forced marches and the long distances were taking their toll on this front too. As early as June 29, the OKH received reports from Leeb's army group that both infantry and the horses were "very tired" (Halder, Journal, VI, 183). By June 30 the Soviet northwestern army group had formed a new front behind the Dvina, and in order to destroy it Leeb's troops had to fight their way across the river and to press toward Leningrad.

By late June, it was clear that Bock's Army Group Center posed the most serious danger for the Russians. Its sheer impetus threatened to carry it to the very gates of Moscow. The *Stavka* relieved General Pavlov and his chief of staff on June 30 (both of whom were subsequently shot on Stalin's orders) and entrusted command of the central front to Marshal Semyon Timoshenko, Commissar for Defense. Timoshenko decided to establish a new front at Smolensk astride the main highway leading east to the Russian capital, an excellent defensive position because it lay in a relatively narrow belt of dry territory between the source of the Dnieper on the south and the banks of the Dvina on the north. With the front fortified and the two rivers to protect its flanks, Timoshenko had reason to believe that the Germans would be forced into fruitless frontal assaults and their advance arrested. The *Stavka* shifted thirty-six divisions (six of them tank divisions) from Marshal Semyon Budenny's Front of Reserve Armies (*i.e.,* the general reserve) to the Smolensk front.[54]

Despite these developments, Halder was confident at the beginning of July that the Red Army everywhere but in the south had been so severely mauled that effective Russian resistance would not be possible against a further German advance. In this optimistic frame of mind, he wrote in his journal on July 3:

On the whole . . . it may be said even now that the objective of shattering the bulk of the Russian Army this side of the Dvina and Dnieper has been accomplished. . . . It is thus probably no overstatement to say that the Russian campaign has been won in the space of two weeks. (VI, 196)

The next task, as Halder saw it, was the destruction of the Russian forces assembling at Smolensk and the establishment of a line from which the final drive on Moscow could be launched. "Once we are across the Dvina and Dnieper," he wrote, "it will be less a question of smashing enemy armies than denying the enemy possession of his production centers" (VI, 197). Clearly, Halder believed at this point that the pursuit phase of the operation had been reached.

The Soviet High Command, too, realized by early July that a crisis was rapidly approaching. Accordingly, the State Defense Committee under Stalin's direction ordered a general reorganization of the embattled Russian army groups. The entire front was redivided into three major sectors, with Marshal Timoshenko confirmed as commander in chief of the Western Front, Marshal Kliment Voroshilov commanding the Northwestern Front, and Marshal Budenny (previously commander of the Front of Reserve Armies) controlling the Southwestern Front. Both Voroshilov and Budenny were old political allies of Stalin, and the Soviet dictator may have wished to assure himself that the army group commanders were thoroughly loyal to him in this moment of extreme crisis.[55]

Guderian's panzer group forged its way across the Dnieper on July 10 by crossing near Orsha, and by July 16 had thrust all the way to Smolensk. The realization that another encirclement maneuver was about to be completed led Timoshenko's command to begin withdrawing their armored and better-quality infantry troops and to throw in less well-trained infantry levies to protect the withdrawal of the better troops. The Germans were now capturing prisoners with as little as two weeks' training, but these inexperienced soldiers made a gallant defense while Timoshenko saved many of his first-line units. Obviously irritated over this development, Halder wrote on July 11:

. . . [T]here is one question which . . . this battle of Smolensk will not settle for us, and that is the question of the enemy's armor. In every instance, large bodies, if not all, manage to escape encirclement, and in the end, their armor may well be the only [quality] fighting force left to the Russians for carrying on the war. The [Russian] strategy . . . would have to be visualized on the basis of operations by two or three major . . . groups of armor, supported by [fortified] industrial centers and peacetime garrisons, and by the remnants of the Russian Air Force. (Journal, VI, 223)

This proved to be a strikingly accurate prophecy of the nature of the fighting in the fall of 1941.

Halder was also disturbed during this battle by reports of new Russian artillery tactics. In the battles of the frontiers the Russians (like the Poles and French before them) had attempted to employ indirect fire. This technique proved highly ineffective against moving targets such as tanks, against which shell splinters were powerless. During the battle of Smolensk, however, Russian artillery was sometimes advanced to as close as 900 yards behind the front lines and fired directly at the target. Although they were not sufficiently equipped with armor-piercing shells, the Russian guns destroyed or disabled numerous German tanks. This new artillery tactic was the first evidence that the Russians were beginning to cope with German armored tactics (Halder, Journal, VI, 226).[56]

The fiercely contested battle of Smolensk was not finally over until August 8. At its close the Germans captured 185,000 prisoners, 2,030 tanks, and nearly two thousand guns. Smolensk was unquestionably a major Russian disaster, but for a second time the German aim of annihilating the main Russian armies had been frustrated. The German forces on this front were now 400 miles from their starting lines and had fought two major battles. Troops were tired, machines were worn, and casualties were high. From June 22 to August 23, according to Halder (VII, 27), German casualties in the East totaled 242,000 officers and men. The logistic system was so strained that as early as July 14 Halder realized that even if the Germans won the battle of Smolensk an immediate advance on Moscow in force was out of the question. At best ten or fifteen divisions could continue on, and Halder doubted that such a small force could either capture or invest Moscow, where the remainder of the Russian armies were sure to fight. (VI, 238) The Germans had no choice but to halt operations along the central front temporarily.

The Crisis in German Strategy

Halder had anticipated a logistic crisis as early as the beginning of the battle of Smolensk, and on July 16 had written:

When the current objectives have been reached, a break will be necessary in order to give the units a rest, and if advisable to merge and refit several units. Guderian thinks [his armor] can do that in three or four days. I believe much more time will be needed. The supply system of Army Group Center will not be functioning at full capacity [because of railroad repairs] before 25 July. (VI, 246)

Halder also saw that the panzer and motorized infantry units would complete recuperation substantially ahead of the infantry divisions, which were not only worn out from marches of unprecedented length, but which had to carry the main burden in the battles of annihilation that followed the armored encirclements. This situation meant that Guderian's and Hoth's armored units would have to wait in idleness for some time if they remained attached to Army Group Center. Halder believed this was an unavoidable delay that should not be permitted to divert German attention from the main objective of Moscow. Hitler believed otherwise.

The Fuehrer as early as July 8 had addressed himself to this problem and late in the afternoon came upon what Jodl described over the telephone to Halder as the "perfect solution." This amounted to detaching Guderian's panzer group from Army Group Center and wheeling it into the rear of Budenny's forces in the Ukraine, where the Russian salient extended west of Kiev. Despite the entry of the Rumanians into the war on July 2, Rundstedt's outnumbered army group had found it hard going in the Ukraine. Hitler believed that by swinging Guderian's armor south he might bag most of Budenny's forces and open Rundstedt's way to the Donets Basin and even perhaps the Caucasus. In a similar fashion the Fuehrer proposed wheeling Hoth's panzer group north to sever contact between Leningrad and Moscow. Then, as a final *coup de grâce,* both Guderian and Hoth would swing inward on Moscow from north and south while the recuperated infantry of Army Group Center would advance on the city from the west. (Halder, VI, 211)

As map strategy, Hitler's idea was not bad, but it completely overlooked the condition that the panzer and motorized infantry divisions would be in after marching back and forth without rest over a distance of 800 miles. It ignored the fact that such operations would extend the delay before Moscow far beyond the time necessary to rest and refit Bock's infantry, repair the rail lines, and build up supply dumps, and that, as a result, the advance on Moscow could not get under way until fall. Timoshenko's central front would be given extra precious weeks to assemble new forces and to prepare defensive positions with the lessons of past defeats to guide the *Stavka.* Halder did not immediately take issue with Hitler's "perfect solution," perhaps hoping that the outcome at Smolensk would permit the capture of Moscow without a major battle. But when, on July 19, Hitler issued a directive [57] that once Guderian's and Hoth's forces were sufficiently rested and refitted the "perfect solution" would be carried out, Halder threw himself into vigorous opposition.

In contrast to Hitler's heady optimism in his East Prussian headquarters, the costly battles, the failure of the encirclements to work perfectly, the delays imposed by poor road and rail communications, and the weariness of troops and animals marching and fighting without a break—all had combined to cast a pall of gloom over the various Army headquarters from the OKH on down. "The most visible expression," Halder wrote on July 20, "is the severe depression into which [Brauchitsch] has been plunged" (VI, 261). But Halder refused to allow himself to be dismayed, for he felt confident that at Moscow the Red Army would fight a decisive action which would permit its final annihilation. The thing now was not to lose sight of the main objective—the capture of Moscow and the destruction of the Russian forces before it.

Halder and Brauchitsch agreed that Halder should attempt to convince Hitler that the best divisions of the Red Army would surely be concentrated before Moscow and that Budenny's forces consisted mostly of unsupported infantry who could be quickly swept up after the Russian first-line units were destroyed. On July 23, Halder met with the Fuehrer, summarized the situation as the OKH saw it, and raised the question of the ultimate objectives of the operation. But Hitler refused to budge from his position. "He has settled in his mind the objectives specified in the OKW directive and sticks to them, enemy or no enemy, or any other consideration," Halder wrote in his journal. The Fuehrer insisted that Bock release his panzer groups to Leeb and Rundstedt and, if able, move on Moscow with infantry divisions alone. If not, the drive on Moscow would have to await the capture of Leningrad and the Donets Basin. Halder wrote:

Moreover, the Fuehrer right now is not interested in Moscow; all he cares about is Leningrad. This sets off a long-winded tirade on how von Leeb's operation ought to have been conducted and why [Hoth's group] now has to be thrown into the battle to destroy the enemy at Leningrad.

The chief object of the operations is viewed by him . . . [as the final] smashing of the enemy, a task which he believes would probably be ac-

complished by the time we are abreast of Moscow [at Leningrad and in
the Donets Basin]. Subsequently (and into the rainy fall season?) he
imagines one could drive to the Volga and into the Caucasus with [panzer
divisions] alone.

Halder concluded this journal entry with the remark, "Let's hope he
is right—but all one can say is that time spent in such a conference
is a sad waste." (VI, 267)

The next few days were spent by the OKH in preparing for the
wheeling movements, the southern one by way of Gomel. Halder
remained strongly opposed to the entire concept of this operation and
at a conference with Brauchitsch warned the Army Commander in
Chief that Hitler's plan would result in "a front expanding in width
at the sacrifice of depth" which would ultimately lead to "position
warfare." Field Marshal Bock agreed with Halder that the wheeling
movements were premature before Moscow was taken, and that "such
a diversion of armor would sabotage the very operational conceptions
underlying the plan." (Halder, VI, 271) Plans were laid, nevertheless, to launch Guderian's armor in a southward direction, while
Hoth was to strike toward the Valdai Hills between Leningrad and
Moscow (VI, 276). Although he believed his efforts futile, Halder
for the last time urged on July 28 that Hitler's scheme be abandoned:

I again point out the absurdity of the operations now decided on. They
are bound to result in dispersion of our strength and checking of the
drive on Moscow, the crucial objective. Von Bock's Group obviously has
been weakened [by Hitler's plan] to a point where he is barely able to
replace his armor with infantry, let alone mount any offensive. Attack
[planned by Hitler] impossible before 10 August. (VI, 278)

At this critical moment, late in the afternoon of July 30, Jodl informed Halder that the Fuehrer had developed still another "new
conception" of the campaign and the OKW had issued a new directive.[58] The Fuehrer ordered Army Group North to attack toward
Leningrad with only the help of the Finns, who had entered the war
on July 10, and Army Group Center to retain all its forces on the
defensive for rest and rehabilitation before driving on Moscow.
There would be no turning movement south, and Rundstedt's forces
would have to await the fall of Moscow before receiving aid from

Bock. Halder was elated over this news, which meant that the OKH's recommendations had been accepted. Halder wrote enthusiastically in his journal:

This decision frees every thinking soldier of the horrible vision obsessing us these last few days, when the Fuehrer's obstinacy made the final bogging down of the eastern campaign appear imminent. At long last we get a break. (VI, 284) [59]

Halder's elation was short-lived, for on August 4, after a conference with the OKW, Heusinger reported that Hitler was again talking in terms of striking toward Leningrad and the Donets Basin. Moscow was being merely "brushed aside" (VII, 17). Halder reacted with considerable irritation to this latest development:

What in fact is our chief object: to capture the Ukraine and the Caucasus as quickly as possible for economic ends, or else to defeat the enemy decisively? If it is the [latter], we should have full liberty in the uses of our resources, without that constant interference from top level. OKH's objective for this year is the area around Moscow, leaving the gaining of more ground to the development of the situation. Under these circumstances naturally we could not expect to reach the Caucasus before the onset of this winter. For the former alternative, we would need strong forces for an invasion of the oil region, and then we would have to go all the way to Baku. (VII, 18)

This time Brauchitsch went to see Hitler, and on his return Halder was cheered to learn that the Fuehrer had agreed to only minor operations in the north and south. This seemed all the more important as the battle of Smolensk came to a close with reports that many Russian armor units had escaped (VII, 20–21, 22).

But Hitler, after visiting the headquarters of his army group commanders for their views,[60] made his third and final decision. Despite the opposition of the OKH, Bock, and even Rundstedt, the Fuehrer decided to make Leningrad in the north and the Donets Basin in the south the next two objectives. Moscow was to be left for the final phase. Halder personally appealed to Jodl to use his influence once more with Hitler, but Jodl replied that Hitler was confident that his strategy would secure both military defeat of the enemy and economic goals. Halder continued to insist that under any plan Moscow must be among the prime objectives to be taken. "We *must* do it," he wrote on August 7, "or else we shall not be able to eliminate this source of the enemy's strength before fall." (Journal, VII, 23, 25)

Halder's next step was to permit Heusinger's operations section to draw up an OKH memorandum which carefully explained in detail the reasons why Moscow had to be seized without further delay.[61] The memorandum stated that, after nearly two months of military operations, the best elements of the Red Army remained largely intact. Until these forces were eliminated, other German goals in Russia could not be achieved. Intelligence indicated that the majority of the best Russian divisions had been deployed to protect the vital political, military, and rail center at Moscow. By advancing on Moscow, by destroying these forces which would have no choice but to stand and fight, and by splitting the front through the capture of the central rail hub of European Russia, the Germans at one stroke would destroy all means of further co-ordinated resistance west of the Volga. Capture of Moscow and destruction of the forces before it, however, would require the entire strength of the Army Group Center and all the reinforcements that the other groups could spare. Halder reckoned the necessary force at forty-two infantry and twelve panzer and motorized infantry divisions.[62]

The early capture of Moscow seemed all the more imperative when, on August 8, Halder received reports of large-scale Russian reorganization along the central front, which indicated that the Soviet High Command was rapidly applying the lessons learned from previous defeats. Intelligence indicated that the Russians were building field fortifications in great depth, behind which mobile reserves were being assembled. Halder commented in his journal that this policy was a clear break with the past and seemed to be "similar to that pursued by the French in the second phase of the Western campaign, that is to form strong islands of resistance . . . which would serve as the backbone of . . . the new defense line." This defense system, which began on the Bryansk-Vyazma line, was apparently being extended back even to Moscow, 200 miles in the rear. Obviously there was no time to waste. Halder saw clearly that Army Group Center "must concentrate its forces to the last man to destroy the main body of the enemy's strength." (VII, 30, 31)

Hitler, however, preferred his intuition to the Army General Staff's advice and rejected the OKH recommendation on August 20.[63] The following day the Fuehrer ordered detailed planning to begin for the southern drive. On September 6, the OKW issued Directive Number Thirty-Five, which set as the aim of the southern sector of the front the annihilation of the enemy forces in the Kremenchug-Kiev-Kanotop triangle by the forces of Army Group South. Army Group Center, according to the directive, was to prepare to resume its eastward advance about the end of September with the aim of destroying the enemy forces in the Vyazma area by pincer movement.[64] A few days later Guderian's panzer units, released from Bock's army group, wheeled south into the Ukraine, behind Budenny. This encirclement maneuver culminated in the battle of Kiev and the largest Kesselschlacht victory of the entire campaign. The Germans captured 665,000 prisoners.[65] But Guderian's armored units were badly worn out by the operation, and it was late in the month before they rejoined Bock's command for the drive on Vyazma and Moscow. Similarly, Leeb's army group in the north had borrowed armored strength from Army Group Center to invest Leningrad. In the meanwhile, Timoshenko's forces had been given precious weeks to recuperate and to improve their defenses covering Moscow. More than a month earlier, Halder had admitted in his journal that the Germans had greatly underestimated the "Russian Colossus" and that even then over three hundred and sixty Soviet divisions had been identified (VII, 36). Now many of those divisions stood ready in prepared positions to contest the way to the Russian capital.

In contrast, the German forces assembling for the decisive drive (Operation Typhoon) had greatly deteriorated since June and were operating on an increasingly precarious logistic system. Since June 22 the blitzkrieg army had already sustained four times the casualties experienced in all its other campaigns put together and had been unable to replace half of them.[66] The losses in matériel, especially tanks and trucks, had been so severe that replacements for all were impossible to secure. The drive on Moscow began with a 40% shortage in tanks, a 22% shortage in trucks, and a 30% shortage in artillery prime movers (Halder, Journal, VII, 91). Only a bare sufficiency in motor fuels and lubricants could be provided, and that only by stripping the last reserves. Despite the frantic efforts of the Eisenbahntruppen, less than 10,000 of the 15,000 miles of Russian railways seized had been converted to narrow gauge. Horse-drawn transport would have to carry the main burden for most of the 200 miles to Moscow. Under these circumstances, the OKH estimated that the German Army's forces deployed in Russia had the effectiveness of only eighty-three full strength divisions.[67]

Despite all these handicaps, the German offensive launched on September 30 was at first a dazzling success. The weather was dry and clear, and by swinging far south of the points where Timoshenko

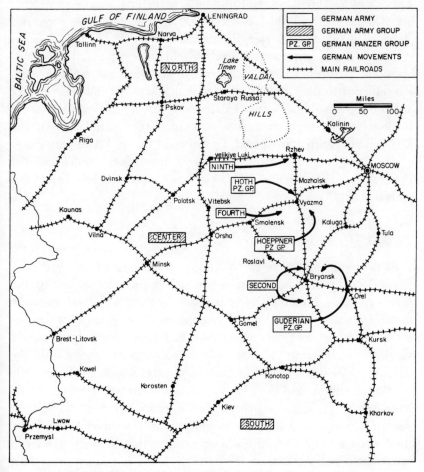

17. The Bryansk-Vyazma Encirclements, October, 1941.

had expected attack and had prepared his best defenses, Guderian's panzer group secured the rear of the Bryansk-Vyazma position. On October 2, Hoth's panzer group enveloped the Russian right wing, and Hoeppner's panzer group (temporarily detached from Leeb's Army Group North) broke through the middle. The initial success of the offensive was mainly due to the fine marching performances of the infantry divisions, which enabled them to keep up with the armored spearheads and to plunge as deep as twenty-five miles into enemy territory by the evening of the second day.[68] On October 7, the trap slammed shut in two major encirclements of a large part of Timoshenko's forces. When this double battle finally ended on October 20, the Russians had lost 663,000 troops, over five thousand pieces of artillery, and over one thousand tanks.[69] Halder's journal is silent on this enormous Kesselschlacht victory; a fall from his horse on October 10 had temporarily paralyzed his writing arm. He returned to duty four days later, but it was not until November 3 that he resumed his journal (VII, 150). Hitler believed the victory so decisive that he prematurely announced the annihilation of the Red Army. Stalin transferred Timoshenko to the Ukrainian front, where Rundstedt was advancing toward the Donets, and appointed General Georgi K. Zhukov in his place as commander in chief of the central front.[70]

To the Gates of Moscow

A desperate situation faced Stalin at the end of the battle of Bryansk-Vyazma. The Germans had wiped out a large part of the forces covering Moscow and, stimulated by their latest victory, were moving on the Russian capital as rapidly as their infantry, horse-drawn transport, and railway repair would allow. Stalin could expect reinforcements from Siberia before many more weeks, but the defense of Moscow would at first fall to the Russian infantry, the territorial militia, and the Moscow workers. Strong defenses would have to ring the city for many miles in every direction, though the dense forests around Moscow would present maneuver problems to the Germans. The Russian dictator realized that his mass conscript army could not yet deal in the open with the blitzkrieg army, but there was reason to think that it might man prepared defenses and turn back an enemy exhausted from a long march and heavy fighting while operating on a precarious supply system. Had the German Army possessed complete motor transport—or, better yet, adequate cross-country motor transport for men and supplies—Stalin's strategy might not have been feasible. But the poor road and rail communications, the exhaustion of the German infantry divisions, the worsening weather (on November 7 the temperature dropped to −7 degrees Fahrenheit), and the wooded terrain, might, if combined with a staunch Russian defense, produce the strain necessary to break the German limits of endurance. The "man of steel" made his decision. By reason, by instinct, or perhaps by force of circumstance, Stalin sought refuge for his battered armies in the defenses of Moscow and prepared to fight to the bitter end.

The German advance after the Bryansk-Vyazma battles was delayed two weeks as the result of the fall rains, which turned the unpaved Russian roads into quagmires after the passage of a few wheeled vehicles or tanks. The tracked vehicles could continue, but the wheeled transport—both motor and horse-drawn—were hopelessly mired until the first freeze on November 7. The whole advance on the central front had to halt for lack of proper cross-country vehicles: the German motorized transport was not only sparse but highly unsuited to Russian conditions. After the freeze the mixed cavalcade of tanks, trucks, horse-drawn wagons and guns—together with marching troops—at last started up again. Already the first snowflakes were falling.[71]

The adverse weather was also beginning to affect the air support of Army Group Center provided by Kesselring's Second Air Fleet. The bombers and fighters of this command had performed in an outstanding fashion in the Bryansk-Vyazma encirclements, both in the roles of interdiction and close support. In addition, the guns of the Second Antiaircraft Artillery Corps had added their firepower to that of the Army in repulsing enemy infantry and tank attempts to break out. But the October rains had made the forward shift of air bases difficult and reduced the numbers of sorties flown in those crucial weeks after the Bryansk-Vyazma victory. The early November freeze eased the problem of ground movement but complicated matters for the Luftwaffe, which was unprepared for winter weather.[72] The liquid-cooled German engines tended to freeze up over night, while snow flurries obscured the vision and navigation of pilots in the air. The quality and precision of air strikes, as well as their number, suffered accordingly.

While the Wehrmacht was immobilized by "General Mud," the Soviet High Command had been rushing to complete the defenses of Moscow and its approaches. General Ivan Konev was appointed Zhukov's deputy front commander, and half a million Muscovites were set to working on the defenses nearly ringing the Russian capital. The outer ring alone eventually contained 1,428 artillery emplacements, 100 miles of antitank ditches and obstacles, 75 miles of barbed-wire entanglements three rows deep, and numerous antitank gun emplacements.[73] Stalin declared a state of siege within the city itself to dampen growing signs of panic among its citizens. Fresh Red Army units from the Far East and Central Asia were routed by rail to the Moscow sector as rapidly as they became available.[74] Halder had hoped to bring the Red Army to a decisive battle before Moscow in September; two months too late and in the harshness of gathering winter the *Stavka* was preparing to grant Halder's wish. Zhukov placed five armies in the defenses to absorb the German drive, while two armies were kept in reserve. Eighteen out of perhaps forty divisions assembled for the climactic battle were fresh from the far East. The remainder were composed of weary but battle-hardened veterans, local militia, and even raw civilians hastily pressed into service for this last-ditch stand. Stalin had earlier approved Zhukov's plan of battle,[75] which envisioned the defenses in depth manned by the forward armies absorbing the German blows and wearing down the Wehrmacht's strength, then a powerful counteroffensive by the armies in reserve to drive back the exhausted Germans. Zhukov's counterattack would be carried out with the eighteen fresh divisions, the last armored formations available to the Russians on the central front, and as many units of the reviving Red Air Force as were available.

As the Russians braced before their capital for the onslaught, Bock's Army Group Center was plunging into the vast forest belt which extends from the White Sea to a line south of Moscow. Immense forests of pine and fir compose a triangle in the middle of European Russia, the corners of which are approximately Leningrad, Ufa (in the southern Urals), and Lvov. In 1941 the countryside around Moscow was slightly undulating, cut by meandering streams, and marked at intervals by ploughed fields in forest clearings.[76] The roads leading to Moscow from the north and west were for the most part narrow forest corridors, ideally suited for defense against a road-bound enemy. To reach Moscow, the blitzkrieg army had to engage the Russians in terrain where maneuver off the highways was difficult at best. Less forestation was found on the southern approach to Moscow, but low, marshy lands around the industrial city of Tula provided an ideal defense against tanks. By mid-November, five lines of fieldworks covered the approaches of Moscow to the north, west, and south.

Even before the Moscow offensive was launched, Halder recorded in his journal the conviction that the battle of Moscow would be a German victory only if the strained German logistic system was able to hold up and if the German troops did not collapse from exhaustion. Because of the infantry divisions, he wrote, the pace of Operation Typhoon would be determined by "railroad capacity and flow of supplies" beyond the railheads. He saw no purpose in advancing beyond the point of adequate sources of supply, and for each step of the way it would be necessary to lay the firmest possible logistic groundwork. "Failure to do that," he wrote on November 4, "would bring fatal reverses . . . upon us." (VII, 152) Yet Halder knew that, even with the most careful preparation possible under the circumstances, the nearly desperate truck and railroad situation made it more than likely that rapid advances could not be supported by adequate supplies. A slower advance would give the Red Army that much more time to strengthen its defenses. Like the Schlieffen Plan of 1914, Operation Typhoon depended on speed for its success, yet lacked the logistic stamina and range to support such a pace.

The OKH plan for the battle of Moscow called for Reinhardt (who had replaced Hoth as commander of the Third Panzer Group on October 5) and Hoeppner to envelop Moscow from the north with their panzer forces, while Guderian's Panzer Army (as it had been retitled on October 5) closed in from the south. General Kluge's Fourth Army would strike at Moscow from the west to close the ring for a final Kesselschlacht. The German offensive first met with sharp resistance on November 16, the date which effectively began the battle of Moscow. This resistance steadily increased in intensity

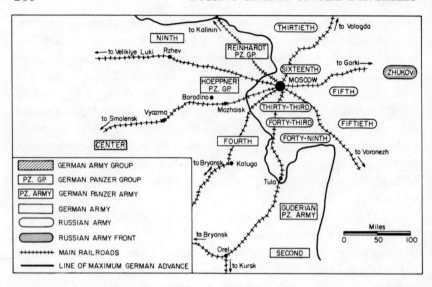

18. The Battle of Moscow, November–December, 1941.

as the Germans pressed deeper into the Russian defenses. Attempts to bypass strong points were repeatedly frustrated by the appearance of other strongly defended positions further to the rear. Predictably, Kluge's infantry divisions suffered the heaviest casualties in what was rapidly developing into a frontal assault, and by November 22 Kluge's forces were stalled in the Russian defenses. At this point, Bock took over personal command and with "enormous energy" drove forward every unit at his disposal. Forward movement resumed, but casualties were severe, especially in the officer ranks. In one regiment the senior officer left on duty was only a Lieutenant. Bock, in reporting to the OKH, compared the frontal fighting with the 1914 battle of the Marne (Halder, VII, 176). The panzer drives north and south of Moscow made better progress, but they couldn't pierce the deep Russian defenses either. At Tula, Guderian's panzer forces were repulsed.

The OKH rushed every available reserve to reinforce Bock's forces, but the tempo of the fighting required greater numbers of men and quantities of matériel than the Germans could bring forward over difficult roads and a faltering rail system. In addition, the supply of reserve equipment had become so depleted by November 27 that

General Eduard Wagner, Chief of the Supply section, warned Halder that the Army was nearly "at the end of [its] . . . resources in both personnel and matériel." The truck situation was "difficult as usual," Halder wrote in his journal the same day, and the "distressing lack of forage" in the wintry forests around Moscow made the condition of the horses in the infantry divisions "very serious." Since the campaign had been planned to terminate before the onslaught of winter, most of the German troops had no winter clothing. Later that day an officer from the front described conditions there for Halder's benefit, and the Chief of the General Staff remarked: "What he has to tell about the state and physical condition of the troops is not . . . pretty. Equipment totally inadequate." Finally, aerial reconnaissance reported the enemy was moving new bodies of troops into the Moscow lines. "They are not large," Halder wrote, "but they arrive in an endless succession and cause delay after delay for our exhausted troops." (VII, 184)

While the German offensive against Moscow was grinding slowly to a halt, further south Rundstedt's army group was meeting with serious difficulties. Following the battle of Kiev, this army group had pressed ahead into the Donets Basin, where it seized Rostov. In so doing, it overstrained its logistic system and exhausted its troops. Timoshenko, who had reorganized the Ukranian forces with reinforcements, struck back and by November 29 threatened to cut off the German forces at Rostov. Rundstedt requested permission from Hitler to pull back behind the Mius River, but the Fuehrer adamantly demanded that Rostov be held. When Rundstedt asked to be relieved of his command, Hitler quickly granted it. Reichenau was sent to replace Rundstedt and found the situation just as Rundstedt had described it. On November 30, Hitler granted permission to retreat only after heavy and largely unnecessary losses had been suffered through his obstinacy (Halder, VII, 196). The dismissal of an excellent field marshal was not the least consequence of the Fuehrer's blunder at Rostov.

The same day that the Rostov crisis arose, November 29, Colonel Greiffenberg, chief of staff of Army Group Center, called the OKH headquarters and pointed out that the German troops before Moscow were nearly exhausted. Halder noted grimly in his journal: "The Supreme Command [i.e., the OKW] insists on carrying on the

offensive even if it means risking the last strength of the troops completely. I have to tell [Greiffenberg] that this is also the view of the
OKH." The German troops gathered themselves for one last try,
and the next day Halder recorded that some progress had been scored
"against the enemy, who, throwing in reinforcements and using
mines [offers] every possible resistance." By this time the German
Army in the East as a whole was 23% below strength,[77] the infantry
divisions at half strength, and entire companies sometimes numbered only fifty or sixty men. (VII, 191, 192, 193)

On December 1, Bock personally called Halder and stressed that
his battered forces were suffering insupportable losses while making
hardly any further headway in their frontal attacks against the stout
Russian defenses. Halder replied:

I emphasize that we, too, are concerned about the casualties suffered.
But an effort must be made to bring the enemy to his knees by applying
the last ounce of strength. Once it is conclusively shown that this is
impossible, we shall make new decisions. (VII, 197)

Halder's requirement was quickly met when the thermometer plum-
meted to −35 degrees Fahrenheit and many German soldiers died
from exposure. Guderian did not even await orders before withdrawing from his forward positions around Tula. Bock's tortured
troops elsewhere received orders to cease making further attacks on
December 5. (Halder, VII, 204) Since November 16, on the Moscow
front the Germans had lost 777 tanks, 55,000 men had been killed,
and 100,000 had been wounded or disabled from frostbite.[78] Some-
infantry divisions were ninety miles from the nearest railhead, almost
double the distance for minimum supply needs, and the last reserves
of men and matériel along the central front were nearly consumed.
Clearly, the blitzkrieg army had failed to capture Moscow or destroy
the enemy defending it, and the initiative passed to the Red Army.

Epilogue

The collapse of the German drive on Moscow on December 5, 1941, was followed a day later by a massive Russian counteroffensive along the central front.[1] By the time the vigor of the Russian blows had spent itself some days later, the German forces had been driven back fifty miles. The German Army never again seriously threatened Moscow. While Zhukov's offensive was only a day old, on December 7 the Empire of Japan launched a surprise air attack on the American fleet at Pearl Harbor. The German and Italian governments declared war on the United States in fulfillment of their pledges made in the Tripartite Pact of 1940, and by December 15 three of the world's greatest industrial powers—the United States, Great Britain, and Soviet Russia—found themselves *de facto* allies against Nazi Germany. As Wladyslaw Anders has written:

For Germany this was "handwriting on the wall" which meant certain defeat. For the engagement of Japan in the Pacific and Southeastern Asia destroyed definitely any hopes of her taking a part in the war against the Soviet Union; while the appearance of an adversary such as the United States made the final defeat of the Third Reich a foregone conclusion.[2]

The defeat at Moscow was also the end for the OKH. Brauchitsch submitted his resignation as Commander in Chief of the Army on the same day that Bock's drive on Moscow collapsed and went into retirement, largely for reasons of health. On December 19, the Fuehrer appointed himself Commander in Chief of the Army, and a reorganization followed in which the OKH was stripped of many of its powers and became merely an adjunct to the OKW. Halder himself became a mere executive tool, though he managed to cling to his post until September, 1942. The OKH remained in name only.

The failure at Moscow was accompanied by a new crisis in North Africa, where in November, 1941, a new British offensive had driven Rommel's forces far back into Cyrenaica and by the end of the year to El Agheila, where Rommel's first offensive had begun. Rommel's desperate situation had forced Hitler to transfer Kesselring and most of his Second Air Force to the Mediterranean theater at the height of the battle for Moscow.[3] Kesselring quickly saw that the key to North Africa was the capture of Malta,[4] but the Luftwaffe was never able to concentrate enough strength in the Mediterranean to achieve that goal and support Rommel's renewed drives into Egypt at the same time. Kesselring, appointed as Commander in Chief, South, at the time of his transfer, was never able to solve Rommel's supply problem, and that factor ultimately doomed the whole North African venture. Although Rommel's return to Egypt in the spring of 1942 earned him a promotion to field marshal, Auchinleck's Eighth Army fought his Axis forces to a standstill in July in an action that one historian has called the "first battle of El Alamein."[5] Auchinleck's successor—General (later Field Marshal) Bernard L. Montgomery —parried Rommel's second thrust in the August–September battle at Alam Halfa Ridge. By the time Montgomery launched the second battle of El Alamein in late October, the British had a crushing superiority in airplanes, tanks, and troops, while the Americans were about to land in Rommel's rear in Algeria and Morocco.

On the Russian front, in the summer of 1942 Hitler launched the famous Stalingrad offensive, which, despite initial successes, finally bogged down and resulted in the November encirclement of General Paulus' Sixth Army at Stalingrad. This effort to invade the Caucasus oil region and the resulting German disaster in the loss of an entire field army is sometimes cited as the turning point of the war in the East. Unquestionably, Stalingrad did mark the turning point for the Red Army. Beginning in 1943, it was powerful enough to launch a series of offensives that eventually carried the Red banner to Berlin. Except for one brief abortive offensive at Kursk in 1943, after Stalingrad the German Army was entirely on the defensive in Russia. The blitzkrieg army had been too depleted in the 1941 operations to have turned the tide by the Stalingrad offensive or any other. Between November, 1941, and the middle of March, 1942, the Germans had lost seventy-five thousand motor vehicles, with only 7,500 replacements. The infantry divisions had to be stripped of the last remnants of their motorization in order to give the motorized divisions even 80% of their requirement. During the winter, 180,000 German horses had perished. Although they were replaced by double that number, the reduction in motor transport resulted in the infantry divisions being even more firmly tied to the railroads than before. George Blau writes that it was no wonder that the Army High Command felt apprehensive about executing Hitler's overambitious plans.[6]

Further, the plan for the summer offensive of 1942 was a confession of German weakness. The blitzkrieg doctrine had been to seek out and destroy the main enemy armies. After 1941 this was clearly impossible, and Hitler had to resort to striking at what he considered the most valuable asset to the German Army and the greatest loss to the Red Army—the Caucasian oil fields. But the plan ignored the danger that, once a deep salient had been driven through to the fields, the Germans would be extremely vulnerable to a Russian pincer to sever the narrow corridor. The capture of the Russian oil supply would take effect only gradually, while a Russian counteroffensive was likely to make the German position untenable long before that time. In the event, Hitler threw away what chance of success there was in the plan in his attempt to capture the oil fields and his megalomaniac desire to capture the "City of Stalin."

Germany's one good chance to defeat the Soviet Union had been in the summer of 1941, when at least the possibility had existed of destroying most of the Red Army while close to the German frontiers and railheads, in a manner for which the German Army was trained and equipped and in which it was experienced. But perfect encirclements proved impossible in the enormous Russian spaces with the semimodern forces available, and the Luftwaffe gravely underestimated the recuperative powers of the Russian rail system. The best elements of the Red Army and Air Force escaped to fight again, with better equipment than that available at the frontiers, while German exhaustion mounted rapidly as the blitzkrieg army pursued the enemy deep into the interior. Logistic collapse threatened the blitzkrieg army long before the battle of Moscow, but had not Hitler altered his course for the Ukraine against the OKH's advice its supply system might have carried it to the Russian capital before the defenders had time to reorganize their forces, to build a defense in depth, and to move reinforcements from Central Asia and the Far East. But the wear on the German forces imposed by the Ukrainian drive, the inadequate road and rail communications leading to Moscow, the deteriorating weather, and the necessity of frontal attacks against fortifications in depth—all combined to put an insupportable strain on the German war machine. The OKH was compelled to employ offensive tactics with the relatively fragile infantry divisions at a time when they were already exhausted from long marches and heavy fighting, an employment quite different from the tactical defensive for which their training, equipment, doctrine, and previous experience had prepared them. The Luftwaffe was hampered by winter conditions, an unprecedented demand for its tactical assistance by the ground forces, and a reduction of its forces by a crisis in the Mediterranean.

Still, in a larger sense, the reasons for German defeat in Russia were endemic to the German system of war. The blitzkrieg army and its doctrine were really based on the nineteenth-century assumption that decisive land battles were the guarantees of final victory. Although the revised doctrine developed between the world wars had drawn upon certain foreign ideas as to the strategic application of new modes of war, its objectives were identical with those of the past: to take the offensive at the outset, to invade the enemy's territory, and to encircle and annihilate his armies near the German frontiers. Such a doctrine and its assumptions proved sound in those areas for which the doctrine was originally developed—Central and Western Europe —and against states with common land frontiers with Germany and with relatively small land areas in which enemy forces could retreat or maneuver. But the 1939 doctrine was no better than that of 1914 in respect to anticipating requirements for waging war successfully against an insular country such as Great Britain or a continental power such as Soviet Russia. The blitzkrieg army and its supporting

Luftwaffe lacked the range, versatility, resources, and naval support to defeat such enemies. Hitler refused to take these weaknesses sufficiently into account in the setting of his political goals, and final German defeat was foreshadowed by the Fuehrer's personality and the character of the German Army.

Notes

Chapter One

1. The *Grosser Generalstab* advised and assisted the King of Prussia in his capacity as Commander in Chief of the Prussian Army. Also subordinate to the Chief of the Great General Staff was the *Truppengeneralstab,* or General Staff with Troops, which advised and assisted higher commanders in the field. For the evolution of the Prussian General Staff system, see Walter Goerlitz, *History of the German General Staff, 1657–1945,* translated by Brian Battershaw (New York and London, 1953), *passim.*

2. Jay Luvaas, *The Military Legacy of the Civil War: The European Inheritance* (Chicago, 1959), p. 126.

3. E. Carrias, *La Pensée militaire allemande* (Paris, 1948), p. 250.

4. *Ibid.* The literal meaning of Kesselschlacht is "cauldron" battle, but I have translated it according to its intended meaning in the German doctrine, "battle of encirclement and annihilation."

5. An excellent discussion of Napoleonic Warfare may be found in David Chandler, *The Campaigns of Napoleon* (New York, 1966), Part III.

6. Eberhard Kessel, *Moltke* (Stuttgart, 1957), pp. 424, 429.

7. Popular summaries of these trends are in Cyril Falls, *The Art of War* (New York, 1961), pp. 63–66; J. F. C. Fuller, *The Conduct of War, 1789–1961* (New Brunswick, N.J., 1961), pp. 103–107; Bernard

and Fawn Brodie, *From Crossbow to the H-Bomb* (New York, 1962), pp. 131–137; and Tom Wintringham, *The Story of Weapons and Tactics* (Boston, 1943), pp. 152 ff. Prussian reaction to these trends may be found in [Friedrich Karl, Prince of Prussia], *The Influence of Firearms upon Tactics,* translated by E. H. Wickham (London, 1876), *passim;* and Prince Kraft zu Hohenlohe-Ingelfingen, *Letters on Artillery,* translated by U. L. Wolford (London, 1898), *passim.*

8. The infantry regulations of 1847 were still in force and called for essentially Napoleonic tactics. In practice, Prussian infantry modified them somewhat by relying little on shock and using their columns mainly to feed their skirmish lines. Gordon Craig, *The Battle of Königgrätz: Prussia's Victory over Austria, 1866* (*Great Battles of History,* Philadelphia and New York, 1964), p. 21.

9. In 1866 the Austrian Army had 736 rifled cannon and 58 smooth-bore cannon to the Prussian Army's 492 rifled cannon and 306 smoothbore cannon. All of the Prussian rifled cannon were breech-loaders, while the Austrian were still muzzle-loaders, but 160 of the Prussian guns were cast steel with defective breech mechanisms. Prussian artillery was also handicapped by a doctrine of extreme caution. Craig, *Königgrätz,* pp. 8, 19.

Each Prussian division was authorized 15,000 men, 700 horses, and 24 guns. (p. 17)

10. Theodore Ropp, *War in the Modern World* (Durham, N.C., 1959), p. 151.

11. "Auszuege aus den Verordnungen fuer die hoeheren Truppenfuehrer von 24 Juni 1869," as printed in *Klassiker der Kriegskunst,* edited by Werner Hahlweg (Darmstadt, 1960), pp. 311–16. A useful source in English is Fuller, *Conduct of War,* pp. 117–18.

12. Herbert Rosinki, *The German Army* (New York, 1966, rev. ed.), p. 83.

13. Michael Howard, *The Franco-Prussian War: The German Invasion of France, 1870–1871* (New York, 1962), p. 5.

14. Hohenlohe-Ingelfingen, *Letters on Artillery,* pp. 165–90.

15. The term *Nation in Arms* as used hereinafter refers to an army organized around a trained civilian reserve which is immediately ready to supplement the standing army at the outbreak of war.

16. Field Marshal Count Helmuth von Moltke, *The Franco-Prussian War of 1870–71,* translated by Clara Bell and Henry W. Fischer (New York, 1892), pp. 15–26; and F. E. Whitton, *Moltke* (New York, 1921), pp. 199–202.

17. A. von Boguslawski, *Tactical Deductions of the War, 1870–71,* translated by Colonel Lumley Graham (Fort Leavenworth, Kans., 1891), *passim.*

18. Howard, *Franco-Prussian War,* pp. 212, 222.

19. For French resistance after Sedan, see Alistair Horne, *The Fall of Paris: The Siege and the Commune, 1870–71* (New York, 1965), *passim.*

20. The term denotes general wartime conscription, usually to repel invasion. Napoleon III's professional army had behind it only a small reserve and a largely untrained *Garde Mobile,* and the mobilization of both was botched.

21. In a letter written to his brother on November 23, 1870, Moltke commented that even after the whole French army had migrated as prisoners to Germany, more men were under arms in France than at the beginning of the war. They were receiving arms from Belgium, Great Britain, and the United States, and if a million arms were brought in, within a few days the Germans would have had a million more French to deal with. Clara Bell and Henry W. Fischer, editors and translators, *Letters of Field-Marshal Helmuth von Moltke* (New York, 1892), p. 203.

22. The whole quotation is "Im Kriege wie der Kunst gibt es keine allgemeine Norm, in beiden kan das Talent nicht durch eine Regel ersetz werden. (In war as in art there is no general rule, in both talent cannot be replaced by a precept.)" Oberkommando des Heeres, *Gedanken von Moltke* (Berlin, 1941), p. 13.

23. Edwin A. Pratt, *The Rise of Rail-Power in War and Conquest, 1833–1914* (London, 1916), p. 110.

24. *Ibid.,* p. 112.

25. The Germans captured a total of 8,500 loaded railway cars around Metz and another 7,500 loaded cars on the Paris-Lyons line. *Ibid.,* p. 147.

26. Writing on October 12, 1870, to his brother, Moltke said: "[T]he railways have all been broken up in places by the Franctireurs. It would take months to repair them where they have been blown up." *Letters,* p. 197.

27. Pratt, *Rise of Rail-Power,* p. 113.

28. Kessel, *Moltke,* pp. 672–74.

29. Gerhard Ritter, *The Schlieffen Plan: Critique of a Myth,* translated by Andrew and Eva Wilson (New York, 1958), p. 20, fn. 7. In the 1879–80 period, Moltke planned to concentrate 360,000 men in the East and 330,000 men in the West. The force in the East, supported

by 600,000 Austro-Hungarian troops, would have a 3–1 superiority over the 315,000 Russians, who could be mobilized by the seventeenth day of mobilization (M+16), and a 3–2 superiority by M+24. But by M+60 the Russians would have 1,200,000 troops mobilized. Hence, the best chance for joint offensive action in Poland for the Austro-German allies would come during the first thirty days. Kessel, *Moltke,* p. 675.

30. Ritter, *Schlieffen Plan,* pp. 21–23. After a brief interval in which Alfred von Waldersee, Moltke's old deputy, was Chief. Waldersee in general followed Moltke's prescriptions, which were too conservative for both the new Kaiser's taste and the tastes of certain of Waldersee's subordinates.

31. "Kriegsspiel November bis Dezember 1905," from *Nachlass Schlieffen* as printed in *Klassiker der Kriegskunst,* pp. 355–56; and "Krieg gegen Frankreich," pp. 356–57 of *Klassiker.*

32. Each active corps numbered 44,000 troops—2 infantry divisions plus heavy artillery, cavalry, supply trains, etc. Each infantry division numbered 17,500 men composed of 2 infantry brigades and 1 artillery. Artillery consisted of 54 77-mm. guns and 18 105-mm. howitzers. Cavalry divisions numbered 7,000 troopers.

33. See "Schlieffen's Great Memorandum of December 1905," translated and printed in Ritter, *Schlieffen Plan,* pp. 131 ff.

34. Ritter, *Schlieffen Plan,* p. 58.

35. G. C. Shaw, *Supply in Modern War* (London, 1938), p. 261.

36. "Organization and Administration of the Theater of Operations: the German First Army, 1914." (Unpublished analytical study, U.S. Army War College, 1931), p. 2. Now in AWC files, Military History Research Collection, Carlisle Barracks, Pa. I have computed these figures on the basis of the authorized ration of 22 pounds of fodder per day per animal. Army wagons on an average could haul about a ton apiece. The small European boxcars could carry about 25,000 pounds.

37. Sherman declared after the Civil War that even in his day no large army could operate more than one hundred miles from its railhead because the teams going and returning consumed the contents of their wagons and left little or nothing for the maintenance of the men and animals at the front who were fully employed in the fighting. As quoted in Pratt, *Rise of Rail-Power,* p. 65.

38. Baron Colmar von der Goltz, *The Nation-in-Arms: A Treatise on Modern Military Systems and the Conduct of War* (London, 1906), pp. 217 ff., presents a full discussion of march limitations.

39. Actually, the increased strength of the left wing came mainly

from 9 new divisions raised before 1914, not transfers from the right wing armies, excepting the Ersatz divisions. But all additional reinforcement was cancelled.

40. A handy summary of Moltke's changes may be found in Robert Asprey, *The First Battle of the Marne (Great Battles of History,* Philadelphia and New York, 1962), pp. 11–12.

41. General [Hermann Joseph] von Kuhl and General [Walter Friedrich Adolf] von Bergmann, *Movements and Supply of the German First Army during August and September 1914,* translated by the Historical Division of the Army War College (Fort Leavenworth, Kans., 1929). The Kuhl-Bergmann manuscript was actually composed in 1923.

42. "Organization and Administration of the Theater of Operations: The German First Army, 1914"; and "March of the German First Army, August 12–24, 1914: Comparison with an Equivalent American Force making the same Movement." (Both unpublished analytical studies, U.S. Army War College, 1931).

43. Kuhl and Bergmann, *Movements and Supply,* pp. 51–52, 62–63. Even after the fall of Namur, the French fortress of Maubeuge continued to keep the short line out of commission through the battle of the Marne and until late September. By the end of the battle of the Marne (September 9), the railhead supplying the First and Second armies had been advanced to Compiègne, a distance of about 35 miles from the battlefront.

44. *Ibid.,* p. 42.

45. *Ibid.,* pp. 42–43.

46. *Ibid.,* pp. 189–196.

47. *Ibid.,* p. 30.

48. Other sources on the condition of the troops and their supplies are Walter Bloem, *The Advance from Mons, 1914,* translated by G. C. Wynne (London, 1930), *passim;* Artur Baumgarten-Crusius, *Deutschen Heerfuehrung im Marnefeldzug* (Berlin, 1921), p. 55; and Alexander von Kluck. *The March on Paris and the Battle of the Marne* (London, 1920), pp. 84–85.

49. The First Army in September, 1914, had veered inward to come down to the Marne east of Paris, and after the retreat to the Aisne the area west of Compiègne was still unoccupied.

50. Good accounts can be found in Edmund Ironside, *Tannenberg: The First Thirty Days in East Prussia* (Edinburgh and London, 1933); and Alfred Knox, *With the Russian Army, 1914–1917* (London, 1921), Volume I, Chapter I.

51. Falkenhayn summed up the matter in a letter to Hindenburg, dated August 13, 1915, when he wrote that the annihilation of the enemy was never hoped for from the current operations in the East. It was impossible, he said, to try to annihilate an enemy who was far superior in numbers, had to be attacked frontally, and who possessed unlimited space in which to maneuver, while the Germans were forced to operate in an area destitute of railways and roads. General [Erich] von Falkenhayn, *The German General Staff and its Decisions, 1914–1916* (New York, 1920), pp. 141–142.

52. Imperial General Staff, *Handbook of the German Army in War* (London, 1918), pp. 32–33.

53. Ludendorff observed a German tank on maneuvers for the first time in February, 1918, at an exercise by one of the new assault battalions. The potentialities of such weapons did not impress him because the Germans could never have been able to produce enough of the machines to put masses of them into action in 1918, and in Ludendorff's view tanks were effective only in masses. Erich Ludendorff, *Ludendorff's Own Story* (New York and London, 1919), II, 204. See also J. F. C. Fuller's *Tanks in the Great War, 1914–1918* (London, 1920), *passim.*

54. Alistair Horne, *The Price of Glory: Verdun, 1916* (New York, 1963), pp. 151, 336.

55. The new assault tactics were prescribed in the *Manual of Positional Warfare for All Arms* issued in January, 1918. D. J. Goodspeed, *Ludendorff: Genius of World War I* (Boston, 1966), pp. 243–244; and Ludendorff, *Ludendorff's Own Story,* II, 200–202.

56. K. Kraft von Dellmensingen, *Der Durchbruch* (Hamburg, 1937), p. 405.

57. Ludendorff, *Ludendorff's Own Story,* II, 232; and Barrie Pitt, *1918: The Last Act* (New York, 1962), pp. 102–103.

58. The Germans inflicted 200,000 casualties and suffered about the same number. They captured 1,100 guns and 70,000 troops.

59. Ludendorff employed 17 divisions and 4,600 guns to attack 8 Allied divisions.

60. Total German casualties between March and July were 800,000; Allied casualties were nearly as severe but more than compensated for by American reinforcements.

61. Appointed at the Doullens Conference in late March and later promoted to the rank of marshal.

62. By July, 25 American divisions were in France and over 40 divisions by November, 1918.

63. Foch's strategy is outlined in *The Memoirs of Marshal Foch,* edited and translated by Colonel T. Bentley Mott (Garden City, N.Y., 1931), pp. 369–72.

Chapter Two

1. The postwar armed forces, collectively titled *Reichswehr,* were divided between the *Reichsheer* and the *Reichsmarine* (Navy), the heads of which were responsible to a single, civilian Reichswehr Minister. Some historians persist in calling the postwar Army the "Reichswehr," but Burkhart Mueller-Hillebrand, *Das Heer bis zum Kriegsbeginn* (*Das Heer, 1933–1945,* Darmstadt, 1954), I, 13, states the "Reichsheer und Reichsmarine bildeten zusammen die Reichswehr. (The Army and Navy together constituted the Reichswehr.)"

2. The old Truppengeneralstab provided operational assistance to higher field commanders but had no direct connection with the Kaiser. Seeckt sought to use it as the principle of staff organization. A good discussion of the origins of Reichsheer organization is in Hans Meier-Welcker, *Seeckt* (Frankfurt-am-Main, 1967), Chapter IX.

3. Edgar Roericht, *Probleme der Kesselschlacht* (Karlsruhe, 1958), p. xv.

4. General [Hans] von Seeckt, *Thoughts of a Soldier,* translated by Gilbert Waterhouse (London, 1930), p. 55.

5. *Ibid.,* p. 63.

6. *Ibid.,* p. 64.

7. *Ibid.,* pp. 61, 62.

8. General Guenther von Blumentritt, "The Dangers of Operational and Tactical 'Systems,'" MS #C-009, Office of Chief of Military History, 1948, pp. 2–3.

9. J. F. C. Fuller, *Memoirs of an Unconventional Soldier* (London, 1936), p. 452.

10. J. F. C. Fuller, *On Future Warfare* (London, 1928), pp. 91, 93.

11. B. H. Liddell Hart, *The Remaking of Modern Armies* (London, 1927), pp. v, 9. After World War II, Liddell Hart wrote that this trend of development facilitated the conversion of the British Army from hoof-and-foot movement to mechanized movement, thus permitting it to be the first to escape many of the troubles that afflicted armies in World War II, which preserved a large proportion of horse-drawn transport in their fighting formations. B. H. Liddell Hart, *The Tanks: The History of the Royal Tank Regiment and its Predecessors Heavy Branch Machine-Gun Corps, Tank Corps, and Royal Tank Corps, 1914–1945* (New York, 1959), I, 236. But Liddell Hart fails to mention

that this was only possible because, relative to Continental armies, the British Army remained small. Actually, the only nearly all-motorized army of World War II of any great size was the American, and the U.S. Army put into the field far fewer divisions than the German and Russian armies.

12. Liddell Hart, *Remaking of Modern Armies,* p. 15.

13. Giffard Martel, *In the Wake of the Tank* (London, 1931), p. 4.

14. Heinz Guderian, *Panzer Leader,* translated by Constantine Fitzgibbon (New York, 1952), pp. 34–35.

15. *Ibid.,* p. 20.

16. *Ibid.*

17. Liddell Hart, *The Tanks,* I, 242.

18. Guderian, *Panzer Leader,* p. 24.

19. Letter, General Hasso von Manteuffel to author.

20. Richard M. Ogorkiewicz, *Armor: A History of Mechanized Forces* (New York, 1960), p. 73.

21. *Ibid.,* p. 74. By 1935 others beside the British pioneers and the Germans had similar ideas. Both Charles de Gaulle in France and General von Einmannsberger in Austria wrote books and articles containing arguments for the concentrated, all-motorized tank force, but neither had any influence on German development. Guderian's basic ideas about armor organization had been formed prior to their time, and German development proceeded independently. (Pp. 20–21)

Moreover, panzer divisions have been sometimes erroneously equated with the cavalry-type mechanized formations of other countries before World War II. Ogorkiewicz comments that what similarities there were were largely superficial and did not extend to the all-important question of operational doctrine (p. 21). The Russians were on the right track for a while in the mid-1930s, but Stalin's purges of the more promising armor experts left Red Army doctrine and armored organization far behind the German by the war's outbreak. See Chapter IX of this book.

22. General Waldemar Erfurth, "The Assistant Chief of Staff for Military History (O.Qu.V)," MS#P-041d,OCMH, n.d., p. 1.

23. Guderian, *Panzer Leader,* p. 32.

24. Reichswehrministerium, *Die Truppenfuehrung* (Berlin, 1933), pp. 75–76. Translation by the U.S. War Department, in the Military History Research Collection, Carlisle Barracks, Pa.

25. Fritsch and Beck planned to strengthen the infantry division's organization by assigning "organic" armor and self-propelled assault-gun batteries. They recognized that under German doctrine tactically strong

infantry divisions were indispensable for defensive purposes, and they hoped to overcome their lack of range and stamina by a gradual transition to all-motorized infantry divisions. But Hitler's rush to rearm forced the concentration of Germany's limited motor resources in a handful of panzer, light-mechanized, and motorized infantry divisions. This was the right decision under the circumstances, but the concentration of resources in all-motorized divisions exacted a price; the infantry divisions were never fully modernized. Friedrich Hossbach, *Infanterie im Ostfeldzug, 1941–1942* (Osterrode am Harz, 1951), pp. 14–15; letter, Field Marshal Erich von Manstein to author.

26. The 1939 infantry division varied from 15,000 to 17,000 men. It was organized into 3 infantry regiments of 3 battalions each [*i.e.,* a "triangular" division], 1 artillery regiment, and supporting services. It had tremendous defensive firepower, with 378 machine guns, 147 mortars, 20 75-mm. guns, 36 105-mm. field howitzers, 12 150-mm. field howitzers, and 6 150-mm. guns. But nearly all the artillery was towed and had to unlimber before firing, and much of it was horse-drawn. Mueller-Hillebrand, *Das Heer bis zum Kriegsbeginn,* I, 72.

27. Hossbach, *Infanterie,* pp. 14–15; and letter, Manteuffel to author.

28. In a letter to the author, Manstein points out that "organic" assault-gun sections planned for the infantry divisions had to be dropped for lack of sufficient quantities of steel.

29. Germany required a minimum of 23 million tons of oil annually at the beginning of the war, of which 10 million tons had to be high-octane aviation fuel. The normal peacetime requirement was 6 million tons, and home production was only 3 million tons annually. Less than 6 months' supply was on hand in September, 1939. For these and other figures, see F. Klein, *Germany's Economic Preparations for War* (Cambridge, Mass., 1959), pp. 174–75; and A. S. Milwood, *German Economy at War* (London, 1965), pp. 7–8, 16.

30. Mueller-Hillebrand, *Das Heer bis zum Kriegsbeginn,* I, 14–19.

31. *Ibid.,* I, 20–21.

32. *Ibid.,* 25; and "Joint Statement of Five German Military Leaders," *Trials of War Criminals (TWC)* (Washington, 1951), X, Doc. 3798-PS, p. 528.

33. For relations between the Army and the Nazi government in this period, see Robert J. O'Neill, *The German Army and the Nazi Party, 1933–1949* (New York, 1966), *passim.*

34. The 1914 class reached 21 years of age in 1935, the age at which they became liable to conscription under Hitler's new law.

35. Mueller-Hillebrand, *Das Heer bis zum Kriegsbeginn,* I, 32. About 600,000 out of 3,800,000 male Germans in this category received some training before the war.

36. "Joint Statement," *TWC,* X, Doc. 3798-PS, p. 528.

37. For example, the divisions assigned to Wehrkreis I composed the I Corps.

38. The XIV Corps (motorized infantry divisions), XV Corps (light divisions), and XVI Corps (panzer divisions). These specialized corps existed only in peacetime. Upon mobilization, the divisions that composed them could be used in any combination desired.

39. More field army headquarters could be improvised from extra Wehrkreis headquarters personnel if needed. After the annexation of Austria in 1938, the number of Wehrkreise reached a peak of 18 just before the war. Mueller-Hillebrand, *Das Heer bis zum Kriegsbeginn,* I, 130–31.

40. *Ibid.,* I, 68. Mueller-Hillebrand actually shows 35 infantry divisions for the active Army and 3 *Gebirgsdivisionen* (mountain divisions), but the mountain divisions were essentially infantry divisions with special equipment for dealing with mountainous terrain. In order to reach a total of 103 divisions, he has counted the cavalry brigade as a division. There were 16 genuine reserve divisions (*i.e.,* composed of troops from the regular training program), 20 former Landwehr divisions reclassified as reserve divisions, 1 Landwehr division, and 14 divisions improvised from extra units and personnel from the training program.

41. Each infantry division was authorized 942 motor vehicles (or as many up to that number as were available), 1,133 horse-drawn vehicles, and 5,375 horses. War Department, *Handbook on German Military Forces* (Washington, 1945), II, 11, Figure 6.

42. In addition to the complete panzer divisions, the composite Fourth Panzer Brigade was improvised on the eve of war by combining an Army tank regiment with SS Regiment "Deutschland," the newly created SS Artillery Regiment, and the SS Reconnaissance Battalion. General Werner Kempf commanded the Fourth Panzer Brigade in the Polish campaign, sometimes identified as *Panzer Verband Kempf.* A few other SS regiments existed in September, 1939, but Himmler's private army was still quite small at the beginning of the war. Burkhart Mueller-Hillebrand, *Die Blitzfeldzüge, 1939–1941 (Das Heer, 1933–1945,* Frankfurt-am-Main, 1956), II, p. 15, Table 6 and p. 17, Table 7; and George H. Stein, *The Waffen SS: Hitler's Elite Guard at War, 1939–1945* (Ithaca, N.Y., 1966), pp. 27–28.

43. Actually, 4 complete motorized infantry divisions and the equivalent of a fifth in Army and SS units. The "light" division was an experimental organization combining 1 light-tank regiment with 2 regiments of motorized infantry. All 4 were converted to panzer divisions in 1940.

44. All figures in this paragraph are drawn from Mueller-Hillebrand, *Die Blitzfeldzüge,* II, 15, Table 6; 17, Table 7, and Stein, *The Waffen SS,* pp. 27–28. The breakdown of the semimotorized divisions on September 9 at full mobilization for the Polish campaign was 36 active infantry and 51 reserve divisions, 3 mountain divisions, and the equivalent of 3 additional divisions composed of frontier security troops, extra SS units, etc., for a grand total of 109 divisions.

45. Robert M. Kennedy, *The German Campaign in Poland, 1939* (Washington, 1956), p. 2.

46. G. C. Shaw, *Supply in Modern War* (London, 1938), p. 261.

47. Roericht, *Probleme der Kesselschlacht,* p. xv.

48. Mueller-Hillebrand, *Das Heer bis zum Kriegsbeginn,* I, 27.

49. Paul Deichmann, *German Air Force Operations in Support of the Army (The German Air Force in World War II, USAF Historical Studies,* New York, 1968), pp. 9–10, 12, 13.

50. Max [Walter] Wever, "Doctrine of the German Air Force," *The Impact of Air Power,* edited by Eugene Emme (New York, 1959), pp. 181–85.

51. Derek Wood and Derek Dempster, *The Narrow Margin: The Battle of Britain and the Rise of Air Power, 1930–1940* (New York, Toronto, London, 1961), pp. 45–46, 49; and Deichmann, *German Air Force Operations,* p. 36.

52. John Killen, *The Luftwaffe: A History* (London, 1967), p. 93. The German air units in Spain were organized into the Condor Legion.

53. Deichmann, *German Air Force Operations,* p. 120; and Hermann Plocher, *The German Air Force Versus Russia, 1941 (The German Air Force in World War II, USAF Historical Studies,* New York, 1965), pp. 248–53.

54. Telford Taylor, *The March of Conquest: The German Victories in Western Europe, 1940* (New York, 1956), p. 35.

Chapter Three

1. So called because the only written record of the conference proceedings is based on notes taken by Hitler's adjutant, Colonel Friedrich Hossbach.

2. "Hossbach Conference Notes," *Trials of War Criminals (TWC)* (Washington, 1951), X, pp. 505–15. See also Trumbull Higgins, *Hitler*

and Russia: The Third Reich in a Two-Front War, 1937–1943 (New York and London, 1966), pp. 10–11.

3. Hitler's bold remilitarization of the Rhineland in 1936 had earlier frightened Blomberg and Fritsch. Walter Goerlitz, *History of the German General Staff, 1657–1945,* translated by Brian Battershaw (New York, 1959), pp. 305–306, 309–11.

4. John Wheeler-Bennett, *Nemesis of Power: The German Army in Politics, 1918–1945* (New York, 1954), p. 362.

5. Fritsch was accused falsely of homosexuality, and Blomberg's recent marriage to an alleged prostitute was deemed to have dishonored the Officer Corps.

6. For details on OKW internal organization, see Walter Warlimont, *Inside Hitler's Headquarters, 1939–1945,* translated by R. H. Barry (New York, 1964), p. 4.

7. Retitled the *Wehrmachtfuehrungsstab* (OKW Operations Staff) in August, 1940.

8. Wheeler-Bennett, *Nemesis of Power,* p. 362.

9. Telford Taylor, *Sword and Swastika: Generals and Nazis in the Third Reich* (New York, 1952), p. 17.

10. OKW Directive No. 1, "Operation Otto," March 11, 1938, *TWC,* X, Doc. C-102, p. 590.

11. "Er fiel stillschweigend unter den Tisch," Peter Bor, *Gespräche mit Halder* (Wiesbaden, 1950), p. 117.

12. "Joint Statement of Five German Military Leaders," *TWC,* X, Doc. PS-3798, p. 528; and Taylor, *Sword and Swastika,* pp. 182–83.

13. John Wheeler-Bennett, *Munich: Prologue to Tragedy* (London, 1948), p. 54.

14. Curiously enough, Hitler may not have intended to attack Czechoslovakia in the spring of 1938. According to E. M. Robertson, *Hitler's Pre-War Policy and Military Plans, 1933–1939* (London, 1963), pp. 106–07, 125, Henlein had been pressuring Hitler to take action since October, 1937, and may have even sparked the Hossbach conference and the new demands on Czechoslovakia in the spring of 1938. But Robertson doubts that Hitler was planning to attack so soon and believes that rumors of a German invasion in May, 1938, probably originated in Prague to test the reactions of France, Britain, and Russia.

15. OKW Directive No. 2, "Case Green," May 30, 1938, *TWC,* X, 603. The West Wall was the code-designation for the German line of fortifications opposite the French border. Work on the West Wall began in 1937 after the remilitarization of the Rhineland.

16. Wolfgang Foerster, *Ein General kaempft gegen den Krieg* (Munich, 1949), p. 98; and Halder Testimony, *TWC,* X, 542.

17. Bor, *Gespräche mit Halder,* p. 118; Halder Testimony, *TWC,* X, 542–43; Wheeler-Bennett, *Nemesis of Power,* pp. 403–04; and Goerlitz, *General Staff,* pp. 328–30.

18. Halder Testimony, *TWC,* X, 543; Goerlitz, *General Staff,* pp. 330–31; Wheeler-Bennett, *Nemesis of Power,* pp. 399–405. The official announcement was not made until October 31.

19. "Biographical Details of Some Senior German Officers," in Robert J. O'Neill, *The German Army and the Nazi Party, 1933–1939* (New York, 1966), Appendix B, p. 189; Halder Testimony, 12–16, April, 1948, *TWC,* X, 533; letter, Halder to author.

20. Halder's appointment led to a reshuffling of positions in the General Staff. After the change, General Karl Heinrich von Stülpnagel was Oberquartiermeister I and General Sixt von Arnim was Oberquartiermeister II. Oberquartiermeister III, Colonel Hans von Greiffenberg, was Chief of the Operations section under Oberquartiermeister I.

21. Halder Testimony, *TWC,* X, 544; Wheeler-Bennett, *Nemesis of Power,* pp. 408–409; Harold C. Deutsch, *The Conspiracy against Hitler in the Twilight War* (Minneapolis, 1968), pp. 31–38 and *passim;* Hans Rothfels, *The German Opposition to Hitler* (Hinsdale, Ill., 1948), pp. 63–75; and Hans Gisevius, *To the Bitter End* (Cambridge, 1947), pp. 283–300.

22. Item 19, File on Case Green, *TWC,* X, Doc. 388-PS, pp. 607–608.

23. *Ibid.,* pp. 608–609.

24. Burkhart Mueller-Hillebrand, *Das Heer bis zum Kriegsbeginn* (*Das Heer, 1933–1945,* Darmstadt, 1954), I, 63.

25. The French war machine was so organized that its peacetime force was merely a training school for recruits and a guard against sudden attack. Richard Challener, *The French Theory of the Nation in Arms* (New York, 1955), pp. 68–74.

26. "Joint Statement," *TWC,* X, Doc. 3798-PS, p. 524.

27. The Welle Plan is fully discussed in Robert M. Kennedy, *The German Campaign in Poland, 1939* (Washington, 1956), pp. 26–27.

28. Mueller-Hillebrand, *Das Heer bis zum Kriegsbeginn,* I, 69–70.

29. Bohemia and Moravia were converted into a Reich Protectorate. Slovakia was given nominal independence, but became in reality a German satellite.

Chapter Four

1. Ribbentrop had succeeded Neurath in early 1938.

2. *Documents on German Foreign Policy, 1918–1945* (Washington, 1957), Series D, VII, 104–107.

3. Signed in 1934.

4. "OKW Case White Directive," April 3, 1939, *Trials of War Criminals (TWC)* (Washington, 1951), X, Doc. C-120, pp. 650–51.

5. Robert M. Kennedy, *The German Campaign in Poland, 1939* (Washington, 1956), p. 58.

6. Erich von Manstein, *Lost Victories,* translated by Anthony G. Powell (Chicago, 1958), p. 34.

7. Kurt von Tippelskirch, *Geschichte des Zweiten Weltkriegs* (Bonn, 1951), p. 14.

8. Edgar Roericht, *Probleme der Kesselschlacht* (Darmstadt, 1958), pp. 1–3.

9. Manstein, *Lost Victories,* p. 44.

10. Kennedy, *Campaign in Poland,* pp. 60–61; and Peter Bor, *Gespräche mit Halder* (Wiesbaden, 1950), pp. 126–37. A weak center as in 1914 would invite the enemy to move deeper into the German trap.

11. Kennedy, *Campaign in Poland,* pp. 60–61; and Bor, *Gespräche mit Halder,* p. 136.

12. Kennedy, *Campaign in Poland,* pp. 60–61; and Bor, *Gespräche mit Halder,* p. 136.

13. "Estimate of the Situation," May 7, 1939, *TWC,* X, Doc. NOKW-2584, pp. 661–662.

14. "OKH Case White Directive," June 15, 1939, *TWC,* X, Doc. NOKW-229, pp. 679–684; and Manstein, *Lost Victories,* p. 49.

15. But Alexander Werth, *Russia at War, 1941–1945* (New York, 1964), pp. 29–32, with the benefit of the Russian archives, shows that even as late as July the Soviet dictator would have reversed his course again if a reasonable chance of an alliance with the West had come about on terms acceptable to Stalin. Molotov's appointment was a warning to the Anglo-French powers, not a complete abandonment of negotiations.

16. "Minutes of the Fuehrer Conference, 23 May, 1939," *TWC,* X, Doc. L-79, pp. 671–79.

17. "OKW Letter Concerning Preparations for Case White," June 22, 1939, *TWC,* X, Doc. C-126, p. 684. Active infantry divisions were composed of 78% active personnel, 12% Category I reservists, 6% Category II reservists, and 4% Landwehr personnel. Burkhart Mueller-Hillebrand, *Das Heer bis zum Kriegsbeginn (Das Heer, 1933–1945,* Darmstadt, 1954), I, 70.

18. Hans Pottgiesser, *Die Deutsche Reichsbahn im Ostfeldzug, 1939–1944 (Der Wehrmacht im Kampf,* Neckargemünd, 1960), p. 16.

19. My figures, computed on the basis of authorized ration and horses per division. The standard German supply train of 40 railroad cars could

haul 80,000 human and 40,000 animal rations. U.S. War Department, *Handbook on German Military Forces* (Washington, 1945), VI, 17. German boxcars could carry about 25,000 lbs.

20. Each mountain division was authorized 3,000 horses. *Ibid.*, p. 11. The average marching distance was assumed to be 14 miles a day.

21. A basic load was 90 rounds per rifleman, 3,750 rounds per machine gun, and 300 rounds per divisional artillery piece.

22. Kennedy, *Campaign in Poland*, pp. 64–65.

23. Robert Jars, *La Campagne de Pologne* (Paris, 1949), p. 51; Manstein, *Lost Victories*, p. 41; Bor, *Gespräche mit Halder*, p. 149; and Tippelskirch, *Geschichte des Zweiten Weltkriegs*, pp. 21–24.

24. Kennedy, *Campaign in Poland*, Map, p. 57; and Jars, *Campagne de Pologne*, Chapter II, *passim*.

25. Franz Halder, "The Private War Journal of Generaloberst Franz Halder," edited and translated under the direction of Arnold Lissance (Unpublished war journal, Duke University, n.d.), I, 1. Halder's italics.

26. Most of these reserve divisions were reclassified Landwehr divisions.

27. Burkhart Mueller-Hillebrand, *Die Blitzfeldzüge, 1939–1941* (*Das Heer, 1933–1945,* Frankfurt-am-Main, 1956), II, p. 15, Table 6, shows that on M+13 in September, 1939, the German forces in the West totaled 42 divisions.

28. Halder, "War Journal," I, 1–5.

29. *Ibid.*, p. 10.

30. Mueller-Hillebrand, *Die Blitzfeldzüge*, II, 16.

31. *Ibid.*

32. Halder, "War Journal," I, 34.

33. Kennedy, *Campaign in Poland*, p. 77.

34. Halder, "War Journal," I, 41.

35. Mueller-Hillebrand, *Die Blitzfeldzüge*, II, 17, Table 7, and 76.

36. Bor, *Gespräche mit Halder*, p. 137.

37. German air fleets 1 and 4 were assigned to the campaign, totalling 700 bombers, 150 dive-bombers, 400 fighters, and 300 transport and reconnaissance aircraft. German air losses amounted to only 126 aircraft for the whole campaign. John Killen, *The Luftwaffe: A History* (London, 1967), p. 100; Werner Baumbach, *The Life and Death of the Luftwaffe,* translated by Frederick Holt (New York, 1949), pp. 32–33; Asher Lee, *The German Air Force* (London, 1946), p. 41; and Paul Deichmann, *German Air Force Operations in Support of the Army* (*The German Air Force in World War II, USAF Historical Studies,* New York, 1968), p. 154.

38. The Mark I was a 2-man light tank, weighed 3 tons, and was armed only with 2 machine guns. The Mark II had a 3-man crew, weighed 6 tons, and was armed with a 20-mm. cannon and machine guns. The Third Panzer also had Mark III and IV tanks, armed respectively with 37-mm. and 75-mm. guns, but 255 out of its 300 tanks were Mark I and II. Kennedy, *Campaign in Poland,* p. 28.

39. Heinz Guderian, *Panzer Leader,* translated by Constantine Fitzgibbon (New York, 1952), p. 70.

40. *Ibid.,* pp. 72–73.

41. *Ibid.,* p. 72.

42. Kennedy, *Campaign in Poland,* pp. 81–83.

43. Mueller-Hillebrand, *Die Blitzfeldzüge,* II, 17, Table 7.

44. Kennedy, *Campaign in Poland,* p. 84.

45. *Ibid.*

46. Letter, Franz Halder to author. An examination of the Allied failure to take the offensive is found in Jon Kimche, *The Unfought Battle* (New York, 1968), *passim.*

47. Manstein, *Lost Victories,* p. 55.

48. *Ibid.*

49. *Ibid.*

50. *Ibid.,* p. 57.

51. Franz Halder, *Hitler as War Lord,* translated by Paul Findlay (London, 1950), p. 4.

52. Halder, "War Journal," II, 16.

53. *Time Magazine* used the term in its September 25 issue. "This was no war of occupation, but a war of quick penetration and obliteration—*Blitzkrieg,* lightning war."

54. Halder, "War Journal," I, 57.

55. Manstein, *Lost Victories,* p. 63.

56. Halder, "War Journal," I, 56.

57. *Ibid.,* I, 47.

58. Manstein, *Lost Victories,* p. 63.

Chapter Five

1. L. F. Ellis, *The War in France and Flanders, 1939–1940 (History of the Second World War, United Kingdom Military Series,* London, 1953), p. 4. Staff discussions had taken place following the German occupation of the remainder of Czechoslovakia in March, 1939.

2. *Ibid.,* pp. 2, 6–7.

3. Colonel A. Goutard, *The Battle of France, 1940,* translated by A. R. P. Burgess (New York, 1959), pp. 23–24.

4. Ellis, *War in France,* p. 7.

5. Goutard, *Battle of France,* p. 24.

6. Ellis, *War in France,* pp. 4–5.

7. Richard M. Ogorkiewicz, *Armor: A History of Mechanized Forces* (New York, 1960), pp. 65, 66.

8. *Ibid.,* p. 67.

9. Jacques Benoist-Méchin, *Sixty Days that Shook the West: The Fall of France, 1940,* translated by Peter Wiles (New York, 1963), p. 35.

10. A good description of the French Army in 1940 is in Alistair Horne, *To Lose a Battle: France 1940* (Boston and Toronto, 1969), pp. 182–90.

11. Goutard, *Battle of France,* p. 30, gives the French 11,500 pieces of artillery to the German 7,700 in the West.

12. Ministry of War, *Instructions for Tactical Employment of Large Units,* translated by U.S. War Department (Paris, 1937), pp. 38, 40. Army War College files, Military History Research Collection, Carlisle Barracks, Pa.

13. Goutard, *Battle of France,* p. 33. Derek Wood and Derek Dempster, *The Narrow Margin: The Battle of Britain and the Rise of Air Power, 1930–1940* (New York, Toronto, and London, 1961), p. 187, gives a total of 1,450 French aircraft on May 10, 1940.

14. For a country supposedly "defensive-minded," France was ill-prepared for defense against air attack. An air defense program was not drawn up until January, 1938, the first 90-mm. AA guns did not start leaving the factories until November, 1939, and the production of the 25-mm. AA gun retarded production of the 25-mm. AT gun. Benoist-Méchin, *Sixty Days,* p. 31.

15. Ellis, *War in France,* p. 19. The BEF was commanded by General the Viscount Gort.

16. Denis Richards, *The Fight at Odds (Royal Air Force, 1939–1945,* London, 1953), I, 32, 108–109. Wood and Dempster, *Narrow Margin,* p. 185.

17. Franz Halder, "The Private War Journal of Generaloberst Franz Halder," edited and translated under the direction of Arnold Lissance (Unpublished war journal, Duke University, n.d.), II, 17.

18. Letter, Franz Halder to author.

19. "OKW Directive No. 6 for the Conduct of the War," October 9, 1939, *TWC,* X, Doc. C-62, pp. 805–806.

20. Hans-Adolf Jacobsen, *Fall Gelb: Der Kampf um den Deutschen Operationsplan zur Westoffensive 1940* (Wiesbaden, 1957), p. 10; and

Helmuth Greiner, *Die Oberste Wehrmachtfuehrung, 1939–1943* (Wiesbaden, 1951), p. 59.

21. Burkhart Mueller-Hillebrand, *Die Blitzfeldzüge, 1939–1941 (Das Heer, 1933–1945,* Frankfurt-am-Main, 1956), II, 46, Table 16.

22. My figures, based on the authorized horse-strength per infantry division (5,375) and the authorized ration per day (22 lbs.). U.S. War Department, *Handbook on German Military Forces* (Washington, 1945), II, 11, Figure 6; and IV, 20.

23. Based on the authorized horse-strength of infantry divisions (5,375) and mountain divisions (3,000).

24. The fact is sometimes overlooked that the Schlieffen Plan called for a massive attack through the Ardennes as part of the wheeling movement in Belgium in order to have a continuous front on both sides of the Meuse. The OKH plan wisely divided its right wing into 2 army groups and avoided the inflexible linear approach used by Schlieffen and the younger Moltke.

25. OKW Directive No. 8, issued on November 20, 1939, provided that precautions were to be taken to enable the main weight of the attack to be switched from Army Group B to Army Group A should the disposition of enemy forces at any time suggest that Army Group A could achieve greater success. *Hitler's War Directives, 1939–1945,* edited by H. R. Trevor-Roper and translated by Trevor-Roper and Anthony Rhodes (London, 1964), p. 16.

26. Ellis, *War in France,* p. 5. By the end of 1939 a fifth motorized infantry division had joined the BEF, and in January, 1940, a sixth motorized infantry division was operational (p. 19).

27. Erich von Manstein, *Lost Victories,* translated by Anthony G. Powell (Chicago, 1958), pp. 99, 103, 104.

28. Letter, Franz Halder to author; letter, Erich von Manstein to author.

29. Manstein, *Lost Victories,* p. 109.

30. Ellis, *War in France,* p. 23.

31. Peter Bor, *Gespräche mit Halder* (Wiesbaden, 1950), pp. 161–62.

32. Manstein, *Lost Victories,* p. 114.

33. Horne, *To Lose a Battle,* p. 157, believes that the Mechelen Incident was "pure gain" for the Germans because it not only confirmed the Allied expectations of an attack centered on the Belgian plain, it also allowed them time to re-examine their strategy at leisure. At any rate, it removed the danger of a premature offensive. A re-examination of German strategy was already planned before the Mechelen Incident, but Hitler might not have stayed his hand that long.

34. Jacobsen, *Fall Gelb*, pp. 107–12; and letter, Manstein to author.

35. Jacobsen, *Fall Gelb*, pp. 112–18.

36. The Allies were counting on aerial reconnaissance to detect any major German build-up opposite the Ardennes, a process they estimated would take at least two weeks. Richards, *Fight at Odds*, p. 108.

37. Franz Halder, "Operational Basis for the First Phase of the French Campaign in 1940," MS#P-151, Office of Chief of Military History, n.d., p. 19.

38. Heinz Guderian, *Panzer Leader*, translated by Constantine Fitzgibbon (New York, 1952), pp. 90–91, 92; letter, Halder to author.

39. Telford Taylor, *The March of Conquest* (New York, 1958), p. 175, reaches the same conclusion.

40. A panzer group ranked between a corps and a field army and from the spring of 1940 on was usually attached to an army group for independent operations. It was a further evolution of Guderian's basic ideas on armor and motorization, and the panzer group amounted to a small, all-motorized, armored army. In October, 1941, the Germans redesignated some of their groups as "panzer armies."

41. Strength figures and deployments based on Mueller-Hillebrand, *Die Blitzfeldzüge*, II, 45, Table 15.

42. Hans-Adolf Jacobsen, *Kriegstagebuch des Oberkommando der Wehrmacht* (Frankfurt, 1965), I, 51. Hereinafter referred to as the OKW War Diary.

43. A British destroyer violated Norwegian coastal waters to intercept the German supply ship *Altmark*, homeward bound after servicing the armored surface raider *Graf Spee*. The *Graf Spee* had been trapped and forced to scuttle in December, 1939, off the South American coast.

44. The most detailed study is Walter Hubatsch, *Weseruebung: Die Deutschen Besetzung von Danemark und Norwegen* (Göttingen, 1960).

45. John Wheeler-Bennett, *The Nemesis of Power* (New York, 1954), p. 494.

46. During the campaign and its aftermath (April–June), 2 battle-cruisers—the *Scharnhorst* and *Gneisenau*—were damaged. The "pocket battleship" *Lützow* (formerly *Deutschland*) was so badly damaged by torpedo that it had to be laid up for a year. The heavy cruiser *Blücher* and 2 light cruisers were sunk. Ten destroyers and 4 submarines were also lost.

Allied naval losses were not light but far from crippling. Only one capital ship was lost—the aircraft carrier *Glorious*, which came off second-best in a duel with the *Scharnhorst*'s guns. In addition, 2 cruisers, 9 destroyers, and 6 submarines were lost. Four cruisers and 8 destroyers were damaged.

47. General Joseph Vuillemin was General in Chief of the Air Force and Admiral Jean Darlan Commander in Chief of the Navy.

48. Goutard, *Battle of France,* p. 77.

49. Ogorkiewicz, *Armor,* pp. 65–67.

50. In his book, *Vers l'armée de métier* (Paris, 1934), De Gaulle did not propose, as sometimes supposed, the abolition of the Nation in Arms. He recognized the latter as the "principal element of national resistance," but one slow to concentrate and maneuver.

51. Charles de Gaulle, *The Call to Honour, 1940–1942 (The War Memoirs of General de Gaulle,* translated by Jonathan Griffin, New York, 1955), I, 9.

52. Actually, 13 divisions were with the BEF, but 3 divisions were without most of their equipment and had been sent over to perform labor duties.

53. In 1939 the "Mobile Division" was renamed the "Armoured Division." It consisted of a light armored brigade (3 battalions of light and cruiser tanks), a heavy armored brigade (3 battalions of cruiser tanks), and a support group (a motorized infantry battalion, a motorized artillery battalion, and an engineer company). Shortages of equipment made this an armored division more on paper than in reality. The British sent several light tank battalions to France and about 100 heavy infantry tanks. At the outbreak of the war the only kind of tank numerous in the British arsenal was the Mark VI, a light reconnaissance machine. British tank design, like the French, was overspecialized. The best British tank in 1939–1940 period was perhaps the infantry tank, Mark II (Matilda II) with 75-mm. of armor around the turret and front, making it the most heavily armored tank in the world at the time. The Matilda II weighed 26½ tons and had a maximum speed of only 15 MPH. Although too slow and with an operating radius of only 60 miles, the Matilda II carried a 40-mm. gun, and its armor was proof against the standard 37-mm. German antitank gun. To stop the Matilda II, the Germans had to turn to their antiaircraft gun—the famous 88-mm. H. C. B. Rogers, *Tanks in Battle (The Imperial Services Library,* London, 1965), III, 97–106; and B. H. Liddell Hart, *The Tanks* (New York, 1959), II, 6–7.

54. Rogers, *Tanks in Battle,* p. 106; and Liddell Hart, *The Tanks,* II, 6–7.

55. Figures vary considerably from one authority to the next, but Goutard, *Battle of France,* pp. 27–28, makes a convincing case that not less than 2,400 and probably in excess of 3,000 modern tanks were available to the Northeast armies. Liddell Hart, *The Tanks,* II, 5–6, gives

800 medium and heavy tanks out of a total of 3,500 tanks. M. Gamelin, *Servir* (Paris, 1947), I, 157, gives 2,507 French tanks and 600 British tanks with the Northeast armies.

56. Liddell Hart, *The Tanks*, II, 5; and Rogers, *Tanks in Battle*, p. 108. Guderian's figures are similar. After the conquest of Poland, the Germans converted their 4 light divisions to panzer divisions by issuing 334 Czech tanks as well as German. The converted Czech machines were designated as 35(t) and 38(t), and both types were armed with 37-mm. guns. Many of the German Mark I light tanks were withdrawn into reserve and replaced by the more powerful Mark II (14-mm. frontal armor and 20-mm. gun) and Mark III (30-mm. frontal armor and 37-mm. gun). The Mark IV was the most powerful German tank in May, 1940 (30-mm. frontal armor and 75-mm. gun). See Goutard, *Battle of France*, pp. 29–30.

57. An average based on cited sources.

58. All French tanks had frontal armor at least 40-mm. thick. The light tanks (H-35 and R-35) had 37-mm. guns, the medium tanks (D and SOMUAs) had 47-mm. guns, and the heavy B tank had a 47-mm. gun in a turret and a 75-mm. gun in the hull. German tanks had better speed (up to 30 MPH) on the average and a greater cruising range, and the provision of radios to every tank insured better command-responsiveness.

59. Liddell Hart, *The Tanks*, II, 5.

60. Wood and Dempster, *Narrow Margin*, pp. 185, 187; and Richards, *Fight at Odds*, p. 113. The principal types were the poorly armed and armored Blenheim and Battle bombers, the ancient Lysander tactical support and reconnaissance aircraft. Only the Hurricane fighters were in a class with the best German aircraft.

61. The German Second (Kesselring) and Third (Sperrle) air fleets were assigned to the West, mustering perhaps 3,500 aircraft. These were divided between 1,400 bombers, 400 dive-bombers, 1,200 fighters, and 500 reconnaissance aircraft. Asher Lee, *The German Air Force* (New York and London, 1946), p. 61. Paul Deichmann, *German Air Force Operations in Support of the Army* (*The German Air Force in World War II, USAF Historical Series*, New York, 1968), p. 155, gives 3,824 aircraft.

62. Richards, *Fight at Odds*, p. 113.

63. Wood and Dempster, *Narrow Margin*, p. 189.

64. Only 2 airborne divisions then existed in the Luftwaffe—the Seventh Air (Parachute) Division and the Twenty-Second Air Assault Division. Since many of the troops were still untrained, only 4,000 para-

chutists were dropped in Holland and 500 troops arrived by glider at Eben Emael. Albert Kesselring, *Kesselring: A Soldier's Record,* translated by Lynton Hudson (New York, 1954), pp. 57–58.

65. Theodore Draper, *The Six Weeks' War: France, May 10–June 25, 1940* (New York, 1944), p. 61.

66. Ellis, *War in France,* p. 40.

67. Generals René Prioux and Georges Blanchard as early as May 11 opposed going forward further than the one day's march to the Escaut River. Gamelin, *Servir,* III, 395.

68. Ellis, *War in France,* p. 38; and Goutard, *Battle of France,* p. 119.

69. Goutard, *Battle of France,* p. 115.

70. F. W. von Mellenthin, *Panzer Battles, 1939–1945,* translated by H. Betzler and edited by E. F. Turner (London, 1956), p. 13.

71. Goutard, *Battle of France,* p. 127; Horne, *To Lose a Battle,* pp. 189–90; and Benoist-Méchin, *Sixty Days,* p. 89.

72. Guderian, *Panzer Leader,* p. 102; Goutard, *Battle of France,* p. 133; and Mellenthin, *Panzer Battles,* pp. 13–15. The German air attacks did not actually knock out the French artillery but forced the gunners to take cover. The lack of AA guns and protected artillery positions proved fatal.

73. Horne, *To Lose a Battle,* pp. 272–277; and Ellis, *War in France,* p. 40.

74. Pierre Lyet, *La Bataille de France* (Paris, 1947), pp. 46–47. Giraud's Seventh Army, recalled from its advance to Holland, was ordered south to plug the hole created by the collapse of the Ninth Army. This involved a long march from Antwerp on the extreme left to the Allied center. The Seventh had gone only as far as Maubeuge by May 16.

75. Guderian, *Panzer Leader,* pp. 107–108.

76. *Ibid.* On May 17 and again on May 19, General de Gaulle's Fourth DC attacked in the Laon area to sever the panzer corridor. But the fourth DC was incomplete, lacked sufficient infantry, and local German forces turned back his attacks. Similar piecemeal attacks elsewhere also failed. De Gaulle, *Call to Honour,* I, 37–42.

77. This incident suggests that French artillery tactics were workable against German armor under certain conditions, especially where the ground was registered. The myth of German tank qualitative superiority was shattered at Merdorp, but German tank tactics were proven sound.

78. Ellis, *War in France,* p. 46.

79. *Ibid.,* pp. 87–88. The attack was made primarily by a British task force composed of 2 tank battalions and part of a third, together with 2 infantry battalions, a field artillery battery and an antitank battery. Ger-

man antitank guns proved ineffective against the heavier British tanks until the 88-mm. guns were brought into play; 37-mm. guns were wholly ineffective. No more than 58 Mark I infantry tanks and 16 Mark II infantry tanks were involved on the British side. Rogers, *Tanks in Battle,* pp. 110–112; and Liddell Hart, *The Tanks,* II, 14–15.

80. Guderian, *Panzer Leader,* p. 117.

81. Bor, *Gespräche mit Halder,* p. 170 states that Halder learned from Kesselring and Erhard Milch later that Goering had been behind the whole business. This view is supported by Walter Warlimont, *Inside Hitler's Headquarters, 1939–1945,* translated by R. H. Barry (New York, 1964), p. 98, but also credits Hitler's and Keitel's concern for the boggy terrain from their World War I experience. Warlimont points out that the terrain had changed since 1918 and that tanks could have been used to good effect (p. 98).

82. J. F. C. Fuller, *A Military History of the Western World* (New York, 1956), III, 404.

83. Ellis, *War in France,* pp. 138–39.

84. Warlimont, *Inside Hitler's Headquarters,* p. 99, does allude to this motive, but perhaps significantly his evidence comes from Rundstedt himself. Rundstedt claimed that he desired only a temporary "halt order" to concentrate his armor (p. 99), and Hitler seized on it as an excuse.

85. Ellis, *War in France,* pp. 145–46.

86. Lee, *German Air Force,* p. 58; Wood and Dempster, *Narrow Margin,* pp. 195–196; Kesselring, *Kesselring,* pp. 58–59.

87. According to Weygand's figures, the French had lost 24 infantry divisions (including 6 out of 7 motorized infantry), all 3 DLMs, 2 out of 5 DCLs, 1 DC and parts of 2 others. Maxime Weygand, *Recalled to Service,* translated by E. W. Dickes (London, 1952), pp. 91–93. Such few planes as there were, according to Weygand, arrived in shipments purchased earlier from the United States.

88. *Ibid.,* pp. 92, 93.

89. *Ibid.,* p. 98.

90. Halder, "War Journal," IV, 48–52; and Günther von Blumentritt, *Von Rundstedt, Soldier and Man* (London, 1952), pp. 79, 80.

91. Only 450 German aircraft had been lost since 10 May. Kesselring, *Kesselring,* p. 59.

92. Blumentritt, *Rundstedt,* p. 80.

93. The Army had only 4 "waves" of trained and semitrained divisions at the outbreak of the war. The induction of large numbers of civilians during the winter of 1939–40 resulted in 24 of 136 divisions in the West having only 9 months' training by May 10, 1940. Mueller-Hillebrand,

Die Blitzfeldzüge, II, 45, Table 15, shows 8 "waves" called up by
May 10.

Chapter Six

1. Franz Halder, "The Private War Journal of Generaloberst Franz
Halder," edited and translated under the direction of Arnold Lissance
(Unpublished war journal, Duke University, n.d.), IV, 91.

2. Expressed to Count Gaetano Ciano. U.S. State Department, *Documents on German Foreign Policy, 1918–1945* (Washington, 1957),
Series D, X, No. 73, p. 79.

3. Ronald Wheatley, *Operation Sea Lion: German Plans for the Invasion of England, 1939–1942* (Oxford, 1958), pp. 15–20.

4. Walter Ansel, *Hitler Confronts England* (Durham, N.C., 1960),
pp. 108–10, suggests that perhaps Schniewind was a bit too eager to
reassure Halder and was responsible for the Army's overconfidence later.

5. Wheatley, *Sea Lion,* p. 32.

6. Derek Wood and Derek Dempster, *The Narrow Margin: The
Battle of Britain and the Rise of Air Power, 1930–1940* (New York,
Toronto, and London, 1961), pp. 110–11. The Luftwaffe estimated British fighter production at 180–300 machines per month when it was
around 450–500 machines per month. The Luftwaffe knew nothing of the
capabilities of the British radar early warning system and underrated
both the crews and machines of the RAF. Chapter 5, *passim.*

7. Actually dated July 16, although not issued until 3 days later. OKW
Directive No. 16, "On Preparations for a Landing Operation against
England," *Hitler's War Directives, 1939–1943,* edited by H. R. Trevor-
Roper, translated by Trevor-Roper and Anthony Rhodes (London,
1964), pp. 34–38.

8. Telford Taylor, *The March of Conquest* (New York, 1958), p. 346.

9. The nearest equivalent American rank is General (4-star).

10. "Fuehrer Conferences on Naval Affairs," edited by Admiral H. G.
Thursfield, *Brassey's Naval Annual, 1948* (London, 1948), p. 120.

11. R. Jouan, *La Marine allemande dans la seconde guerre mondiale*
(Paris, 1949), p. 65.

12. Arthur Bryant, *The Turn of the Tide, 1939–1943: A Study based
on the Diaries and Autobiographical Notes of Field Marshal the Viscount
Alanbrooke* (London, 1957), p. 217. General Alan Francis Brooke was
Chief of the Imperial General Staff during the summer of 1940.

13. Thursfield, "Fuehrer Conferences," pp. 120–21.

14. *Scharnhorst* and *Gneisenau* were battle-cruisers and the *Lützow*
(formerly *Deutschland*) and *Admiral Scheer* were "pocket battleships."

The battleships *Bismarck* and *Tirpitz* were not ready for sea and Germany's one aircraft carrier—*Graf Zeppelin*—was never finished.

15. Basil Collier, *Defense of the United Kingdom* (*History of the Second World War, United Kingdom Military Series,* London, 1957), p. 122.

16. Halder's italics. There is a queer illogic here too. If the Russian campaign was to be scheduled in the spring of 1941, it would be *taking the place of,* rather than *preceding,* the invasion of England. These remarks may have been concocted to convince the military of the need to attack Russia for "military" reasons, while Hitler's real reasons were ideological and connected with his belief in German expansion in the East.

17. Werner Baumbach, *The Life and Death of the Luftwaffe,* translated by Frederick Holt (New York, 1949), p. 79.

18. The Second (Kesselring and later Felmy), Third (Sperrle), and Fifth (Stumpff) air fleets were assigned to Operation Eagle Attack. Their forces totaled 3,500 aircraft with 50% reserves: 1,000 fighters, 1,800 bombers, and 700 reconnaissance aircraft. Asher Lee, *The German Air Force* (New York and London, 1946), pp. 72–73. Denis Richards, *The Fight at Odds* (*Royal Air Force, 1939–1945,* London, 1953), I, 157–58 gives similar figures. A good discussion of RAF and Luftwaffe organization is found in Telford Taylor, *The Breaking Wave: The Second World War in the Summer of 1940* (New York, 1967), Chapter 3. In the summer of 1940 the British Anti-Aircraft Command had some 1,300 heavy and 700 light guns. Taylor, p. 86.

19. Wood and Dempster, *Narrow Margin,* p. 463, give the Fighter Command 1,106 fighters on hand and 749 immediately operational.

20. Richards, *Fight at Odds,* I, 170.

21. Wood and Dempster, *Narrow Margin,* pp. 472, 474.

22. Collier, *Defense of the United Kingdom,* pp. 177–78.

23. Richards, *Fight at Odds,* I, 180–181.

24. Wood and Dempster, *Narrow Margin,* pp. 463, 470, 474. Actually, the low point in numbers for RAF Fighter Command had come before the August–September air battles. On June 22, the day of the French armistice, Fighter Command had only 565 operational fighters. (P. 463.)

25. Albert Kesselring, *Kesselring: A Soldier's Record,* translated by Lynton Hudson (New York, 1954), p. 73.

26. Thursfield, "Fuehrer Conferences," pp. 133, 136.

27. Werner Kreipe *et al., The Fatal Decisions* (New York, 1956), p. 20. British losses were 26 aircraft.

28. Thursfield, "Fuehrer Conferences," p. 138.

29. Lee, *German Air Force,* p. 83.

30. *Ibid.;* Wood and Dempster, in *Narrow Margin,* p. 463, give 732 serviceable RAF fighters.

31. Lee, *German Air Force,* p. 85; Wood and Dempster, in *Narrow Margin,* p. 474, give a total German loss of 1,733 aircraft.

Chapter Seven

1. A top secret OKW order of October 12, 1940, postponed further preparations for Operation Sea Lion until the spring of 1941. The text of that order is contained in "Fuehrer Conferences on Naval Affairs," edited by H. G. Thursfield, *Brassey's Naval Annual, 1948* (London, 1948), pp. 139–140.

2. Franz Halder, "The Private War Journal of Generaloberst Franz Halder, edited and translated under the direction of Arnold Lissance (unpublished war journal, Duke University, n.d.), IV, 144–145.

3. The Nationalist fort in Toledo which held out against repeated Republican attacks in 1937 during the Spanish Civil War. The best study of Felix and other planned German operations against Gibraltar is in Charles Burdick, *Germany's Military Strategy and Spain in World War II* (Syracuse, N.Y., 1968).

4. Thursfield, "Fuehrer Conferences," p. 146.

5. P. K. Kemp, *Key to Victory: The Triumph of British Sea Power in World War II* (Boston and Toronto, 1957), pp. 94–95.

6. "OKW Directive No. 18," November 12, 1940, as printed in *Hitler's War Directives, 1939–1945,* edited by H. R. Trevor-Roper and translated by Trevor-Roper and Anthony Rhodes (London, 1964), pp. 40–43.

7. Thursfield, "Fuehrer Conferences," pp. 170–171.

8. General Alexander Papagos, *The Battle of Greece, 1940–1941* (Athens, 1949), pp. 322–25. Papagos claims that it was firmly understood that he would not begin the withdrawal until informed by the British. British notes on the conference stated that preparations were to be made at once and put into execution to withdraw the Greek troops in Thrace and Macedonia to the Vermion line, which the British would be obliged to hold if the Yugoslavs did not join the Allies. I. S. O. Playfair, *The Mediterranean and Middle East (History of the Second World War, United Kingdom Military Series,* London, 1954–56), I, 379–80.

9. Papagos, *Battle of Greece,* 324–25.

10. It will be remembered that Operation Marita originally called only for the occupation of Greece north of the Aegean Sea. Hitler's new decision probably reflected a decision to obtain as much use of Greece as a

German air base as possible, perhaps with a view of attacking British east Mediterranean bases, but more likely with the intention of dominating British Mediterranean sea lanes. As Rommel had not yet turned the tide in North Africa, it is doubtful that Hitler at this time saw Greece as a base from which to strike at Alexandria or Suez.

11. Halder seems to have had no idea that Rommel's limited offensive would lead to a general British retreat from Cyrenaica. Prior to Rommel's launching of the Agedabia offensive, Halder did not think the Afrika Korps could move to Tobruk before the fall of 1941.

12. Halder Testimony, April 12–16, 1948, *Trials of War Criminals* (Washington, 1951), X, 927.

13. *Ibid.*

14. Paulus had become First Deputy in September. At the same time, Colonel Adolf Heusinger relieved Greiffenberg as Chief of the Operations section of the OKH. Walter Goerlitz, *History of the German General Staff, 1657–1945,* translated by Brian Battershaw (New York, 1959), p. 386.

15. The SS motorized infantry division "Das Reich" and the SS motorized infantry regiment "Adolf Hitler" also participated. George E. Blau, *The German Campaign in the Balkans* (Washington, 1953), pp. 39–40, 81; and George Stein, *The Waffen SS: Hitler's Elite Guard at War* (Ithaca, N.Y., 1966), pp. 115–16.

16. F. W. Mellenthin, *Panzer Battles,* translated by H. Betzler and edited by E. J. Turner (London, 1956), p. 35.

Chapter Eight

1. "Fuehrer Conferences on Naval Affairs," edited by H. G. Thursfield, *Brassey's Naval Annual, 1948* (London, 1948), p. 170.

2. The Fifth Light Division and the Fifteenth Panzer Division. It will be recalled that the first 4 light divisions had been converted to panzer divisions in 1940. The Fifth Light Division was improvised to meet special conditions and consisted of 1 tank regiment of 2 battalions, 3 motorized machine-gun battalions, 1 artillery regiment of 2 battalions, and a battalion each of antitank guns and engineers. Richard M. Ogorkewicz, *Armor: A History of Mechanized Forces* (New York, 1960), p. 77.

3. Franz Halder, "The Private War Journal of Generaloberst Halder," edited and translated under the direction of Arnold Lissance (unpublished war journal, Duke University, n.d.), V, 105–106.

4. *The Rommel Papers,* edited by B. H. Liddell Hart and translated by Paul Findlay (New York, 1953), pp. 98, 99.

5. *Ibid.,* p. 101.

6. Halder estimated on March 14 that there were between 4 and 8 British divisions in Libya. Actually, there were no more than 4, perhaps less since the British transfer to Greece began on March 5. By the end of March there were only 2 divisions in Egypt. I. S. O. Playfair, *The Mediterranean and the Middle East* (*History of the Second World War, United Kingdom Military Series* (London, 1956), II, 33.

7. Liddell Hart, *Rommel Papers,* p. 106.

8. Playfair, *Mediterranean,* II, 1–2, 33.

9. *Ibid.,* 53.

10. *Ibid.,* 58 (tonnage sunk) ; and M. A. Bragadin, *The Italian Navy in World War II,* translated by Gale Hoffman (Annapolis, 1957), p. 72 (percentage figures).

11. Liddell Hart, *Rommel Papers,* pp. 106, 107.

12. *Ibid.,* p. 109.

13. *Ibid.,* p. 111.

14. It is significant that when Rommel asked permission on April 14 to make a drive on Suez, the defenses of Tobruk had not been tested. Over the next three days the Afrika Korps strove without success to break Tobruk's resistance. After that time, Rommel made no more requests to invade Egypt.

Rommel's forces were quite small ; only the Fifth Light Division, the Italian Ariete Armored Division, the Trento Motorized Division, and 70 airplanes from the X Air Corps in Sicily. Once he was forced to split his command to lay siege to Tobruk, he certainly lacked the forces to invade Egypt.

15. The British attempts to use subs in this manner had also failed. See S. W. Roskill, *The War at Sea* (London, 1954), I, 375.

16. Playfair, *Mediterranean,* II, 34–37.

17. *Ibid.,* p. 36.

18. The dispatch of a General Staff officer to advise and assist a commander in the field had been a not unusual practice for the German General Staff since the days of the elder Moltke.

19. Playfair, *Mediterranean,* II, 36.

20. Hitler refused to put pressure on the French, which I. S. O. Playfair believes was a blunder. "This was very fortunate for the British," he writes, "for if Axis ships had merely to dart across the Narrows it is difficult to see how they could have been much interfered with." *Ibid.,* p. 53. The French did grant the use of Bizerta and the coastal railroad as far as Gabès on May 27.

21. Walter Warlimont, *Inside Hitler's Headquarters, 1939–1945,* translated by R. H. Barry (New York, 1964), p. 131; and B. H. Liddell Hart, *The Other Side of the Hill* (London, 1951), p. 238.

22. Warlimont, *Inside Hitler's Headquarters,* p. 131; Liddell Hart, *Other Side of the Hill,* p. 238; and Alan Clark, *The Fall of Crete* (New York, 1962), p. 24.

23. Directive No. 28, *Hitler's War Directives, 1939–1945,* edited by H. R. Trevor-Roper and translated by Trevor-Roper and Anthony Rhodes (London, 1964), pp. 68–79.

24. Clark, *Fall of Crete,* pp. 53–54.

25. The British had landed about 5,000 troops on Crete as early as November, 1940, and by early May, 1941, their numbers had risen to nearly 30,000. But most of them were from the defeated Australian and New Zealand units earlier sent to Greece, without sufficient weapons and ammunition and serving under a divided command. The British Air Officer Commanding, Middle East, had only 90 bombers and 43 single-engined fighters in the whole eastern Mediterranean, 23 bombers and 20 fighters in Crete. *Ibid.,* p. 39.

26. Playfair, *Mediterranean,* II, 159, 163–164.

27. Liddell Hart, *Rommel Papers,* p. 139.

28. F. W. von Mellenthin, *Panzer Battles, 1939–1945,* translated by H. Betzler and edited by E. J. Turner (London, 1956), p. 42.

29. Employed in operation Mercury were the Luftwaffe's Seventh Air (Parachute) Division, its only glider regiment, and the Army's Fifth Mountain Division, which had no previous experience in airborne operations. These units were to be reinforced by elements of the Army's Sixth Mountain Division and the Fifth Panzer Division, moved by sea and air. The Twenty-Second Air Assault Division was guarding the Ploesti oil fields and was not available. Air transport was provided by the troop carriers of the XI Air Corps, while air support was provided by Wolfram von Richthofen's VIII Air Corps, which disposed of 280 bombers, 150 dive-bombers, and about 200 single and twin-engined fighters. I. McD. G. Stewart, *The Struggle for Crete, 20 May–1 June 1941: A Story of Lost Opportunity* (London, New York, Toronto, 1966), p. 79.

30. P. K. Kempf, *Key to Victory: The Triumph of British Sea Power in World War II* (Boston and Toronto, 1957), p. 135.

31. Bragadin, *Italian Navy,* p. 72. In May, the Italians transported only 49,304 tons to Rommel's forces, the least since the Afrika Korps arrived in Libya.

32. Enough armor was eventually moved to the Afrika Korps to permit the conversion of the Fifth Light Division to the Twenty-First Panzer Division, based on OKW Directive No. 32, June 11, 1941, *Hitler's War Directives,* p. 79. In late November, 1941, Kesselring, the headquarters of the Second Air Fleet, and the II Air Corps were transferred to the Mediterranean. With the X and II air corps, Kesselring (as Commander in Chief, South), managed briefly to neutralize Malta in the spring of 1942, but never managed to supply Rommel's drive on El Alamein from Crete. Malta revived and an aerial invasion planned for June had to be cancelled to supply and reinforce Rommel in Egypt. "With the revival of Malta's potency and the strengthening of [the British Eighth Army in Egypt] . . . the hour of disaster loomed perceptibly near." Albert Kesselring, *Kesselring: A Soldier's Record,* translated by Lynton Hudson (New York, 1954), p. 151.

33. Playfair, *Mediterranean,* II, 59, and chart on 58.

34. The Fifteenth Panzer Division had 2 tank battalions, 2 motorized infantry battalions, and the usual complements of artillery and supporting services.

35. Tactical command was actually in the hands of Beresford-Peirse.

36. The British launched tank-supported infantry assaults on positions backed up by the formidable German 88-mm. antitank guns. German armor counterattacked when the enemy armor was decimated and the infantry helpless. The failure was Beresford-Peirse's, but Churchill sacked Wavell and replaced him with Claude Auchinleck. Correlli Barnett, *The Desert Generals* (New York, 1961), pp. 68–72. Rommel supposedly learned these tactics while repelling the 1940 British tank attack at Arras. Ronald Lewin, *Rommel as Military Commander* (London, 1968), p. 22.

37. Liddell Hart, *Rommel Papers,* p. 146, corrected figures. Also Playfair, *Mediterranean,* II, 171.

Chapter Nine

1. Franz Halder, "The Private War Journal of Generaloberst Franz Halder," edited and translated under the direction of Arnold Lissance (unpublished war journal, Duke University, n.d.), IV, 128; and Halder, Testimony, April 12–16, 1948, *Trials of War Criminals* (Washington, 1951), X, 1014.

2. Warlimont Testimony, June 21–25, 1948, *TWC,* X, 1026–27; Warlimont Affidavit, November 21, 1945, *TWC,* X, Doc. 3023-PS, p. 995; and Walter Warlimont, *Inside Hitler's Headquarters, 1939–1945,* translated by R. H. Barry (New York, 1964), pp. 135–36.

3. George Blau, *The German Campaign in Russia: Planning and Operations, 1940–1942* (Washington, 1955), pp. 6–12.

4. *Ibid.,* p. 6.

5. *Ibid.,* pp. 19–20.

6. *Ibid.,* pp. 20–21.

7. Wladyslaw Anders, *Hitler's Defeat in Russia* (Chicago, 1953), p. 20, points out that while Moscow has no natural resources, its district at that time produced a third of the output of Soviet heavy industry. He believes that the Urals were less important in 1941 than now. John Erickson, *The Soviet High Command: A Military-Political History, 1918–1941* (London, 1962), p. 575, analyzes industrial distribution in Russia and tends to support Anders' view. All three aircraft fuselage building centers were located around Moscow, for instance. Tank production was more widely spread on both sides of the Urals, in Leningrad, in Kharkov, and in Stalingrad.

8. See also Blau, *Campaign in Russia,* pp. 18–19.

9. Directive No. 21 is quoted in full in Blau, *Campaign in Russia,* pp. 22–25; and in *Hitler's War Directives,* edited by H. R. Trevor-Roper and translated by Trevor-Roper and Anthony Rhodes (London, 1964), pp. 49–52.

10. Blau, *Campaign in Russia,* p. 24.

11. Anders, *Hitler's Defeat in Russia,* pp. 23–24, suggests that operations should have been planned over several summers. He agrees with J. F. C. Fuller, *The Second World War, 1939–1945: A Strategical and Tactical History* (London, 1948), p. 117.

12. Paul Leverkuehn, *German Military Intelligence,* translated by R. H. Stevens and Constantine Fitzgibbon (London, 1954), pp. 155–61, and *passim.*

13. Blau, *Campaign in Russia,* p. 7.

14. The official Soviet *Istoriya Velikoi Otechestvennoi Voiny Sovetskogo Soyuza* (*History of the Great Patriotic War of the Soviet Union*) 5 vols., Moscow, 1960–1963, abounds with statistics on the state of obsolescence in the Red Army in June, 1941. Although 7,000 tanks were with the frontier armies on June 22, only about 1,500 were modern T-34 and KV models. So many tanks were undergoing major and minor repairs that only about 27% were actually operational. Soviet production of modern tanks in 1940 amounted to only 243 KVs and 115 T-34s. During the first half of 1941 an additional 393 KVs and 1,110 T-34s were manufactured, but only 508 KVs and 967 T-34s had joined the frontier armies by June 22. Even units equipped with the newer tanks had had little time to train in them. The great majority of the Russian

tanks were obsolescent T-26 and BT types. (Figures cited from the official Soviet *History* in Alexander Werth, *Russia at War, 1941–1945,* New York, 1964, p. 139.) A total of 2,413 armored fighting vehicles were produced by the Russians during the first half of 1941, but 6,590 were produced by the end of 1941. See Martin J. Miller, Jr., *Red Armor in Combat* (Canoga Park, Calif. [1969]), p. 76. Soviet frontier aviation was in a similar state (Werth, *Russia at War,* p. 137).

15. The T-34 was in a class with the American M-4 Sherman tank, but had a more modern hull design and a powerful 76-mm. gun. The KV-2 heavy tank mounted a 152-mm. howitzer. I. G. Andronikow and W. D. Mostowenko, *Die roten Panzer: Geschichte der sowjetischen Panzertruppen 1920–1960,* translated into German by Dr. F. M. von Senger und Etterlin (Munich, 1963), p. 235.

16. Soviet fighter units were still equipped with the obsolescent I-15, I-16, and I-153 types. New Soviet fighters—the YAK-1 and MIG-3— were in production, but only a few had joined the frontier forces by June, 1941. Bomber units were usually equipped with the SB-3 and DB-3 aircraft, the former a twin-engined mid-range bomber and the latter a twin-engined long-range bomber. Both lacked strong defensive armor and armament. The more powerful PE-2 bomber was in production but not delivered in quantity by June, 1941. Of about 7,300 Soviet aircraft in European Russia, perhaps 2,000 were of modern design. Nearly all of these were massed on 66 airfields because they required longer runways. Werth, *Russia at War,* p. 137; and Hermann Plocher, *The German Air Force versus Russia (The German Air Force in World War II, USAF Historical Studies),* New York, 1968, pp. 19–20.

17. Raymond L. Garthoff, *Soviet Military Doctrine* (Glencoe, Ill., 1953), p. 67. The 1939 Draft Field Regulations, still in force in 1941, declared, "Any enemy attack on the Soviet Union will be met by a smashing blow from its armed forces. We shall conduct the war offensively, and carry it into enemy territory." Quoted in the official Soviet *History* and cited in Werth, *Russia at War,* p. 133.

18. *Stavka Glavnovo Komandovaniya Vooruzhennykh Sil SSSR.* The *Stavka* was the Soviet equivalent of GHQ and subordinate to the State Defense Committee (GOKO) headed by Stalin. In June, 1941, it was headed by Marshal Semyon Timoshenko, the Defense Commissar, and consisted of about a dozen higher officers. General Georgi Zhukov, the head of the operational General Staff, was a member of the *Stavka.* Erickson, *Soviet High Command,* p. 598.

19. "Fortifications," MS#P-203, Office of Chief of Military History, pp. 22–24. A published description of the Stalin Line may be found in Alan Clark, *Barbarossa: The Russian-German Conflict, 1941–1945* (New York, 1965), pp. 30–31; and in Erickson, *Soviet High Command,* pp. 569–70.

20. According to Werth, *Russia at War,* p. 138, the entire Soviet Union had only about 800,000 motor vehicles in June, 1941.

21. The standard rifle division was similar to its German counterpart in organization, but not so well equipped. Its authorized strength in June, 1941, was 14,300 men, 25–30 motor vehicles, 600 horsedrawn wagons, and about 2,000 horses. Later rifle divisions were reduced to 10,000 men each. Malcolm Mackintosh, *Juggernaut: A History of the Soviet Armed Forces, 1918–1966* (New York, 1966), pp. 133–34, 224.

22. Each tank division consisted of 2 tank regiments, a motorized rifle regiment, an artillery regiment, and an AA battalion. The motorized rifle division consisted of 2 rifle regiments, a tank regiment, an AA battalion, and an AT battalion. Erickson, *Soviet High Command,* p. 571.

23. Other useful works on the Red Army are Augustin Guillaume, *Soviet Arms and Soviet Power* (Washington, 1949); B. H. Liddell Hart, *The Red Army* (New York, 1956); Louis B. Ely, *The Red Army Today* (Harrisburg, Pa., 1956); and Michel Garder, *A History of the Soviet Army* (New York, 1966).

24. The OKH was greatly concerned about the possibility of succesful withdrawals of Russian armor into the interior and gave their encirclement and destruction top priority in its instructions to its panzer leaders. Hermann Hoth, *Panzer-Operationen: Die Panzergruppe 3 und der operative Gedanke de deutschen Fuehrung Sommer 1941 (Der Wehrmacht in Kampf,* Heidelberg, 1956), p. 42.

25. Blau, *Campaign in Russia,* pp. 26–27.

26. Burkhart Mueller-Hillebrand, *Die Blitzfeldzüge, 1939–1941 (Das Heer, 1933–1945,* Frankfurt-am-Main, 1956), II, 107; and R. M. Ogorkiewicz, *Design and Development of Fighting Vehicles* (Garden City, N.Y., 1968), p. 36, shows total German tank production for 1940 as 1,460 and for 1941 as 3,256.

27. Both Mark III and Mark IV were more than a match for the Soviet T-26 and BT tanks but inferior to the later T-34 and KV tanks. Richard M. Ogorkiewicz, *Armor: A History of Mechanized Forces* (New York, 1960), pp. 73–79, 220; and Andronikow and Mostowenko, *Die Roten Panzer,* Chapter II, *passim.*

28. Halder Testimony, April 12–16, 1948, *TWC,* X, 1017–18. Nor was Hitler entirely wrong. The Germans would have 3,000 modern tanks against about 1,500 modern Soviet tanks, not to mention a vastly greater technological and tactical experience in June, 1941; and Mueller-Hillebrand, *Die Blitzfeldzüge,* II, 105.

29. Halder Testimony, *TWC,* X, pp. 1012–13.

30. Hans Pottgiesser, *Die Deutsche Reichsbahn im Ostfeldzug, 1939–1944 (Der Wehrmacht im Kampf,* Neckargemünd, *1960*), pp. 21–23, 64.

31. Mueller-Hillebrand, *Die Blitzfeldzüge,* II, 102, 109, 111, Table 29; and George H. Stein, *The Waffen SS: Hitler's Elite Guard at War* (Ithaca, N.Y., 1966), p. 120. This 142-division total does not include 9 Security divisions or 1 SS Police Division, or 1 SS motorized infantry division, 2 mountain divisions, and 1 infantry division in Finland.

32. Mueller-Hillebrand, *Die Blitzfeldzüge,* II, 109–112.

33. Kurt von Tippelskirch, *Geschichte des Zweiten Weltkriegs* (Bonn, 1951), p. 204.

34. "Letter from the OKW Department of National Defense concerning Conference with Finland," May 22, 1941, *TWC,* X, Doc. 883-PS, p. 999.

35. Blau, *Campaign in Russia,* p. 41.

36. Warlimont, *Inside Hitler's Headquarters,* p. 141.

37. Blau, *Campaign in Russia,* p. 34.

38. Paul Deichmann, *German Air Force Operations in Support of the Army (German Air Force in World War II, USAF Historical Studies,* New York, 1968), pp. 158–59.

39. Plocher, *The German Air Force,* pp. 5, 9–10, 14–15.

40. The First Air Fleet consisted of 270 bombers, 110 fighters, 30 air transports, 160 reconnaissance planes, and 50 liaison planes; the Second, of 240 bombers, 250 dive bombers, 330 fighters, 60 ground attack planes, 60 transports, 180 reconnaissance planes, and 60 liaison planes; the Fourth, of 360 bombers, 210 fighters, 60 transports, 220 reconnaissance planes and 80 liaison planes (*Ibid.,* pp. 33–35). For total, see Deichmann, *German Air Force Operations,* p. 158. On June 22, 1941, the Luftwaffe had a total of 3,340 combat aircraft. Besides those in the East, the others were deployed as follows: 190 for home defense, 370 in the Mediterranean, 660 in the West, 120 in Norway (not counting units to be used there for Barbarossa).

41. The Russians had no radar system. Their 2,400 heavy and light antiaircraft guns were located around their principal cities instead of being concentrated around their airfields. Plocher, *The German Air Force,* pp. 19–20.

42. Deichmann, *German Air Force Operations,* pp. 159–160.

43. The theoretical deployment is more certain than the actual strengths and capabilities of units identified as "tank divisions," "motorized rifle divisions," and the like. My figures are consensus estimates and should be considered as only approximate. Halder's journal never refers to Russian tank or armored divisions but only to "armored brigades," although his figures make clear that he is referring to tank divisions. Some estimates on numbers are contained in Clark, *Barbarossa,* pp. 40–43; Garder, *A History of the Soviet Army,* p. 105; and Mackintosh, *Juggernaut,* pp. 133–136. Andronikov and Mostowenko, *Die roten Panzer,* pp. 33–35, is especially good on the organization of Soviet armor and motorized infantry, but the best source in English is Erickson, *Soviet High Command,* pp. 568–72.

44. For instance, the XIV Mechanized Corps of the Fourth Army in the Western District had its Twenty-Second Tank Division on the frontier, its Thirtieth Tank Division 24 miles behind the frontier, and its 205th Motorized Rifle Division still further to the rear. The XIV Mechanized Corps was authorized 1,025 tanks on June 22 but actually possessed only 508 obsolescent T-26 tanks. Andronikov and Mostowenko, *Die roten Panzer,* p. 34.

45. Plocher, *The German Air Force,* p. 30.

46. Blau, *Campaign in Russia,* p. 37.

47. Warlimont, *Inside Hitler's Headquarters,* pp. 172–73.

48. Plocher, *The German Air Force,* p. 39.

49. Actually, the Luftwaffe's count was low. By noon 1,200 Soviet aircraft had been destroyed or disabled, three-fourths of them on the ground. The Western Military district lost 528 on the ground and 210 in the air. Werth, *Russia at War,* p. 156.

50. Maximilian Tretter-Pico, *Missbrauchte Infanterie: Deutsche Infanteriedivisionen im Osteuropaeischen Grossraum 1941 bis 1944* (Frankfort, 1957), p. 26.

51. *Ibid.*

52. The Second Air Fleet had 16 mixed battalions and 7 light antiaircraft artillery battalions. Plocher, *The German Air Force,* p. 34.

53. As a result, according to the Soviet claim, only 8 rifle, 3 tank, and 2 motorized rifle divisions were finally destroyed at Minsk.

54. Mackintosh, *Juggernaut,* p. 146.

55. For organizational and high command changes in detail, see Erickson, *Soviet High Command,* pp. 597–604.

56. Garthoff, *Soviet Military Doctrine,* p. 305, claims that 25% of Soviet artillery was used in this fashion by the end of 1941.

57. OKW Directive No. 33, "Continuation of the War in the East," *Hitler's War Directives, 1939–1945,* edited by H. R. Trevor-Roper and translated by Trevor-Roper and Anthony Rhodes (London, 1964), pp. 85–89.

58. OKW Directive No. 34, *Hitler's War Directives,* pp. 91–93.

59. See Warlimont, *Inside Hitler's Headquarters,* pp. 185–86. Warlimont believes that Jodl used his influence to bring Hitler around to the OKH view.

60. *Ibid.,* p. 186.

61. A. Heusinger, *Befehl im Widerstreit* (Tübingen and Stuttgart, 1950), pp. 132–35.

62. Blau, *Campaign in Russia,* pp. 66–67.

63. Heusinger, *Befehl im Widerstreit,* pp. 132–35.

64. OKW Directive No. 35, *Hitler's War Directives,* pp. 96–97.

65. Blau, *Campaign in Russia,* p. 73.

66. *Ibid.,* p. 71, gives 409,000 casualties by 31 August.

67. *Ibid.,* pp. 72, 78, 83. See also Pottgiesser, *Deutsche Reichsbahn,* p. 26.

68. Anders, *Hitler's Defeat in Russia,* pp. 57–58.

69. *Ibid.,* p. 58. Blau, *Campaign in Russia,* p. 79 gives 658,000 troops.

70. Anders, *Hitler's Defeat in Russia,* pp. 58, 59. Zhukov had earlier turned over his duties as Chief of the General Staff to Marshal Boris Shaposhnikov and gone to Leningrad to assist Voroshilov. He was transferred to the central front on October 7 and appointed commander on October 10. Georgi K. Zhukov, *Marshal Zuhkov's Greatest Battles,* translated by Theodore Shabad (New York, 1969), pp. 35, 45.

71. Blau, *Campaign in Russia,* p. 80.

72. Plocher, *The German Air Force,* pp. 231–233.

73. Zhukov, *Greatest Battles,* p. 61.

74. During November and December, a total of 15 rifle divisions, 3 cavalry divisions, and 7 tank brigades were transferred from the Far East. Still, in the critical period from November 16 to December 5, Zhukov's armies did not have over 800 operational tanks. Clark, *Barbarossa,* p. 170, fn. 4.

75. Zhukov, *Greatest Battles,* p. 55.

76. Nicholas Mikhailov, *Soviet Russia: The Land and its People* (New York, 1948), p. 41.

77. Total German casualties in the East since June 22 had soared to 743,112. Even after all available replacements had been sent, the forces in the East were short 340,000 men.

78. Werth. *Russia at War,* p. 259.

Epilogue

1. Georgi K. Zhukov, *Marshal Zuhkov's Greatest Battles,* translated by Theodore Shabad (New York, 1969), p. 84.

2. Wladyslaw Anders, *Hitler's Defeat in Russia* (Chicago, 1953), p. 80.

3. OKW Directive No. 38, December 2, 1941, *Hitler's War Directives,* edited by H. R. Trevor-Roper and translated by Trevor-Roper and Anthony Rhodes (London, 1964), pp. 105–106.

4. Albert Kesselring, *Kesselring: A Soldier's Record,* translated by Lynton Hudson (New York, 1954), pp. 116, 124, and Chapter IV.

5. Correlli Barnett, *The Desert Generals* (New York, 1961), Part V, Chapter IV.

6. George Blau, *The German Campaign in Russia: Planning and Operations, 1940–1942* (Washington, 1955), p. 138.

Selected Bibliography

I. Unpublished Sources and Printed Sources of Limited Circulation
   A. Foreign Military Studies, Office of Chief of Military History
       (OCMH), Department of the Army, Washington, D.C.
       Blumentritt, Guenther von. "The Dangers of Operational and
           Tactical 'Systems.'" MS#C-009, OCMH, 1948.
       Erfurth, Waldemar. "The Assistant Chief of Staff for Military
           History (O.Qu.V)." MS#P-041d, OCMH, n.d.
       Feige, Richard. "Relationship between Operations and Supply in
           Africa." MS#D-125, OCMH, 1947.
       "Fortifications." MS#P-203, OCMH, n.d.
       Halder, Franz. "Control of the German Army General Staff."
           MS#P-041d, OCMH, 1952.
       ———. "Operational Basis for the First Phase of the French
           Campaign in 1940." MS#P-151, OCMH, n.d.
       "Military Improvisations during the Russian Campaign." MS-
           #20-201, OCMH, 1951.
       Mueller-Hillebrand, Burkhart. "Horses in the German Army,
           1941–1945." MS#P-090, OCMH, n.d.
       Reinhardt, Helmuth. "Utilization of Captured Material by Ger-
           many in World War II." MS#P-103, OCMH, n.d.
       "Supply for Modern Infantry." MS#P-085, OCMH, n.d.
       "Supply in Far-Reaching Operations." MS#T-8, OCMH, n.d.
   B. Sources in the Military History Research Collection, Carlisle
       Barracks, Pa.

Kuhl, General [Hermann Joseph] von and General [Walter Friedrich Adolf] von Bergman. *Movements and Supply of the German First Army during August and September 1914.* Fort Leavenworth, Kansas, 1929.

"March of the German First Army, August 12–24, 1914: Comparison with an Equivalent American Force making the same Movement." Unpublished analytical study, U.S. Army War College, 1931.

Ministry of War. *Instructions for Tactical Employment of Large Units.* Translated from the French by U.S. War Department. Washington, D.C., 1937.

"Organization and Administration of the Theater of Operations: The German First Army, 1914." Unpublished analytical study, U.S. Army War College, 1931.

Reichswehrministerium, *Die Truppenfuehrung.* Translated by the U.S. War Department. Berlin, 1933.

C. Other

Halder, Franz. "The Private War Journal of Generaloberst Franz Halder." Edited and translated under the direction of Arnold Lissance. Unpublished war journal, Duke University, n.d. 9 vols.

U.S. War Department. *Handbook on German Military Forces.* Washington, 1945.

II. Published Sources

Anders, Wladyslaw. *Hitler's defeat in Russia.* Chicago, 1953.

Andronikow, I. G., and W. D. Mostowenko. *Die roten Panzer: Geschichte der sowjetischen Panzertruppen, 1920–1960.* Edited and translated from Russian into German by Dr. F. M. von Senger und Etterlin. Munich, 1963.

Ansel, Walter. *Hitler Confronts England.* Durham, N.C., 1960.

Asprey, Robert. *The First Battle of the Marne.* (*Great Battles of History.*) Philadelphia and New York, 1962.

Barnett, Correlli. *The Desert Generals.* New York, 1961.

Baumbach, Werner. *The Life and Death of the Luftwaffe.* Translated by Frederick Holt. New York, 1949.

Baumgarten-Crusius, Artur. *Deutschen Heerfuehrung im Marnefeldzug.* Berlin, 1921.

Beck, Ludwig. *Studien.* Edited by Hans Speidel. Stuttgart, 1955.

Bell, Clara, and Henry W. Fischer, editors and translators. *Letters of Field-Marshal Helmuth von Moltke.* New York, 1892.

Benoist-Méchin, Jacques. *Sixty Days that Shook the West: The Fall of France, 1940.* Translated by Peter Wiles. New York, 1963.

Blau, George E. *The German Campaign in the Balkans.* Washington, 1953.

———. *The German Campaign in Russia: Planning and Operations, 1940–1942.* Washington, 1955.

Bloem, Walter. *The Advance from Mons, 1914.* Translated by G. C. Wynne. London, 1930.

Blumentritt, Guenther von. *Von Rundstedt, Soldier and Man.* London, 1952.

Boguslawski, A. von. *Tactical Deductions of the War of 1870–71.* Translated by Colonel Lumley Graham. Fort Leavenworth, Kansas, 1891.

Bor, Peter. *Gespräche mit Halder.* Wiesbaden, 1950.

Bragadin, A. *The Italian Navy in World War II.* Translated by Gale Hoffman. Annapolis, Md., 1957.

Brodie, Bernard and Fawn. *From Crossbow to the H-Bomb.* New York, 1962.

Bryant, Arthur. *The Turn of the Tide, 1939–1943: A Study based on the Diaries and Autobiographical Notes of Field Marshal the Viscount Alanbrooke.* London, 1957.

Burdick, Charles. *Germany's Military Strategy and Spain in World War II.* Syracuse, N.Y., 1968.

Carrias, E. *La Pensée militaire allemande.* Paris, 1948.

Challener, Richard. *The French Theory of the Nation in Arms.* New York, 1955.

Chandler, David. *The Campaigns of Napoleon.* New York, 1966.

Clark, Alan. *Barbarossa: The Russian-German Conflict, 1941–1945.* New York, 1965.

———. *The Fall of Crete.* New York, 1962.

Collier, Basil. *Defense of the United Kingdom.* (*History of the Second World War, United Kingdom Military Series.*) London, 1957.

Craig, Gordon. *The Battle of Königgrätz: Prussia's Victory over Austria, 1866.* (*Great Battles of History.*) Philadelphia and New York, 1964.

De Gaulle, Charles. *The Call to Honor, 1940–42* (*The War Memoirs of Charles de Gaulle,* Vol. I.) Translated by Jonathan Griffin. New York, 1955.

———. *The Army of the Future.* London and Melbourne, 1940.

Deichmann, Paul. *German Air Force Operations in Support of the Army. (The German Air Force in World War II. USAF Historical Studies.)* New York, 1968.

Dellmensingen, K. Kraft von. *Der Durchbruch.* Hamburg, 1937.

Deutsch, Harold C. *The Conspiracy against Hitler in the Twilight War.* Minneapolis, 1968.

Draper, Theodore. *The Six Weeks' War: France, May 10–June 25, 1940.* New York, 1944.

Ellis, L. F. *The War in France and Flanders, 1939–1940. (History of the Second World War, United Kingdom Military Series.)* London, 1953.

Ely, Louis B. *The Red Army Today.* Harrisburg, 1956.

Emme, Eugene, ed. *The Impact of Air Power.* New York, 1959.

Erickson, John. *The Soviet High Command: A Military–Political History, 1918–1941.* London, 1962.

Falkenhayn, [Erich] von. *The German General Staff and its Decisions, 1914–1916.* New York, 1920.

Falls, Cyril. *The Art of War.* New York, 1961.

Foch, Ferdinand. *The Memoirs of Marshal Foch.* Translated by Colonel T. Bentley Mott. Garden City, N.Y., 1931.

Foerster, Wolfgang. *Ein General kaempft gegan den Krieg.* Munich, 1949. [The Beck papers.]

[Friedrich Karl, Prince of Prussia]. *The Influence of Firearms upon Tactics.* Translated by E. H. Wickham. London, 1876.

Fuller, J. F. C. *A Military History of the Western World.* Vol. III. New York, 1956.

———. *Memoirs of an Unconventional Soldier.* London, 1936.

———. *On Future Warfare.* London, 1928.

———. *Tanks in the Great War, 1914–1918.* London, 1920.

———. *The Conduct of War, 1789–1961.* New Brunswick, N.J., 1961.

———. *The Second World War, 1939–1945: A Strategical and Tactical History.* London, 1948.

Gamelin, M. *Servir: La Guerre (Septembre 1939–19 Mai 1940).* Paris, 1947. 3 vols.

Garder, Michel. *A History of the Soviet Army.* New York, 1966.

Garthoff, Raymond L. *Soviet Military Doctrine.* Glencoe, Ill., 1953.

Gisevius, Hans. *To the Bitter End.* Translated by Richard and Clara Winston. Cambridge, Mass., 1947.

Goerlitz, Walter. *History of the German General Staff, 1657–1945.* Translated by Brian Battershaw. New York, 1953.

Goodspeed, D. J. *Ludendorff: Genius of World War I*. Boston, 1966.

Goutard, A. *The Battle of France, 1940*. Translated by R. P. Burgess. New York, 1959.

Greiner, Helmuth. *Die Oberste Wehrmachtfuehrung, 1939–1943*. Wiesbaden, 1951.

Guderian, Heinz. *Panzer Leader*. Translated by Constantine Fitzgibbon. New York, 1953.

Guillaume, Augustin. *Soviet Arms and Soviet Power*. Washington, 1949.

Hahlweg, Werner, ed. *Klassiker der Kriegskunst*. Darmstadt, 1960.

Halder, Franz. *Hitler as War Lord*. Translated by Paul Findlay. London, 1950.

Heusinger, A. *Befehl im Widerstreit*. Tübingen and Stuttgart, 1950.

Higgins, Trumbull. *Hitler and Russia: The Third Reich in a Two-Front War, 1937–1943*. New York and London, 1966.

Hohenlohe-Ingelfingen, Kraft zu. *Letters on Artillery*. Translated by U. L. Wolford. London, 1898.

Horne, Alistair. *The Fall of Paris: The Siege and the Commune, 1870–71*. New York, 1965.

———. *The Price of Glory: Verdun, 1916*. New York, 1963.

———. *To Lose a Battle: France 1940*. Boston and Toronto, 1969.

Hossbach, Friedrich. *Infanterie im Ostfeldzug, 1941–1942*. Osterrode am Harz, 1951.

———. *Zwischen Wehrmacht und Hitler*. Hanover, 1949.

Hoth, Hermann. *Panzer-Operationen: Die Panzergruppe 3 und der operative Gedanke der deutschen Fuehrung Sommer 1941. (Der Wehrmacht im Kampf.)* Heidelberg, 1956.

Howard, Michael. *The Franco-Prussian War: The German Invasion of France, 1870–1871*. New York, 1962.

Hubatsch, Walter. *Weseruebung: Die Deutschen Besetzung von Danemark und Norwegen. (Studien und Dokumente zur Geschichte des Zweiten Weltkriegs.)* Göttingen, 1960.

Imperial General Staff. *Handbook of the German Army in War: April 1918*. London, 1918.

Ironside, Edmund. *Tannenberg: The First Thirty Days in East Prussia*. Edinburgh and London, 1933.

Jacobsen, Hans-Adolf. *Fall Gelb: Der Kampf um den Deutschen Operationsplan zur Westoffensive 1940*. Wiesbaden, 1957.

———, ed. *Generaloberst Halder: Kriegstagebuch*. Band I. Stuttgart, 1962.

————, ed. *Kriegstagebuch des Oberkommando der Wehrmacht.* Band I. (OKW War Diary.) Frankfurt-am-Main, 1965.

Jars, Robert. *La Campagne de Pologne.* Paris, 1949.

Jouan, R. *La Marine allemande dans la seconde mondiale.* Paris, 1949.

Kemp, P. K. *Key to Victory: The Triumph of British Sea Power in World War II.* Boston and Toronto, 1957.

Kennedy, Robert M. *The German Campaign in Poland, 1939.* Washington, 1956.

Kessel, Eberhard. *Moltke.* Stuttgart, 1957.

Kesselring, Albert. *Kesselring: A Soldier's Record.* Translated by Lynton Hudson. New York, 1954.

Killen, John. *The Luftwaffe: A History.* London, 1967.

Kimche, Jon. *The Unfought Battle.* New York, 1968.

Klein, F. *Germany's Economic Preparations for War.* Cambridge, Mass., 1959.

Kluck, Alexander von. *The March on Paris and the Battle of the Marne.* London, 1920.

Knox, Alfred. *With the Russian Army, 1914–1917.* Vol. I. London, 1921.

Kreipe, Werner, *et al. The Fatal Decisions.* New York, 1956.

Lee, Asher. *The German Air Force.* London, 1946.

Levin, Donald. *Rommel as Military Commander.* London, 1968.

Liddell Hart, B. H. *The Other Side of the Hill.* London, 1951.

————. *The Red Army.* New York, 1956.

————. *The Remaking of Modern Armies.* London, 1927.

————, ed. *The Rommel Papers.* Translated by Paul Findlay. New York, 1953.

————. *The Tanks: The History of the Royal Tank Regiment and its Predecessors Heavy Branch Machine-Gun Corps, Tank Corps and Royal Tank Corps 1914–1945.* Vol. I. New York, 1959.

Ludendorff, Erich. *Ludendorff's Own Story.* Vol. II. New York and London, 1919.

Luvaas, Jay. *The Military Legacy of the Civil War: The European Inheritance.* Chicago, 1959.

Lyet, Pierre. *La Bataille de France.* Paris, 1947.

Mackintosh, Malcolm. *Juggernaut: A History of the Soviet Armed Forces, 1918–1966.* New York, 1966.

Manstein, Erich von. *Lost Victories.* Translated by Anthony G. Powell. Chicago, 1958.

Martel, Giffard. *In the Wake of the Tank.* London, 1931.

Meier-Welcker, Hans. *Seeckt*. Frankfurt-am-Main, 1967.

Mellenthin, F. W. von. *Panzer Battles, 1939–1945*. Translated by H. Betzler and edited by E. F. Turner. London, 1956.

Miller, Martin, Jr. *Red Armor in Combat*. Canoga Park, Calif. [1969].

Milwood, A. S. *German Economy at War*. London, 1965.

Moltke, Field Marshal Count Helmuth von. *The Franco-Prussian War of 1870–71*. Translated by Clara Bell and Henry W. Fischer. New York, 1892.

Mueller-Hillebrand, Burkhart. *Das Heer bis zum Kriegsbeginn. (Das Heer, 1933–1945.)* Band I. Darmstadt, 1954.

———. *Die Blitzfeldzüge, 1939–1941. (Das Heer, 1933–1945.)* Band II. Frankfurt-am-Main, 1956.

Nuremberg Military Tribunal. *Trials of War Criminals*. Vols. X, XI. Washington, 1951.

Oberkommando des Heeres. *Gedanken von Moltke*. Berlin, 1941.

Ogorkiewicz, Richard M. *Armor: A History of Mechanized Forces*. New York, 1960.

———. *Design and Development of Fighting Vehicles*. Garden City, N.Y., 1968.

O'Neill, Robert J. *The German Army and the Nazi Party, 1933–1939*. New York, 1966.

Papagos, Alexander. *The Battle of Greece, 1940–1941*. Athens, 1949.

Pitt, Barrie. *1918: The Last Act*. New York, 1962.

Playfair, I. S. O. *The Mediterranean and Middle East. (History of the Second World War, United Kingdom Military Series.)* London, 1954–56.

Plocher, Hermann. *The German Air Force versus Russia, 1941. (The German Air Force in World War II, USAF Historical Studies.)* New York, 1968.

Pottgiesser, Hans. *Die Deutsche Reichsbahn im Ostfeldzug, 1939–1944. (Der Wehrmacht im Kampf.)* Neckargemünd, 1960.

Pratt, Edwin A. *The Rise of Rail-Power in War and Conquest, 1833–1914*. London, 1916.

Richards, Denis. *The Fight at Odds. (Royal Air Force, 1939–1945.)* Vol. I. London, 1953.

Ritter, Gerhard. *The Schlieffen Plan: Critique of a Myth*. Translated by Andrew and Eva Wilson. New York, 1958.

Robertson, E. M. *Hitler's Pre-War Policy and Military Plans, 1933–1939*. London, 1963.

Roericht, Edgar. *Probleme der Kesselschlacht*. Karlsruhe, 1958.

Rogers, H. C. B. *Tanks in Battle.* (*The Imperial Services Library.*) Vol. III. London, 1965.

Ropp, Theodore. *War in the Modern World.* Durham, 1959.

Rosinski, Herbert. *The German Army.* New York, 1966, rev. ed.

Roskill, S. W. *The War at Sea.* Vol. I. London, 1954.

Rothfels, Hans. *The German Opposition to Hitler.* Hinsdale, Ill., 1948.

Seeckt, [Hans] von. *Thoughts of a Soldier.* Translated by Gilbert Waterhouse. London, 1930.

Shaw, G. C. *Supply in Modern War.* London, 1938.

Stein, George H. *The Waffen SS: Hitler's Elite Guard at War, 1939–1945.* Ithaca, N.Y., 1966.

Stewart, I. McD. G. *The Struggle for Crete, 20 May–1 June 1941: A Story of Lost Opportunity.* London, New York, Toronto, 1966.

Taylor, Telford. *Sword and Swastika: Generals and Nazis in the Third Reich.* New York, 1952.

——. *The Breaking Wave: The Second World War in the Summer of 1940.* New York, 1967.

——. *The March of Conquest: The German Victories in Western Europe, 1940.* New York, 1956.

Thursfield, Admiral H. G., editor. "Fuehrer Conferences on Naval Affairs." *Brassey's Naval Annual, 1948.* London, 1948.

Tippelskirch, Kurt von. *Geschichte des Zweiten Weltkriegs.* Bonn, 1951.

Tretter-Pico, Maximilian. *Missbrauchte Infanterie: Deutsche Infanteriedivisionen im Osteuropaeischen Grossraum 1941 bis 1944.* Frankfurt-am-Main, 1957.

Trevor-Roper, H. R., editor. *Hitler's War Directives, 1939–1945.* Translated by Trevor-Roper and Anthony Rhodes. London, 1964.

U.S. State Department. *Documents on German Foreign Policy 1918–1945.* Series D, Vol. VII.

Von der Goltz, Baron Colmar. *The Nation-in-Arms: A Treatise on Modern Military Systems and the Conduct of War.* London, 1906.

Werth, Alexander. *Russia at War, 1941–1945.* New York, 1964.

Weygand, Maxime. *Recalled to Service.* Translated by E. W. Dickes. London, 1952.

Wheatley, Ronald. *Operation Sea Lion: German Plans for the Invasion of England, 1939–1942.* Oxford, 1958.

Wheeler-Bennett, John. *Munich: Prologue to Tragedy.* London, 1948.

——. *Nemesis of Power: The German Army in Politics, 1918–1945*. New York, 1954.

Wintringham, Tom. *The Story of Weapons and Tactics*. Boston, 1943.

Wood, Derek, and Derek Dempster. *The Narrow Margin: The Battle of Britain and the Rise of Air Power, 1930–1940*. New York, Toronto, and London, 1961.

Young, Desmond. *Rommel, the Desert Fox*. New York, 1950.

Zhukov, Georgi K. *Marshal Zhukov's Greatest Battles*. Translated by Theodore Shabad. New York, 1969.

Index

Aachen, Germany, 98

Abbeville, France, 16, 26, 97, 113

Acropolis, The, 157

Admiral Hipper (vessel), 130

Admiral Scheer (vessel), 130, 242*n*14

Advanced Air Striking Force (AASF), of Britain, 86

Aegean Sea, 143, 244*n*10

Agedabia, Libya, 151, 161, 162, 164–65, 245*n*11

aircraft, 25, 29, 30, 38, 42–46, 68–69, 79, 80, 81–82, 85, 171; of Britain (1939–1941), 86–87, 102, 107, 125, 133, 134–37, 163, 214, 239*n*60, 242*n*6, 247*n*25; in British attack (1940), 126–27, 131, 132, 133–37, 138, 190, 243*n*18; in Cretan invasion, 173–74, 247*n*29; of France (1939–1940), 86, 102, 106, 107, 119, 123, 235*n*13, 239*n*60, 241*n*87; in French invasion (1939), 83, 102, 104, 112, 114, 115, 116, 122, 123, 239*n*61, 241*n*91; in Gibraltar attack, 141; North African campaign and, 164, 166, 246*n*14; in Norwegian invasion, 99; of Poland, 64, 65, 74; in Polish invasion, 79, 80, 81–82, 85, 233*n*37; of Russia, 183, 190, 191, 194, 250*n*16, 252*n*40, 253*n*49; in Russian invasion, 189–90, 193–94, 207–208, 211; in Yugoslavian invasion, 152

Aisne River, 23, 27, 109, 111, 119, 120

Alam Halfa Ridge, 214

Albania, 142, 145, 148, 149, 152, 154, 155, 158

Alcazar, battle of, 140

Alexandria, Egypt, 146, 172, 173, 244*n*10

Algeria, 214

Aliakmon River, 148

alliances, 10–11. *See also specific nations*

Allied High Command, 91, 105, 106, 123

Allies, The, 98, 99–102. *See also specific nations*

Alps, The, 83, 84, 121, 122

Alsace-Lorraine, 11

Altmark (vessel), 99, 237*n*43

Alzette River, 107

American Civil War, 3, 4, 5, 222n37

Amiens, France, 26, 97

ammunition wagons, 7, 9, 10, 15, 26, 37, 41. *See also* horses

Anatolia, 141, 142

Anders, Wladyslaw, quoted, 213

Angerburg, East Prussia, 193

Anschluss, *see* Austria, Hitler and

antiaircraft guns, 64, 74, 157, 252n41; French (1939–1940), 86, 107, 235n14

antitank weapons, 33, 75, 81, 107, 157; German, 35, 71, 72, 238n53, 240n79, 248n36; Russia and, 184, 198, 208

Antonescu, Jan, 187

Antwerp, Belgium, 15, 105, 111, 240n74

Appomattox, surrender at, 4

Archangel, Russia, 178, 182

Ardennes, The: in French invasion (1939), 71, 84, 88, 89, 90, 91–93, 96–97, 105–106, 107–10, 236n24, 237n36

armament, 3, 4–5, 6, 25; Versailles Treaty on, 29, 30, 38, 42–43. *See also specific weaponry*

armored divisions, 29, 70, 251n26; Austria and, 50, 226n21; British, 25, 32–33, 101, 161, 162, 168, 172, 174, 214, 225n11, 238nn52–53, 55, 240n79, 248n36; in Czech invasion, 56, 57; of France, 31, 84–85, 86, 100–102, 110, 118, 119, 122–23, 239n58; in French invasion, 88, 90, 91–92, 95, 96, 97, 101, 104, 106, 107–108, 109–10, 112, 113, 114–16, 119, 120–21, 122–23, 238n55, 239n56, 240nn76–77, 79, 241nn81, 84; German organization of, 34–38, 39, 40–42, 224n53, 234n38, 237n40; in Greek campaign, 149, 154, 155, 157, 158, 193, 247n29; in North African campaign, 141, 147, 151–52, 159–76, 214, 245n2, 246-

n14, 248nn32, 34, 36; in Polish invasion, 64, 65, 68, 73, 74, 75, 76, 78–79, 80, 81, 228n42; in Russian invasion, 180, 183, 184–85, 186, 187, 188–89, 191, 192, 194–95, 197, 198–99, 200–201, 202, 203, 204, 206, 207, 208–209, 210, 212; in Yugoslavian invasion, 150, 151, 152, 154, 157

Arnim, Sixt von, 231n20

Arras, France, 112–13, 248n36

artillery, 3–6, 8, 23, 24–25, 26, 36, 220n9, 222n32, 240n72; assault gun sections, 227n28; for home defense (1939), 71, 72; horse-drawn, 7, 85, 95, 184, 185, 227n26; rapid-fire, 16; of Russia, 191, 192, 193–94, 195, 197–98, 206, 208, 251n22, 253–56; tanks and, 31, 32, 34, 35, 37, 75, 81, 85, 107, 108, 110, 184, 195, 198, 240nn77, 79; Versailles Treaty on, 29

Athens, Greece, 148, 157

attrition, 27, 28, 44, 135–36, 182

Auchinleck, Claude, 214, 248n36

Australia, 162, 247n25

Austria, 5–6, 9, 10, 11, 221n29, 226-n21, 228n39; Hitler and, 47, 48, 49–50, 51, 56, 117; in World War I, 25, 27; Yugoslavia and, 150, 151, 154

Austro-Prussian War of 1866, 5–6, 9, 10

Axis, The, 187. *See also specific nations*

Baku, Russia, 202

Balkans, The, 27, 125, 130, 138–58, 159, 165–66, 168, 193. *See also specific nations*

Baltic, The, 98, 138, 178, 184, 188, 191, 195. *See also specific nations*

Bardia, Libya, 167, 169, 170

Basel, Switzerland, 71

Bastogne, Belgium, 107
Bavaria, 54
Bay of Biscay, 38, 150
bayonets, 6
Beachy Head, England, 133
Beck, Ludwig, 35–38, 50, 54, 56, 226n25; Czech invasion and, 48–49, 52–53
Belgium, 52, 71, 84, 87, 221n21; Moltke the younger and, 17, 19–21, 22, 80; Nazi invasion of, 88–89, 90, 91–93, 96–98, 102, 104–11, 113, 114–15, 117, 123, 125; Schlieffen and, 14–15, 16, 236n24
Belgium. Air Force, 133, 190
Belgium. Army, 14–15, 20, 26; World War II and, 105–106, 110, 117
Belgrade, Yugoslavia, 150, 152, 154, 155, 166
Benghazi, Libya, 161, 162, 166, 171
Beresford-Peirse, Noel, 168, 248n36
Berghof conferences, 127–28, 130, 132, 146
Bergmann, Friedrich Adolf von, cited, 19, 20, 21, 22
Berlin, Germany, 6, 127, 128, 157
Berry-au-Bac, France, 120
Bessarabia, 187
Biggin Hill, England, 134
Billotte, Gaston, 105, 106
Bismarck, Otto von, 10, 11, 12
Bismarck (vessel), 242n14
Bizerta, Tunisia, 246n20
Black Sea, 178
Blanchard, Georges, 240n67
Blaskowitz, Johannes, 76
Blau, George, 215
blitzkrieg, 28–46; in British attack, 134–37, 138; in French invasion, 90–91, 92–93, 100–101, 102–23; in Greek invasion, 155–58; in Poland, 69, 73–79, 80, 85, 234n53; in Russia, 183, 188–89, 192–93; in Yugoslavia, 150–51, 152, 157
blockades, 27, 141, 147

Blomberg, Werner von, 36, 43, 47–48, 49
Blücher (vessel), 237n46
Blumentritt, Guenther von, 66, 120
Bock, Feodor von, 65, 77, 78; in French invasion, 88, 110, 111, 113–14, 115, 116, 117, 119, 120; in Russian invasion, 188, 195, 196, 199, 200, 201, 202, 204, 208, 210, 212, 214
Bohemia, 52, 56, 231n29
bombers, 44–46, 239n61, 243n18; British (1939–1940), 86, 134, 247–n25; of France, 86, 118, 239n60; in French invasion, 116, 120; German losses in Britain, 136, 137; in Malta, 174; in Polish invasion, 65, 73–74, 79, 81; of Russia, 250n16; in Russian invasion, 193–94, 252n40
Brauchitsch, Walter von, 49, 53, 54, 56; Balkan operations and, 144, 147, 150, 151, 152, 154, 155, 156, 157, 165, 167; British attack and, 130, 135; French invasion and, 87, 91, 111, 113–14, 115, 116, 117, 119, 121, 128; North African campaign and, 162, 166, 167, 169, 170, 172; Norwegian invasion and, 99; Polish invasion and, 62, 67, 76, 78, 79; Russian invasion and, 130, 140, 177, 180, 185, 200, 201, 202, 213–14
Breslau, Germany, 154
Britain, 47, 48, 51, 52, 221n21, 230n14; attack (1940) on, 45, 87, 125–38, 139, 140, 142, 144, 145, 146, 157, 177, 178, 216, 243nn16, 18, 244n1; Austrian Anschluss and, 49; Balkans and, 142, 144, 146, 148–49, 155–56, 157, 158, 244nn8, 10, 246n6; conscription in, 60, 83; Crete and, 247n25; Franco-Soviet negotiations, 62, 67, 232n15; French invasion and, 117, 123,

Britain (cont.)
124, 125–26, 248n36; mechanized
warfare and, 31–33; Munich Conference and, 57–58, 59, 61–62;
North Africa and, 130, 135, 139,
140, 141, 145, 146, 149, 151–52,
161–76, 214, 245n11, 246nn6, 15,
20, 248nn32, 36; Polish invasion
and, 67, 70, 72, 73, 76–77, 125;
Schlieffen and, 14–15, 19; United
States war entry and, 213; war
declaration (1939) and, 77, 83, 125
Britain. Air Force (RAF): French
invasion and, 83–84, 86–87, 102,
104, 116, 125; German attack and,
126, 127, 131, 133–37, 242n6
Britain. Air Force (RAF) Fighter
Command, 133, 134, 137, 243-
nn19, 24
Britain. Army (British Expeditionary Force, BEF), 33, 83–84, 86,
90, 129, 131, 225n11; French in-
vasion and, 101, 105, 113, 115, 116,
118, 235n15, 236n26, 238nn52–53;
World War I and, 19, 26
Britain. Navy, 27, 83, 125, 246n15;
Crete and, 173; French invasion
and, 113, 116; German attack and,
126, 127; Gibraltar and, 140, 141;
Norway and, 99, 237nn43, 46
British Defence Committee, 162
British Expeditionary Force (BEF),
see Britain. Army
Brno, Czechoslovakia, 56
Brooke, Alan Francis, 242n12
Brussels, Belgium, 16, 20, 109
Bryansk-Vyazma line, 203, 204, 206,
207
Budenny, Semyon, 196, 197, 199,
200, 204
Bulgaria, 27; World War II and,
142, 143, 144, 146, 148, 149, 150
bullets, 4, 233n21
Busch, Ernst, 188

Calais, France, 114
Cambrai, France, 20, 111, 112
cannon, 220n9
"cap and ball" rifle, 4
Caporetto, battle (1917) of, 25
Capuzzo, Libya, 169
Carpathians, The, 70
Case Green, 51–53, 55. See also
Czechoslovakia
Case White, 61–62. See also Poland
Case Yellow, 88, 95, 98. See also
France
casualties, 4, 5, 30, 43; in Crete, 173;
in Franco-Prussian War (1870),
8; in Netherlands, 117; in North
Africa, 175; in Russia, 195, 198,
204, 206, 210, 212, 214, 254n77;
in World War I, 23, 224nn58, 60
Caucasus, The, 180, 199, 201, 202,
214, 215
cavalry, 7, 14, 33–34, 35, 40, 73, 187,
222n32; Belgian, 106; French, 84,
85, 106; Polish, 64, 70, 74, 75;
Russian, 183, 185, 191, 192, 254-
n74; Versailles Treaty on, 29. See
also horses
Chamberlain, Neville, 58
Charleville, France, 114
Château-Porcien, France, 120
Château-Thierry, France, 120, 121
Chauny, France, 20
Cherbourg, France, 129
Churchill, Winston, 172, 193, 248n36
civilian populations: air warfare and,
30, 43, 79; in Moscow defense,
208; as "Nation in Arms," 7, 11,
30, 100, 220n15, 238n50; in Paris
defense (1871), 8, 221nn20–21
Coblentz, Germany, 21
Compiègne, France, 120, 121, 122,
223nn43, 49
Conduct of Air War, The (Luft-
waffe Field Manual No. 16) 43–44
conscription, 8, 38, 39–40, 87, 221n20,

227n34, 228n35, 241n93; British, 60, 83; Russian, 206–207
convoys, 163, 164, 167, 172, 174
Corap, André, 105–106
Corinth, Greece, 156
Cracow, Poland, 70, 76
Crete, 142, 170–74, 176, 247n25, 248n32
Crimean War, 3
Croatia, 151, 154
Cyrenaica, Libya, 161, 162, 165, 166, 168, 170, 175, 214, 245n11; Italian Army in, 145, 146, 159, 160
Czechoslovakia, 45, 239n56; invasion of, 47, 48, 50–53, 55–58, 59–60, 61, 62, 117, 230n14, 231n29, 234n1
Czechoslovakia. Army, 52, 57
Czestochowa, Poland, 76

Danish War (1864), 3–4, 5
Danzig, 61, 62, 67, 81
Darlan, Jean, 238n47
"defense in depth," 118–19, 123, 203, 208, 210, 216
Demer River, 105
demotorization, 94–95
Denmark, 3–4, 5, 98–100, 125
Deutsches Afrika Korps, 147, 149, 151–52, 159–76, 245n11, 246n14, 247n31, 248n32. See also Rommel, Erwin
Dieppe, France, 135
Dinant, Belgium, 106, 107, 108
dive-bombers, 44, 45, 81
Division Cuirasée (DC), 85. See also infantry, of France
Divisions Légères Mécaniques (DLM), see armored divisions, of France
Dnieper River, 179, 185, 188, 189, 196, 197
Dniester River, 189
Donets Basin, Ukraine, 179, 180, 182, 199, 200, 201, 202, 206, 211
Dornier 17 bomber, 45

Doullens Conference (1918), 224n61
Drava River, 151
Dreyse rifle, 6
Dunkirk, France, 26, 113–17, 118, 119, 129, 157
Dvina River, 179, 185, 188, 189, 195, 196
Dyle River, 91, 105, 107, 108, 110

East, The, 47. See also specific nations
East Prussia, 23–24; Polish invasion and, 61, 62, 65, 69, 74, 75–76; Russian invasion and, 188, 193, 200
Eben Emael, 104, 239n64
Egypt, 130, 139, 141, 162; Rommel and, 161, 166–67, 168, 169, 170, 174, 176, 214, 244n10, 246n14, 248n32
Einmannsberger, General L. von, 226n21
Eisenbahntruppen (Railroad Troops), 16, 20, 205
El Agheila, Libya, 160, 161, 164, 214
El Akhdar, Libya, 170
El Alamein, Egypt, 214, 248n32
El Gazala, Libya, 170
Ellis, L. F., 115
El Mekili, Libya, 166
encirclement, 6, 7, 9, 11, 12–17, 30, 42, 219n4; aircraft in, 46, 79, 80; in Czech invasion, 52, 56–57; Egypt and, 141; in French invasion, 90–91, 92, 111, 113–14, 117, 119, 120–21, 123; in Greece, 152, 154, 158; in Poland, 63, 64–65, 69, 74–75, 77–78, 79–80, 81–82; in Russian invasion, 144, 179, 180, 182, 184, 185, 188–89, 190, 193, 194–95, 197, 199, 200, 204, 206, 207, 209, 215, 216, 251n24; Russian use of, 214, 215; tanks and, 31, 37, 38, 90; World War I and, 23–24, 26, 29; in Yugoslavia, 150–51

England, see Britain
English Channel, 23, 90, 118, 126–27, 137, 138
Erfurth, Waldemar, 187–88
Escaut River, 91, 240n67
Etzdorf, Hasso von, 147
Exercise Weser (Weseruebung), 99
exhaustion, 4, 17, 19, 22, 27, 42; in Russian invasion, 195, 196, 198, 199, 200, 207, 208, 209, 211, 216

Falkenhayn, Erich von, 23, 24, 224n51
Falkenhorst, Nicholas von, 99
Felmy, Helmuth, 243n18
Fighter Command (British), 133, 134, 137, 243nn19, 24
Finland, 98; in Russian invasion, 184, 187–88, 190, 191, 201, 252n31
Flakartillerie (antiaircraft artillery), 43. See also antiaircraft weapons; artillery
flamethrowers, 25, 81, 108
Flanders, see Belgium
flanking, 6, 8, 22, 23, 31
Foch, Ferdinand, 27, 118, 122
Fontainebleau, France, 127, 128, 130, 132
food, 15, 21, 27, 68, 180, 232n19
Forsyth, Alexander, 4
fortifications, 14, 29; in Belgium, 20, 104, 107–108; Czech invasion and, 52, 56, 58; French, 11, 84, 89, 100, 108, 118, 119; German (see West Wall); Greek, 148–49, 156; North African, 167, 168; Polish, 64, 75, 79, 81; Russian, 184, 203
France, 31, 49, 197; Anglo-Soviet negotiations (1939), 62, 67, 232n15; Czechoslovakia and, 48, 50–51, 52, 57, 58, 59, 60, 62, 230n14; Moltke the elder and, 4, 6, 7–8, 9, 10–11; Moltke the younger and, 17–22, 28–29, 80; Nazi attack on Britain

and, 129, 134; Nazi invasion of, 47, 83–124, 125–26, 127–28, 131, 176, 184, 203, 235n14, 236n24, 238nn52–53, 239n60, 240nn74–79, 248n36; North Africa and, 145, 246n20; Polish invasion and, 45, 67, 69, 70, 71–72, 73, 77, 85, 125; Schlieffen and, 12, 14–17
France. Air Force (Armée de l'Air), 86, 102, 104, 118, 120, 133, 190, 235n13, 238n47
France. Army, 83, 231n25; Czechoslovakian invasion and, 57; home defense (1940) and, 86, 117, 118, 119, 120; mechanization and, 31, 34, 36, 84, 85, 100, 185; Moltke the elder and, 8, 10; Moltke the younger and, 19; Netherlands invasion (1940) and, 105–106, 113, 117; Polish invasion and, 70; Schlieffen and, 14, 17; the Somme and, 26
France. Army High Command, 84, 85, 100, 117–19
France. Navy, 145, 146, 238n47
France. Vichy government, 121–22, 145–46
Franco, Francisco, 125, 142, 144, 145
Franconia, 56
Franco-Prussian War (1870–1871), 7–12
Fritsch, Werner von, 36, 48–49, 226n25
fronts, 30, 59, 64; in Russian invasion, 191–93, 194, 196, 197–98, 201, 203; trench warfare and, 23; in two-front warfare, 10–11, 12, 14, 17, 19, 25, 52, 70
Fuller, J. F. C., 31, 32, 34, 114
fulminate of mercury, 4

Galicia, Poland, 79
Gamelin, Maurice, 100, 108, 111
Gariboldi, Italo, 160, 165, 169, 172
gas, 25

Gaulle, Charles de, 100, 226*n*21, 238*n*50, 240*n*76

Gause, Alfred, 173

Gembleaux Gap, 105

Georges, Alphonse, 105

Genoa, Italy, 144

Germany: Anglo-French ultimatum (1939), 76–77; Franco-Russian alliance and, 10–11, 17, 19; Italian alliance of, 121, 122, 123–24, 139, 140–42, 146, 154, 156, 159–60, 187, 213; Japanese alliance of, 187, 213; Nazi resistance movement in, 53, 54–55, 57–58; post-World War I rearmament of, 29, 30, 35–38; Russian alliance of, 67, 72, 79, 130, 131, 140, 149; territorial conquest and, 47–49, 58, 59, 123–24; unification of, 6, 8–9

Germany. Air Force (*Luftwaffe*), 35, 38, 42–46, 94; Balkan campaigns and, 143, 152; in British attack, 126–27, 129, 131, 132, 133–37, 138, 242*n*6; Crete and, 171, 173–74, 247*n*29; in Czech invasion, 52; French invasion and, 96, 102, 104, 108, 114, 115, 116, 119 120, 123, 239*nn*61, 64; North African campaign and, 160, 164, 165, 214; in Norway, 99; parachute troops, 43, 99, 156, 167, 173, 239*n*64, 247*n*29; in Polish invasion, 65, 73–74, 79, 81–82, 233*n*37; in Russian invasion, 182, 183, 189–90, 193–94, 207–208, 215, 216, 252*n*40, 253*nn*49, 52

Germany. Air Ministry, 43

Germany. Armed Forces (*Wehrmacht*), 35, 43, 49, 102, 123, 138, 174; French victory celebration, 127–28; Hitler's expansion of, 38–39, 45, 87

Germany. Armed Forces High Command, *see* OKW (*Oberkommando der Wehrmacht* . . . High Command of the Armed Forces)

Germany. Army (*Heer*), 35, 38–39, 48, 87, 124; Air Force interaction and, 43–45, 46, 94, 123, 152, 189–90, 207–208, 216–17; British attack and, 126, 129, 131, 132–33, 137, 138; motorization shortages (1939–1940) of, 93–95, 117, 122, 226*n*25; North Africa and, 135; planning staffs, 65–66; reorganization (1939) of, 40–42, 43, 58–60, 80, 122, 185, 226*n*25, 227*nn*26, 28; Russian defeat of, 213; Yugoslavian invasion and, 150

Germany. Army (post-World War I), *see* Germany. *Reichsheer* (post-World War I German army)

Germany. Army Command (*Heeresleitung*), 28, 35, 38. *See also* OKH (*Oberkommando des Heeres* . . . Army High Command)

Germany. Army General Staff (*Generalstab des Heeres*), 35, 36, 48, 49, 53–55, 59, 95, 231*n*20; Balkan campaign and, 144, 156; British attack and, 126, 127, 129, 132–33, 137; Czechoslovakia and, 51, 53, 56, 58; French invasion and, 96; North Africa and, 172, 175; Poland and, 65–66, 68; Russian invasion and, 139, 186, 254*n*70

Germany. Army Group Commands (*Heeresgruppenkommandos*), 40

Germany. Army High Command, *see* OKH (*Oberkommando des Heeres* . . . Army High Command)

Germany. Foreign Office, 126, 147

Germany. Imperial Army (*Kaiserheer*), 9, 12–29, 40, 43, 54

Germany. Military Districts (*Wehrkreise*), 39–40, 41, 50, 228*nn*37, 39

Germany. Militia Divisions (*Landwehr*), 39, 40, 58

Germany. Navy (*Kriegsmarine*), 35, 38, 43; British attack and, 126–27, 129–31, 132–33, 135, 137–38; Norway invasion and, 98, 99–100, 130, 138

Germany. Railroad Troops (*Eisenbahntruppen*), 16, 20, 205

Germany, *Reichsheer* (post-World War I German army), 28–35, 38, 54, 82

Germany. Troop Office (*Truppenamt*), 28, 29, 35, 54. *See also* Germany. Army General Staff (*Generalstab des Heeres*)

Germany. Waffen SS, 38

Germany. War Ministry (*Kriegsministerium*), 36, 43, 48, 49, 50. *See also* OKW (*Oberkommando der Wehrmacht* . . . High Command of the Armed Forces)

Gestapo, 182

Gette River, 20

Gibraltar, 130, 140, 142, 143, 144–45, 146

Giraud, Henri, 240n74

Glorious (vessel), 237n46

Gneisenau (vessel), 130, 237n46, 242n14

Goering, Hermann, 38, 43, 44, 94, 116, 128, 152, 171, 241n81

Gomel, Russia, 201

Gort, John, 113, 235n15

Gott, W. H. E., 168, 169

Graf Spee (vessel), 237n43

Graf Zeppelin (vessel), 242n14

Graziani, Rodolfo, 147, 160

Great Britain, *see* Britain

Greece, 159, 162, 246n6; Crete and, 170–74, 247nn25, 29; invasions (1940) of, 142, 143, 144–45, 146–47, 148–49, 244nn8–10; surrender of, 155–57, 167, 168, 193; Yugoslavian invasion and, 150, 151, 152, 154, 155, 166

Greece. Army, 156, 158, 244n8

"Green Plot," 55, 57–58

Greiffenberg, Hans von, 62–63, 130, 132, 211, 212, 231n20, 245n14

grenades, 108

Grudziadz, Poland, 74, 75

Guderian, Heinz, 33–35, 50, 75, 80, 226n21, 237n40; Beck and, 36–37; French invasion and, 91, 96–97, 107, 108, 109, 114, 119, 123; Russian invasion and, 188, 194, 195, 198, 199, 200, 201, 204, 206, 209, 210, 212

Gulf of Sirte (Sidra), 160

Haase, Wilhelm, 66

Halder, Franz, 49, 50, 53–55, 231-n20; British attack and, 125–26, 127, 128–30, 132, 135, 136, 137, 140, 142, 144, 145, 146, 177; Czechoslovakia and, 55–58; estimate of French threat (1939) and, 70–71, 77; French invasion and, 87, 90–91, 96–97, 104, 106, 108, 109–10, 111, 112, 113–17, 119, 120, 121, 122, 125, 176; Gibraltar and, 140–41, 142, 143, 144–45, 146; Greek surrender (1941) and, 156–57, 159, 167, 168; motorization crisis (1940) and, 93–95; North African campaign and, 147, 149, 151, 152, 161–63, 165–66, 167–68, 169–70, 171, 172–73, 174, 175–76; Norwegian invasion and, 99; Polish invasion and, 62, 65, 66, 67, 68, 70, 76, 77, 78, 79, 80, 81, 95, 176; Russian invasion and, 132, 139–40, 143, 144, 147, 175, 176, 177, 178–79, 180, 185, 186, 192, 193, 194, 195, 196–97, 198–99, 200–201, 202–203, 204, 206, 209, 211–12, 214; Vichy and, 145–46; Yugoslavia and, 149–50, 151, 154, 155, 165–66

Halfaya Pass, 168, 174

"Halt Order" (May, 1940), 114–16, 241nn81, 84

Hannut, France, 110

Hapsburg dynasty, 50

Hawker aircraft, 134

Heer, see Germany. Army (*Heer*)

Heinkel 111 bomber, 45

Henlein, Konrad, 51, 230*n*14

Heusinger, Adolf, 155, 156, 202, 203, 245*n*14

Himmler, Heinrich, 38, 228*n*42

Hindenburg, Paul von, 23, 25, 224*n*51

Hindersin, Gustav Eduard von, 6–7

Hitler, Adolf, 47–49, 229*n*1; Balkan campaigns and, 141, 142, 143, 144–45, 146–47, 149, 150, 151, 152, 154–55, 156–57, 244*n*10; British attack and, 126, 127, 128, 131, 135, 136–37, 139, 140, 144, 145, 146, 178, 243*n*16; Cretan invasion and, 171, 176; Czechoslovakian invasion and, 50–51, 53, 55–58, 230*n*14; French invasion and, 87, 91, 92–93, 96–97, 104, 109–10, 111, 112, 114–17, 122, 123, 128, 241*nn*81, 84; German resistance to, 53, 54–55, 57–58; military expansion and, 34, 38–39; 42–43, 87, 138, 226*n*25, 230*n*3; North African campaign and, 147, 152, 159, 161, 165, 166, 172–73, 175, 176, 214; Poland and, 61, 62, 65, 67, 71–73, 79; Russian invasion and, 132, 139–40, 147, 176, 177, 178, 180, 182, 186, 189, 193, 195, 199–203, 204, 206, 211, 214, 215, 216, 217, 243-*n*16, 254*n*59; Scandinavia and, 98–100; Vichy France and, 145

Hoeppner, Erich, 188, 195, 209

Holland, 14, 17, 52, 71; Nazi invasion of, 87, 88, 89, 91, 92, 97–98, 104–105, 106, 107, 117, 125, 131, 239*n*64, 240*n*74

Holland. Air Force, 133, 190

Holland. Army, 104, 117

Hornchurch, England, 134

horses, 7, 9, 10, 15–16, 37, 220*n*9, 222*n*36; army reorganization (1939) and, 40, 41, 42, 94–95, 228*n*41; Marne march and, 19, 20, 21, 22, 29; Poland invasion and, 68, 233*n*20; World War II use of, 85, 88, 89, 184, 188, 195, 196, 200, 205, 206, 207, 211, 215, 225*n*11, 236*nn*22–23, 251*n*21

Hossbach, Friedrich, 229*n*1

Hossbach Conference, 47–49, 229*n*1, 230*n*14

Hoth, Hermann, 97, 116, 120; in Russian invasion, 188, 194, 199, 200, 201, 206, 209

howitzers, 81, 227*n*26

Hungary, 27, 151, 154

Huntziger, Charles, 106, 107, 109

Hurricane fighter planes, 86, 102, 133, 239*n*60

Hutier, Oskar von, 25

Iberian peninsula, *see* Spain

Imperial Guard, 40

India, 33

industry, Russian, 45, 179, 180, 182, 183, 185, 189, 190, 197, 249*n*7

infantry, 3, 7, 24, 29, 36, 38, 39, 128, 151, 226*n*25; in Czech invasion, 51–52, 56, 57; of France, 84, 85–86, 100, 108, 118, 236*n*26, 240*n*76, 241*n*87; in French invasion, 88, 89, 91, 96, 97, 98, 104, 108, 109–10, 112, 115, 122; in Greek invasion, 156, 158; horse strength authorization, 236*nn*22–23; motor vehicle authorization, 228*n*41; in Norway, 99; of Poland, 64, 70, 74, 75, 77; in Polish invasion, 65, 68, 73, 74, 75, 76, 78–79, 80, 232*n*17; Prussian, 6, 14, 220*n*8, 222*n*32; reorganization (1939) of, 40–42, 227*nn*26, 28; of Russia, 183, 185, 187, 191, 192, 197, 200, 207; in Russian invasion, 187, 188, 194–

infantry (cont.)
96, 199, 200, 201, 203, 205–206,
207, 209, 212, 215, 216, 252n31;
storm troops, 25–26, 34, 40, 187,
228n42, 229n43, 245n15, 252n31
infiltration, 25–26
*Instructions for Tactical Employ-
ment of Large Units,* 85–86
intelligence, 59, 63, 107, 109, 119,
129, 149; Allied (1939), 91, 92,
236n33; on Russia, 178, 182–83,
191, 203
Inter-Allied Military Control Commission, 29
interdiction: blitzkrieg as, 43–44, 45,
65. *See also* blitzkrieg
iron, 98–99
Iron Cross, Order of the, 128
Italian Unification, Wars of, 3
Italy, 3, 25, 27, 187, 213; Austrian
Anschluss and, 49, 50; French invasion and, 83, 84, 121, 122, 123–
24, 126; Greek invasions and, 142–
43, 145, 146, 147, 152, 154, 156,
173, 174; North Africa and, 130,
139, 140, 141, 142, 145, 146, 147,
159–60, 161, 162, 165, 171, 246n14,
247n31
Italy. Navy, 171, 173, 175, 246n10

Jacobsen, Hans-Adolf, 93
Japan, 131–32, 183, 187, 213
Jebel el Akhdar area, Libya, 161
Jeschonneck, Hans, 152
Jodl, Alfred, 49, 50, 166, 172, 173;
Russian invasion and, 199, 201,
202, 254n59
Joffre, Joseph Jacques Césaire, 118
Junkers, 44, 45

Kaiserheer, see Germany. Imperial
Army (*Kaiserheer*)
Kanotop, Russia, 204
Kaupisch, Leonhard, 99

Keitel, Wilhelm, 49, 56, 145, 241n81
Keller, Alfred, 190
Kempf, Werner, 228n42
Kesselring, Albert, 44, 73–74, 243-
n18, 248n32; French invasion and,
104, 120, 239n61, 241n81; Russian
invasion and, 190, 207, 214
Kesselschlacht doctrine, 3–27; World
War I defeat and, 29, 38. *See also*
encirclement
Ketrzyn, Poland, 193
Kharkov, Russia, 249n7
Kiev, Russia, 185, 189, 191, 199, 204,
211
Kinzel, Eberhardt, 178
Kirponos, M. P., 191, 194
Kleist, Ewald von, 150, 154, 188–
89; in French invasion, 97, 106,
108, 109, 110, 111, 116
Kluck, Alexander von, 19
Kluge, Günther von, 74, 75, 188,
209, 210
Konev, Ivan, 208
Königgrätz, battle of, 5–6
Kotowice, Poland, 76
Kremenchug, Russia, 204
Kriegsmarine, see Germany. Navy
(*Kriegsmarine*)
Kriegsministerium, see Germany.
War Ministry (*Kriegsminister-
ium*)
Kroll Opera House, Berlin, 127
Krupp, 7
Küchler, Georg von, 74, 75, 104, 188
Kuhl, Hermann Joseph von, cited, 19,
20, 21, 22
Kursk, Russia, 215
Kuznetsov, F. I., 191, 195

La Fère, France, 111
Lake Ladoga, 188
Landwehr (militia divisions), 39, 40,
58
Laon, France, 240n76

Larissa, Greece, 156
leadership, 8, 10, 11, 28; in Czech invasion, 52–53; in North African campaign, 172–73, 174, 175–76; in Polish invasion, 82; of Russia, 191, 196, 197, 206, 208; in Russian invasion, 188, 192, 214. *See also individual leaders*
Le Cateau, Belgium, 20
Lee, Robert E., 4
Leeb, Wilhelm Ritter von, 73, 79, 88, 119; in Russian invasion, 188, 196, 200, 204, 206
Lemnos, Island of, 142
Leningrad, Russia, 188, 191, 196, 199, 200–201, 204, 208; industries of, 179, 180, 182, 202, 249n7
Libya, 139, 143, 145, 146, 246n6; Rommel in, 151, 159–76, 214, 245–n11, 246n14, 247n31
Liddell Hart, B. H., 31, 32, 33, 34
Liège, Belgium, 14, 17, 20, 71, 72, 88; invasion (1940) and, 97, 104
List, Wilhelm, 76; Balkan campaigns and, 148, 151, 152, 154, 155, 156
Litvinov, Maxim, 67
Lodz, Poland, 70, 77, 78
Loehr, Alexander, 74, 190
logistics, *see* supply
Loire, The, 121
London, England, 136
Lorenz rifle, 6
Lorraine Gap, 8, 11
Lossberg, Bernhard von, 177
Louvain, Belgium, 20, 105, 110
Ludendorff, Erich, 23, 25–26, 27, 224n53
Luftkriegfuehrung (The Conduct of Air War), 43–44
Luftwaffe, see Germany. Air Force (*Luftwaffe*)
Lützow (vessel), 130, 237n46, 242n14
Luxembourg, 14, 70–71, 97, 107
Lvov, Russia, 208
Lyme Bay, England, 128–29

Maastricht Appendix, 14, 88, 97, 104
Macedonia, 244n8
machine guns, 16, 23, 25, 33, 81, 227n26, 233n21
Maginot Line, 84, 88, 89, 92, 98, 102, 105; fall of, 118, 119–20
Main River, 6
Malta, 146, 163, 170–74, 176, 214, 248n32
maneuver, *see* tactics
Mannstein, Erich von, 49, 50, 82, 227n28; French invasion and, 90, 91, 92, 97; Polish invasion and, 66, 77–78, 80
map exercises, 92, 93, 179
Marada Oasis, Libya, 164
marches, 15–16, 105; the Marne, 17–22, 27, 29, 80, 81, 223nn43, 49; in Russian invasion, 194–96, 199, 205–206, 207, 216; standard speeds of, 75, 80, 233n20; tank support and, 31, 32, 37, 109
Marcks, Erich, 132, 178–79, 183, 186
Maria Theresa Academy, Vienna, 154
Mark tanks, 74, 186, 234n38, 238n53, 239n56, 240n79
Marne River, 17, 118, 119, 210; Moltke the younger and, 17–22, 29, 80, 81, 223nn43, 49
Martel, Giffard, 31, 32–33
Masurian Lakes, 23
matériel, see supply
Maubeuge, France, 20, 111, 223n43, 240n74
mechanized warfare, 30–35, 39, 100–101, 225n11; costs of, 34, 37–38, 93–95, 117, 226n25, 227n29. *See also specific war machinery*, e.g., armored divisions
Mechelen Incident (1940), 92, 236–n33
Mediterranean area, 138, 139, 176, 214; Britain and, 140, 141, 142–43, 145–46, 163, 171

Mellenthin, F. W. von, 173
Memel, Lithuania, 184
Merdorp, Belgium, 110, 240*n*77
Mersa el Brega, Libya, 164
Mersa Matruh, 141
Messerschmidts, 45
Metaxas line, 148–49
Metz, France, 8, 14, 17
Meuse River, 14, 20, 71, 72; Nazi invasion (1939) and, 88, 89, 90, 91, 93, 96–97, 105–106, 107, 108, 109, 110, 236*n*24
Middle East, 140, 162, 178
Mikosch, Lieutenant Colonel, 140
Milch, Erhard, 241*n*81
Minié, Claude, 4
Minsk, Russia, 188, 194–95, 253*n*53
Mius River, 211
Mlawa, Poland, 75, 81
mobilization, 8, 14, 17, 22, 29, 30, 31, 39; Allied (1939), 77, 83; Austrian Anschluss and, 50; for Czech invasion, 51–52, 55–56, 57, 58; of Poland, 69, 70, 73, 81; for Polish invasion, 62, 64–65, 67–68, 70, 71, 72–73, 75, 80, 229*n*44; of Russia, 191–92; for Russian invasion, 186–87, 192; Welle Plan for, 58–60, 73, 75, 241*n*93; for Yugoslavian invasion, 150, 157
Modlin, Poland, 69, 79
Moldavia, 189
Molotov, Vyacheslav, 67, 232*n*15
Moltke, Helmuth von, the elder, 3–12, 15, 29, 36, 187, 221*nn*25–26
Moltke, Helmuth von, the younger, 17–23, 29, 80, 91
Monastir Gap, 152, 155, 158
Mons, Belgium, 20
Monschau, Germany, 97
Montcornet, Belgium, 109
Montgomery, Bernard L., 214
Moravia, 52, 56, 231*n*29
Morocco, 214
Morshead, L. J., 168

mortars, 25, 227*n*26
Moscow, Russia, 180, 182, 199–201, 202, 203, 216, 249*n*7; German drive on, 178, 179, 196, 198, 204–205, 206–12, 213–14
motor cycle troops, 35
motorized divisions, *see* armored divisions; motor vehicles
motor vehicles, 22, 29, 30, 32, 228-*n*41; armored divisions and, 33, 34–35, 37, 40, 56, 57, 64, 65; British, 118; French, 84–85, 100, 117; German shortages in (1939–1940), 41–42, 93–95, 98, 112, 117, 122, 226*n*25; North African campaign and, 167; oil supply and, 37, 39, 68–69, 80; Polish invasion and, 73, 80; Russian, 184, 191, 192, 249*n*14, 251*nn*20–21; in Russian invasion, 186, 187, 188, 198–99, 203, 204–205, 207, 215
mountain divisions, 73, 76, 99, 128, 228*n*41; in Greece, 151, 156, 247-*n*29; horse strength authorization, 236*n*23; marching speed, 233*n*20; in Russia, 187
Mount Grammosi, 149
Mount Olympus, 148, 149, 155
Munich Conference, 55, 57–58, 59, 61, 71
Münstereiffel, Germany, 104
Mussolini, Benito, 49, 121, 142

Namur, Belgium, 20, 223*n*43
Napoleon Bonaparte, 4, 32, 193
Napoleon III, 7, 8, 221*n*20
Napoleonic Wars, 4, 5
Narew, Russia, 69
Narvik, Norway, 98, 126
Nation in Arms, 7, 11, 30, 100, 220*n*15, 238*n*50
Nazi Party, 43, 51, 55, 56; military strategy and, 114, 115
Nazi-Soviet nonaggression pact, 67, 72, 79, 232*n*15

Neame, P., 166
Netherlands, 14, 17. *See also* Holland
Neurath, Constantine von, 48, 231*n*1
New Zealand, 162, 247*n*25
Nieuport, Belgium, 23
Nile River, 141
Nish, Yugoslavia, 150, 154
North Africa, 84, 118, 124, 135, 139, 245*n*2; Gibraltar campaign and, 140, 141, 142, 145, 146; Rommel in, 147, 149, 151–52, 159–76, 214, 244*n*10, 246*nn*6, 14. *See also specific nations*
North German Confederation, 6, 7–8
North Sea, 23, 83, 90, 98, 138, 150
North Weald, England, 134
Norway, 98–100, 125, 126, 130, 138, 173, 237*nn*43, 46; Nazi invasion of Russia, 190, 252*n*40
Norway. Air Force, 133, 190
Nuremberg, Germany, 56
Nuremberg Trials, 150

Odessa, Russia, 192
offensives, 4–5, 6, 8, 11; air, 30, 43–46, 73–74, 79, 80, 81–82, 85, 99, 102, 104, 114, 116, 120, 131, 133–37, 171, 173, 182, 189, 193–94; amphibious, 127, 129–33, 134, 135, 136, 137–38, 141, 144, 171, 173, 178, 244*n*1; in Czechoslovakia, 51–52, 56; in French invasion, 87–88, 89, 90–91, 104, 106, 108–10, 114, 120–21, 236*nn*24–25; German estimate (1939) of French threat of, 70–71; in North African campaign, 161, 164–65, 166–68, 169–70, 171, 172–73, 174, 175–76, 214, 245*n*11; in Norway, 98–100; in Polish invasion, 64, 67–68, 69, 73–74, 75–76, 80, 85; Russian counteroffensives, 213, 215, 250*n*17; in Russian invasion, 178, 179, 180, 182, 183, 188–89, 193–95, 199–202, 204–206, 209–11, 214–15, 216;

tank, 32, 34, 36–37, 75–76, 81, 86, 100–102, 106, 107–108, 109–10, 112, 114–15, 116, 120–21, 161, 163, 164, 174–75, 180, 194–95, 206; Welle Plan and, 59; in World War I, 23, 25–26, 27
Ogorkiewicz, Richard, 35, 84, 226*n*21
oil, 37, 39, 68–69, 80, 88, 227*n*29; the Balkans and, 142, 143, 157, 171, 247*n*29; Russia and, 180, 202, 204, 214, 215
Oise River, 120, 121
OKH (*Oberkommando des Heeres . . .* Army High Command), 36, 38–39, 40, 41, 42, 58–59; Austria and, 49–50; the Balkans and, 142, 143, 147, 149–50, 151, 152, 154–55, 156, 157, 158, 159; British attack and, 125–30, 132–33, 135, 136, 137; Czechoslovakia and, 51, 52, 56; French invasion and, 87–93, 95–98, 104, 106–107, 108, 110, 111, 112, 113–14, 115, 119, 120, 121, 122, 123, 236*n*24; Intelligence Division of, 178; North Africa and, 145, 147, 159, 160, 161, 162, 163, 165, 167, 168, 169, 173, 175; Norway and, 99; Poland and, 62, 63, 65, 68, 72–73, 78, 79, 80, 87; Russia and, 177–79, 180, 182, 183–84, 185–86, 187, 188, 189, 190, 193, 195, 200, 201, 202, 203, 204, 205, 209, 210, 211*n*12, 213–14, 216. *See also* Halder, Franz
OKW (*Oberkommando der Wehrmacht . . .* High Command of the Armed Forces), 49, 51, 52, 55, 62, 99; British attack and, 127, 132, 133, 136, 137, 244*n*1; Economics Section of, 87, 180; French invasion and, 104, 112, 115, 122, 236*n*25; Gibraltar and, 143, 144–45; Intelligence Division of, 182; Malta and, 171; North Africa and, 166, 172, 173, 248*n*32; Operations

OKW (cont.)
Office of, 49, 50; Russia and, 177–78, 180, 190, 193, 200, 201, 202, 204, 211–12, 214
Olomoue, Czechoslovakia, 56
Operation Attila, see Vichy France
Operation Barbarossa, see Russia
Operation Battle-Axe, see Crete
Operation Dynamo, see Dunkirk, France
Operation Eagle Attack, see Britain, attack (1940) on
Operation Felix, see Gibraltar
Operation Marita, see Greece
Operation Mercury, see Crete
Operation Otto, see Austria, Hitler and
Operation Sea Lion, see offensives, amphibious
Operation Sunflower, see North Africa, Rommel in
Operation Twenty-Five, see Yugoslavia
Operation Typhoon, see Moscow, Russia
Orsha, Russia, 197
Ostend, Belgium, 135

panzer divisions, see armored divisions
Papagos, Alexander, 148, 244n8
parachute troops, 43, 99, 156, 167, 173, 239n64, 247n29
Paris, France, 111, 119, 120, 121; Prussian siege (1870), 8, 10; Schlieffen and, 14, 16–17
Paris Peace Conference (1919), 47
Paul, Prince Regent of Yugoslavia, 149–50
Paulus, Friedrich, 151, 169–70, 172, 214, 245n14
Pavlov, D. G., 191, 196
Pearl Harbor, Hawaii, 213
Peloponnesos, Greece, 156, 157
Péronne, France, 109, 120

Pétain, Henri Philippe, 121–22, 145
Peter, king of Yugoslavia, 150
pincer movements, see encirclement
Pindus Mountains, 155, 156
Piraeus, Greece, 157
planning staffs, 65–66
Playfair, I. S. O., quoted, 246n20
Ploesti, Rumania, 142, 247n29
Poland, 11, 24, 45, 162, 197, 221n29; Czechoslovakia and, 52, 60; invasion of, 61–82, 83, 87, 95, 125, 133, 137, 176, 184, 228n42, 229n44, 232n17, 233n37; Russian campaign and, 178, 179, 184, 187, 188, 189, 191, 193
Poland. Air Force, 64, 65, 74, 133, 190
Poland. Army, 64, 65, 66, 69–70, 73, 74, 77, 81
Polish Corridor, 61, 65, 66, 67, 69, 74–75
Pomerania, 64, 65, 66, 67, 69, 74, 75
Popov, M. M., 191
Pottgiesser, Hans, 187
Poznan, Poland, 70, 74, 76, 77–79
Prague, Czechoslovakia, 62
Prioux, René, 240n67
Pripet Marshes, 179, 182
prisoners: in Franco-Prussian War, 8, 221n21; in Greek invasion, 155, 157; in North African campaign, 166; in Polish invasion, 79; in Russian invasion, 195, 197, 198, 204; in World War I, 224n58
Prussia, 3–12, 219n1, 220nn8–9
Prussia. General Staff, 3–9, 10, 25, 27, 28, 219n1; Moltke the younger and, 17, 21, 23; Schlieffen and, 12
Prussia. Route Inspectorates, 9, 10
Prussia. Supply Transportation Inspectorate, 9
Przymsyl, Poland, 184
Ptolomais, Greece, 155
pursuit, 11; in Russia, 179, 180, 182, 186, 197

"Race to the Sea" (1914), 23
radar, 45, 102, 133, 242n6, 252n41
Radom, Poland, 76, 77
Raeder, Erich, 38, 98; British attack and, 130–31, 136
RAF, see Britain. Air Force (RAF)
railroads, 40–41, 42, 222nn36–37, 246n20; bombing of, 46, 74; Czechoslovakian invasion and, 51–52, 56; French invasion and, 88–89, 96, 107, 109, 112, 119, 123; Greek invasion and, 158, 171; Moltke the elder and, 3, 4, 5, 9–10, 11, 221-nn25–26; Polish invasion and, 61, 64, 65, 68, 69, 70, 74, 77, 81, 232-n19; Russian invasion and, 179, 180, 184, 186–87, 188, 189, 190, 198, 199, 200, 203, 205, 206, 207, 208, 209, 210, 212, 215, 216; Schlieffen and, 14, 15, 16; World War I and, 19, 20–21, 22, 23–24, 26, 223n43, 224n51; Yugoslavian invasion and, 150, 151
Ramsgate, England, 128–29
Ras el Ali, Libya, 160
Rastenburg, East Prussia, 193
reconnaissance, aerial, 106, 163, 164, 211, 237n36, 239nn60–61, 243n18, 252n40
Red Army, see Russia. Army
Regulations for the Higher Troop Commanders (Moltke), 6, 8
Reichenau, Walther von, 76, 104, 120, 188, 211
Reinhardt, Georg-Hans, 97, 109, 209
Remaking of Modern Armies, The (Liddell Hart), 32
reserves, 7, 8, 17, 22, 30, 39, 40, 100, 220n15, 238n50; in Czech invasion, 51–52, 57; French (1940), 84, 85, 100, 107–108, 111; of Poland, 64, 69, 70, 73, 77, 81; in Polish invasion, 64, 65, 68, 73, 232-n17; of Russia, 206–207, 211, 212;

in Russian invasion, 210, 211; Welle Plan and, 58
Rethel, France, 109
Reynaud, Paul, 121
Rhineland, The, 8, 11, 48, 71, 88, 230nn3, 15
Rhine River, 11
Ribbentrop, Joachim von, 61, 72, 231n1
rifles, 3, 16, 233n21; breechloading, 4, 6, 7; Russian rifle divisions, 184, 191, 192, 251nn21–22, 253-nn43–44, 53, 254n74
Ritter, Gerhard, 15
Ritterkreuz, 128
roads, 80, 88–89, 119, 123, 158, 171; Russian invasion and, 179, 188, 189–90, 194, 195, 196, 200, 207, 209, 210, 216
Robertson, E. M., 230n14
Rome, Italy, 159
Rommel, Erwin, 147, 149, 159–76, 214, 244n10, 245n11, 246n14, 247n31, 248n32
Rosinski, Herbert, 6
Rostov, Russia, 211
Rouen, France, 120
rubber, 94
Ruhr Valley, 87
Rumania, 142, 143, 146, 157, 171; in Russian invasion, 187, 188, 189, 192–93, 199
Rumania. Army, 187, 189
Rundstedt, Gerd von, 66, 76, 77, 78; French invasion and, 88, 89, 111, 114, 115, 116, 119, 120, 241n84; in Russian invasion, 188, 189, 199, 200, 201–202, 206, 211
Russia, 10–11, 12, 14, 17, 19, 47, 138, 221n29; Czechoslovakia and, 51, 52, 58, 62, 230n14; Finnish invasion and, 98, 184, 187; German alliance (1939) with, 67, 72, 79, 125, 130, 131–32, 140, 149, 232n15; German British attack and, 127,

Russia (cont.)
    131–32, 243*n*16; invasion of, 45–
    46, 117, 119, 124, 130, 132, 139–40,
    143, 144, 146, 147, 157, 174, 175,
    176, 177–212, 213–17, 243*n*16,
    249*n*14, 250*n*17; Polish invasion
    and, 63, 64, 67, 68, 72, 79, 184
Russia. Air Force, 45, 182, 183, 190,
    197, 208, 215, 253*n*49
Russia. Army, 23–24, 226*n*21; Ger-
    man strategy (1941) and, 178, 179,
    180, 182–84, 186, 187, 188–89, 194,
    196, 200, 203, 204, 206, 212; de-
    fense of Moscow and, 208, 209;
    Poland and, 67, 72, 182, 184; re-
    organization (1940) of, 184–85,
    191–92, 249*n*14; Stalingrad and,
    214–15
Russia. Army High Command
    (*Stavka*), 183, 184, 185, 191, 193,
    203, 250*n*18; defense of Moscow
    and, 208; Timoshenko and, 196,
    197, 199
Russia. State Defense Committee
    (GOKO), 250*n*17
Russian Revolution, 25

Saar, 8
Saarbrucken, Germany, 71
sabotage, 10
Saint-Omer, France, 109
Saint-Quentin, France, 109, 111, 112
Salmuth, Hans von, 65
Salonika, Greece, 152, 154, 155, 156
San River, 76
Sava River, 151
Scandinavia, 98–100
Scharnhorst (vessel), 130, 237*n*46,
    242*n*14
Schlieffen, Alfred von, 12–17, 36, 88,
    91, 193, 209, 236*n*24; Moltke the
    younger and, 17, 19, 21, 22, 23, 29
Schniewind, Otto, 126, 127, 242*n*4
Schobert, Eugen, 188
Schuschnigg, Kurt von, 50
Sedan, France, 7–8, 9, 14; Nazi in-

vasion and, 90, 91, 97, 106, 107,
    108, 109
Seeckt, Hans von, 28–31, 34, 37, 38,
    40, 59, 74
Seine River, 16, 119, 120
Shaposhnikov, Boris, 254*n*70
Shaw, G. C., 16, 41
Sherman, William Tecumseh, 222*n*37
shipping: Balkan campaign and, 144;
    in British attack, 129, 130, 132–
    33, 134, 137–38, 242*n*14; in Dun-
    kirk evacuation, 116; North
    African campaign and, 141, 163,
    170–71, 246*n*20; Norwegian in-
    vasion and, 98, 99, 237*nn*43, 46;
    pneumatic boats and, 108
Siberia, 183, 206
Sicily, 163, 171, 172, 176, 246*n*14
Sidi Barrani, battle of, 145, 162
Silesia, 56, 64, 65, 67
"sitzkrieg," 100
Skoplje, Yugoslavia, 150, 152
Slovakia, 52, 56, 62, 65, 66, 231*n*29
Smolensk, Russia, 195, 196, 197, 198,
    199–200, 202
Sollum, Libya, 166, 167, 169, 170,
    174–75
Somaliland, 130
Somme River, 26, 90, 118, 119, 120
Soviet Union, *see* Russia
Spain, 130, 147; pro-German sym-
    pathies of, 125, 142, 143, 144, 145
Spanish Civil War, 44, 184, 244*n*3
Sperrle, Hugo, 104, 239*n*61, 243*n*18
Spicheren, battle of, 8
Spitfire fighter planes, 102, 133
"square" divisions, 24
Stalin, Joseph, 67, 72, 226*n*21, 232-
    *n*15, 250*n*18; invasion and, 197,
    206–207, 208
Stalingrad, Russia, 214–15, 249*n*7
"Stalin Line," 184
steel, 37, 39, 227*n*28
storm troops, 25–26, 34, 40, 187,
    228*n*42, 229*n*43, 245*n*15, 252*n*31

Strasbourg, France, 10
strategy: Allied (1939–1940), 83, 89–90, 98, 104–106, 107, 110, 111, 113, 122; blitzkrieg, 28–29, 43–46, 69, 73–79, 192–93; of British attack (1940), 126–27, 128–33, 135–38; "defense in depth" as, 118–19, 123, 203, 208, 210, 216; diplomacy and, 10–11, 12, 62, 67, 72–73, 79, 140; of French invasion, 87–93, 95–98, 100–101, 106, 107, 109–10, 111, 113, 114–17, 123–24, 236nn24–25, 33; in Gibraltar attack, 140, 141, 142, 143, 145, 146; in Greek defenses, 148–49, 158, 244n8; of North African campaign, 161, 165, 166–67, 170, 175–76; of Polish invasion, 63–67, 69; Russian, 183–84, 185, 191–92, 196, 197, 203, 206–207, 208, 216; of Russian invasion, 144, 177–90, 192–93, 194, 196–97, 198–206, 208, 214–16; of Scandinavian invasion, 98–99; technology and, 3–10, 16, 22, 23, 30–33, 35, 100–101
Strauss, Adolf, 188
Struma River, 149
Student, Kurt, 171
Stülpnagel, Karl Heinrich, 56, 62, 188, 231n20
Stumpff, Hans-Juergen, 243n18
submarines, 87, 167; British, 163, 174, 237n46, 246n15
Sudetenland, Czechoslovakia, 51, 58, 61
Suez, Egypt, 141, 146, 166–67, 171, 176, 244n10, 246n14
supply, 3, 7, 9–10, 222n37; in French invasion, 88–89, 96, 106–107, 112, 122; motorization and, 37–38, 40–42, 80, 89, 93–95, 112; in North African campaign, 141, 161, 162–63, 165, 166–67, 169, 170–71, 172, 173, 174, 175–76, 214, 247n31, 248n32; in Polish invasion, 64, 67–69,

232n19; in Russian invasion, 179, 180, 187, 192, 194, 198–99, 204, 207, 209, 210–11, 212, 216; World War I and, 15–16, 19, 20–22, 23–24, 26–27, 30, 222n36, 223n43
Switzerland, 14, 23
Syria, 141, 142

tactics, 6, 8, 9, 24–25; air warfare and, 43, 44–46; mechanization of warfare and, 30–33, 37, 192–93; of Napoleon, 4, 5. See also specific battles
tanks, see armored divisions
Tannenberg, Germany, 23, 72
Taranto, Italy, 143
Taylor, Telford, quoted, 46
Tczew, Poland, 65
telegraphy, 3, 5
territorial conquest, 11, 47–49, 58, 59, 123–24. See also specific regions.
Thebes, Greece, 157
Thermopylae, Greece, 155–56, 157
Thessaly, Greece, 148, 155, 156, 158
Thionville, France, 14, 17
Thomas, Georg, 87, 180
Thomsen, Hermann (von der Lieth-), 43
Thrace, Greece, 148, 149, 152, 155, 158, 244n8
Thuringia, Germany, 56
Time Magazine, 234n53
Timoshenko, Semyon, 196, 197, 199, 204, 205, 211, 250n18; Bryansk-Vyazma and, 206
Tippelskirch, Kurt von, 59, 63
Tirpitz (vessel), 242n14
Tobruk, Libya, 151, 166; Rommel attack on, 161, 162, 167, 168, 169–70, 172, 245n11, 246n14
Toledo, Spain, 244n3
"total victory" see blitzkrieg
Toulon, France, 145, 146
Tours, France, 121

training, 80, 82, 85, 228n35, 231n25; conscription and, 8, 39, 87, 227-n34, 241n93; of parachute troops, 239n64; professionalism and, 12; reserves and, 14, 17, 30, 84, 220n15

trench warfare, 23, 26

"triangular" divisions, 24–25

Trieste, 144

Tripartite Pact, 187, 213

Tripoli, Libya, 147, 159, 160, 162, 163, 171

troop numbers, 14; Allied losses in Netherlands (1940), 117; Bry-ansk-Vyazma Russian losses, 206; conscription and, 39, 83–84, 221-n21; in Czechoslovakian invasion, 57; in Dunkirk evacuation, 116; German infantry divisions, 227-n26; German losses in Crete, 173; German losses in Russia, 254n77; Moltke Russian campaign plans and, 221n29; in Polish invasion, 73; Prussian infantry divisions, 222n32; of rifle divisions, 251n21; in Russian invasion, 187; Versailles limitations on, 29, 38

trucks, 29, 32, 68, 164; German supply (1940), 93–95, 112, 188; in Russian invasion, 204, 207, 209, 211

Truppenfuehrung (*Troop Command* . . . Beck), 36, 86

Tula, Russia, 209, 210, 212

Tunis, Tunisia, 171

Tunisia, 163, 171

Turkey, 143, 171

Udet, Ernst, 44

Ufa, Russia, 208

Ukraine, 178, 179, 180, 189, 202, 204, 216; defense of, 184, 191, 194, 199, 200, 206, 211

United States of America, 124, 125, 221n21; British attack and, 127, 131–32; Civil War of, 3, 4, 5; Czechoslovakian invasion and, 52; French aircraft and, 241n87; North African campaign and, 214; Pearl Harbor attack and, 213; World War I and, 27, 224nn59, 62

United States. Army, 225n11

United States Army War College, 19

Ural Mountains, 179, 182, 189, 190, 208, 249n7

Valdai Hills, Russia, 201

Valenciennes, France, 20, 111

Vardar River, 149

Venice, Italy, 144

Verdun, France, 25, 119, 121

Vermion Mountains, 148, 149, 152, 154, 155, 158, 244n8

Versailles Treaty, 28, 29, 30; Hitler and, 38, 39, 42–43

Vichy France, 121–22, 145–46

Vickers Aircraft, 134

Vienna, Austria, 151, 154, 156, 166

Vistula River, 64, 65, 66, 76, 77, 78, 79

Vitebsk, Russia, 191

Volga River, 178, 179, 189, 193, 201, 203

Voroshilov, Kliment, 197, 254n70

Vuillemin, Joseph, 238n47

Vyazma, Russia, 204, 206

Wagner, Eduard, 211

Waldersee, Alfred von, 222n30

Warlimont, Walter, 177, 241nn81, 84

Warsaw, Poland, 65, 66, 75, 76, 77, 78, 193; bombing of, 79

warships, 98, 99, 130–31, 137–38, 237nn43, 46, 242n14; British, 173; Italian, 143

Warta River, 76, 77

Wavell, Archibald, 146, 162, 168, 172, 174; dismissal of, 248n36

Wavre, Belgium, 110

Wegorzewo, Poland, 193

Weichs, Maximilian von, 150–51, 154, 193

Weizsaecker, Ernst von, 126

Wehrmacht, see Germany. Armed Forces (*Wehrmacht*)

Welle Plan, 58–60, 73, 75, 241n93

Wellington, Arthur Wellesley, Duke of, 4

Weseruebung (Exercise Weser), 99

West, The, *see specific European nations*

West Wall, 52, 57, 58, 59, 230n15; Allied war declarations and, 77, 83; French invasion (1940) and, 96; Poland invasion and, 62, 70, 71, 73

Wever, Walter, 44

Weygand, Maxime, 111, 118–19, 121, 241n87

White Russia, 178

White Sea, 208

Wilberg, Helmuth, 43

William I, Kaiser of Germany and King of Prussia, 5, 12

William II, Kaiser of Germany and King of Prussia, 12, 27, 222n30

Winterswijk, Holland, 98

"Winter War" of 1939–1940, 98, 184, 187

World War I, 19–27, 32, 36, 40, 80, 85, 89, 241n81; aircraft in, 43; casualties in, 224nn58, 60; Foch in, 118, 122; Halder in, 54; Seeckt's view of, 28–29, 30

World War II, 16, 22, 34, 35, 41, 42, 43, 45, 225n11; Czechoslovakian invasion and, 52–53; declarations of, 77, 121, 213. *See also specific nations*

Wörth, battle of, 8

Yugoslavia, 52, 147–48, 149, 244n8; invasion of, 150–51, 152, 154–55, 165–66

Zagreb, Yugoslavia, 151, 154

Zhukov, Georgi K., 206, 208, 213, 250n18, 254nn70, 74

Zossen, Germany, 73, 78, 104, 168, 169

ABOUT THE AUTHOR

Professor Addington received his M.A. and B.A. in History at the University of North Carolina and his Ph.D. in History at Duke University, where he studied under Theodore Ropp. He taught two years at San Jose State College and has been attached to The Citadel in Charleston, S.C., since 1964, where he is currently Associate Professor of History. A lieutenant in the U.S. Air Force for nearly three years, he also spent some time in the Strategic Air Command. He served as historical consultant to the Army War College's Institute of Advanced Study in Carlisle, Pa., in 1968–69, and has contributed to numerous publications on military affairs.